AOLY

Design

Fractal Geometry

Applications of Fractals and Chaos

A. J. Crilly
R. A. Earnshaw
H. Jones

Editors

Applications of Fractals and Chaos

The Shape of Things

With 163 Figures
in 259 Parts,
20 in Colour

Springer-Verlag
Berlin Heidelberg New York
London Paris Tokyo
Hong Kong Barcelona
Budapest

A. J. Crilly
Middlesex University
Trent Park
Bramley Road
London N14 4XS, U.K.

Rae A. Earnshaw
Head of Computer Graphics
University of Leeds
Leeds LS2 9JT, U.K.

Huw Jones
Middlesex University
Bounds Green Road
London N11 2NQ, U.K.

ISBN 3-540-56492-6 Springer-Verlag Berlin Heidelberg New York
ISBN 0-387-56492-6 Springer-Verlag New York Berlin Heidelberg

Library of Congress Cataloging-in-Publication Data
Applications of fractals and chaos/A. J. Crilly, R. A. Earnshaw, H. Jones, editors. p. cm.
Includes bibliographical references and index.
ISBN 0-387-56492-6
1. Fractals. Chaotic behavior in systems. I. Crilly, A. J. II. Earnshaw, Rae A., 1944- . III. Jones, H. (Huw)
QA614.86.A67 1993 514'.74–dc20 93-8105 CIP

© Springer-Verlag Berlin Heidelberg 1993
Printed in Germany

Cover Design: Design & Concept, Heidelberg
Typesetting: Camera-ready by editors
Printing: Druckhaus Beltz, Hemsbach
Binding: J. Schäffer, Grünstadt
33/3140 - 5 4 3 2 1 0 - Printed on acid-free paper

Preface

This volume is based upon the presentations made at an international conference in London on the subject of 'Applications of Fractals and Chaos'. Its objective was to bring together some of the leading developers and practitioners in the fields of fractals and chaos and their applications in the fields of scientific. investigation and modelling of phenomena. Based on this initial conference and subsequent exchanges between the editors and the authors, revised and updated papers were produced. These papers are contained in the present volume.

We thank all those who contributed to this effort by way of planning and organisation, and also all those who helped in the production of this volume. In particular, we wish to express our appreciation to Gerhard Rossbach, Computer Science Editor, and David and Nancy Rogers, who did the typesetting.

A. J. Crilly
R. A. Earnshaw
H. Jones
March 1993

Contents

Introduction

Beautiful and fascinating images generated by applying computer graphics to fractal methods rightly generate enormous interest in this recently 'rediscovered' area. The mathematical theory underlying these developments was a matter of much dispute early in the twentieth century, but became accepted as part of the core of mathematical theory before the mid-century. Fractal effects of patterns with infinitesimal subdivisibility and self-similarity have been observed in many artificially generated sets. Recently, observers and researchers have become excited over similarities between the properties of such sets and those of naturally occurring phenomena, such as growing plants, clouds and coastlines.

Before the last third of this century, physicists, biologists and mathematicians had treated as spurious, observations and calculations that led to apparent unpredictability from the application of deterministic laws, explaining them away by talk of experimental error or ill-conditioned equations. This scepticism occurred in spite of the fact that very basic models in population studies and in physical kinematics exhibited such behaviour. Since then, the presence of such effects has been accepted, sometimes reluctantly, as a feature of recursive processes. Fractal geometry has found an application as a tool to describe and analyse the apparent unpredictability of such chaotic phenomena. Although the papers presented here are grouped under the general areas of fractals and chaos, there is inevitable overlap in such intrinsically interwoven studies.

Study of the symbiotic subjects of fractals and chaos is expanding rapidly as their fascinating properties are seen to be applicable to a wide range of problems. Theories of fractals and chaos are becoming more thoroughly understood and form bases for aesthetic and scientific exploration. There are strict conditions pertaining to whether an object can be considered truly a fractal or a phenomenon chaotic, or whether the apparent unpredictability is totally due to random factors. The papers collected here, first presented to an international conference in London organised by the British Computer Society, investigate a number of cases of claims of fractal or chaotic behaviour and look to how knowledge of the subject matter can be put to use in understanding, predicting or simulating such effects. Many of the investigations involve looking at the mathematical properties of sequences of numbers that encode information on kinematic, musical, pictorial and other information. Readers unfamiliar with this area will find excellent introductions to the study of fractal signals and noise and their spectral analysis in the first chapter in this text by Richard F. Voss, and the chapter by Dietmar Saupe in *Fractals and Chaos*, Crilly, Earnshaw and Jones, Eds., published by Springer-Verlag in 1991.

Dr. Richard F. Voss is one of the pioneers of the modern study of fractals, and continues to investigate a bewildering variety of applications of the method from his work base at the IBM Thomas J. Watson Research Center in New York State, USA. He presents an introduction to spectral density methods for investigation of various forms of 'noise', and applies these techniques to the investigation of DNA sequences, indicating that different animal and plant species have characteristic values of fractal dimension for these sequences. He also comments on the similarity of this work to fractal investigations of music.

These comments lead naturally into the collaborative work of Professor Kenneth J. Hsü of the Zurich Technische Hoschule, and his son, Andrew J. Hsü of the Konservatorium Zurich, Switzerland, academic geologist and concert pianist, respectively. Their thoroughly researched study of discrete sequences of musical intervals analyses a number of musical forms. With the exception of the diminished fifth, or 'devil's note', the lower intervals from Swiss children's songs, Bach and Mozart exhibit fractal features that are absent in the dissonance of Stockhausen. A striking example of self-similarity in Bach's BWV 776 is beautifully illustrated, and the same method is applied to investigate the musicality of bird song.

The theme switches back to biology in the work of Jaap A. Kaandorp of the University of Amsterdam's Department of Computer Science, The Netherlands. He investigates fractal shapes and textures in marine sessile organisms, such as sponges and corals, and develops methods for convincing simulation of these forms. The work extends the previous two-dimensionally based model developed by Dr. Kaandorp into a more realistic three-dimensional domain, with results that can be used to simulate growth of organisms with 'radiate accretive growth'.

Drs. Stephen R. Bishop and Mohamed S. Soliman of the Centre for Nonlinear Dynamics, at University College London, UK, are more concerned with the surface of the sea than what goes on below it. They investigate the way in which fractal measurements of the chaotic nature of ship behaviour when driven by ocean waves can be used to avoid potentially catastrophic situations. Their work should have an effect on ship design and is poignantly applied to the tragedy of the Gaul, a trawler that foundered with the loss of 36 lives in February 1974.

Ships are also illustrated in the work of Dr. Jonathan M. Blackledge, of Cranfield Institute of Technology's Applied Mathematics and Computing Group, UK. He describes methods for simulating and processing signals of the form that are commonly used to transmit visual information. The elimination of noise through use of fractal dimension evaluation and power spectra is again a theme in this work, and Dr. Blackledge shows how his work can be applied to identification of features, such as ships, from noisy radar images.

The next presentation is more concerned with obscuring features rather than exposing them. Dr. Lewis F. Jardine of the Royal Military College of Science (Cranfield), Shrivenham, UK, shows how image textures are simulated by synthesizing sections with equivalent fractal dimensions. The work presented has potential applications in camouflage or in the completion of damaged or incomplete images. Dr. Jardine's illustrations of images with artificial inserts have the fascination of children's puzzles — find the deliberate mistake!

Another paper concerned with analysing the form of fractal signals and images is presented by Graham H. Watson of SD-Scicon UK, Ltd. and J. Glynn Jones of the Defence Research Agency, Farnborough, UK. They use the positive wavelet transformation to analyse fractal patterns generated using pseudorandom processes, from records of atmospheric turbulence and for identification of features from LANDSAT survey images.

Fractal features in the geosciences are investigated by Michael D. Impey and Peter Grindrod of Intera Information Technologies, Henley-on-Thames, UK. They analyse data from geological site investigations to measure the characteristics of rock structures, in particular the transmission of particles through such features. Their model, based on statistically self-affine fractals, is used to generate a transmissivity field from scattered field data. This work has important applications in the disposal of nuclear and other forms of toxic waste.

In a transatlantic collaboration, Maaruf Ali, Michael Gennert and Trevor Clarkson have applied fractal techniques to the analysis and compression of images of roadway cracks. Further development of these methods could lead to early identification of severe pavement distress, enabling highway authorities to schedule repair programmes efficiently and leading to smoother travel for all of us.

Dr. Richard F. Voss presents his second contribution, entitled "Multifractals and the Local Connected Fractal Dimension: Classification of Early Chinese Landscape Paintings". He applies multifractal analysis to digitised forms of Chinese paintings, establishing a method that distinguishes between the more complex forms of the few extant early examples of the genre, which appear to exhibit some fractal features to the trained eye, and the less detailed modern equivalent. This fascinating work has recently been applied with some success to the analysis of mammograms — a fast and accurate method of analysing these images is of vital importance.

The first paper in the section on chaos, "Chaotic bursts in complex dynamical systems" by one of the meetings's keynote speakers, Robert L. Devaney of Boston University, USA, outlines some of the discoveries that led to the exposure of the theory of chaos. Professor Devaney explains the concept of strange attractors and uses the modern tools of computer graphic-generated fractal images to investigate and extend the range of the Julia sets that were studied by French mathematicians during the first world war.

Professor John Lansdown of the Middlesex University Centre for Advanced Studies in Computer Aided Art and Design, UK, examines "Chaos, Complexity and Design Applications" from the viewpoint of utilising computers to manage complexity rather than reduce it. In highly complex imagery, temporal randomness combines with spatial order to produce patterns of a form different from those normally arising by use of conventional geometry or in natural pictures. Current images differ from the interesting images of classical art in being low in narrative and structural content. He concludes that reality is chaotic and complex, 'our perceptions create the image'.

How we perform such perception is investigated by Dr. Arun V. Holden, Julie Hyde and Henggui Zhang of the University of Leeds Departments of Physiology and Applied Mathematical Studies, UK. They present their work on "Computing with the Unpredictable: Chaotic Dynamics and Fractal Structures in the Brain". They show the fractal-like, branching, neurophysiological structures of neurones in the brain. They then extend their discussion to generating phase state images and bifurcation diagrams of brain activity from theoretical considerations and from EEG observations. Concepts from neural network theory and diffusion-limited aggregation are used to develop their thesis.

Two models used to describe road traffic flow are analysed by David Jarrett and Zhang Xiaoyan of the Road Traffic Research Centre and School of Mathematics, Statistics and Computing at Middlesex University, UK. They fail to find evidence of chaos in the car-following model, although it has been claimed by others in similar circumstances. Chaotic features are demonstrated in a dynamic trip-distribution model, although the authors comment that the parameters of this model are not practically realistic. The question of identifying chaos in other aspects of road traffic research is opened.

A similar search for chaos by Dr. J.C. Vassilicos of the University of Cambridge and London School of Economics and Political Science, UK, and his collaborator, F. Tata of Hochschule St. Gallen, Switzerland, proves fruitless. They investigate two series of economic time series, using a battery of mathematical tests. But they fail to find evidence of the chaotic behaviour claimed by other researchers. The suggestion is that earlier claims for chaos were made from relatively short data sets, and that very long sequences are needed to investigate this feature.

The chaos theory tool of phase portrait reconstruction is used by Dr. Jonathan J. Healey of the University of Cambridge Department of Engineering, UK. He investigates the behaviour of controlled disturbances introduced into the boundary layer near the leading edge of a flat plate in a low turbulence intensity wind tunnel. Spectral analysis also crops up again in this study, which uses a novel signal processing technique based on radial basis functions to generate a successful model of the phenomenon.

Dr. Richard D. Neilson and Miss Diane H. Gonsalves of the Department of Engineering, University of Aberdeen, Scotland, UK, are researching chaos in mechanical engineering systems. They observed chaotic behaviour in the contra-rotatory parts of aeronautic turbine engines. They describe a theoretical study of a simplified version of this problem, using a range of chaos theory techniques to demonstrate these effects.

The papers presented here show only some of the applications areas for the still developing theories of fractals and chaos. They cover the visual and musical arts; biology, physiology, medicine and psychology; aeronautical, mechanical, nautical and electronic engineering; image processing for camouflage and enhancement of features; perhaps in the behaviour of road traffic but possibly not economic indicators. The richness of this collection, when considered alongside other developments that are not represented, indicate that study of fractals and chaos is soundly based. The current wave of interest may be faddish, but there is enough solid theoretical material to ensure that the topic's importance will extend beyond any fashionable peak. They continue to have value both for technical and aesthetic applications. Fractals and Chaos are here to stay.

A.J. Crilly
R.A. Earnshaw
H. Jones
March 1993

1 Applications of Fractals

$1/f$ Noise and Fractals in DNA-base Sequences

Richard F. Voss

Abstract

Standard spectral density measurement techniques are applied in a new manner to individual base positions in DNA sequences. The measurements demonstrate the ubiquity of low frequency $1/f^\beta$ noise and long-range fractal correlations as well as prominent short-range periodicities. Large averages over classifications in the GenBank data bank (primate, invertebrate, plant, ...) show systematic changes in spectral exponent β with evolutionary category.

Introduction: the Genetic Code

Genetic information is stored in the sequence of nucleotide bases (A, C, G and T) that are attached to the DNA sugar-phosphate backbone [Frie85]. Improvements in sequencing techniques and heightened interest have greatly increased the combined volume of available DNA sequences. The GenBank Release 68 database contains approximately 200 Mbytes of sequence and annotation data sorted according to organism category (primate, invertebrate, plant, ...) and contains some sequences with well over 10^5 bases (see Bilofsky and Burkes [Bilo88]).

Numerous attempts have been made to characterize and graphically portray the genetic information stored in DNA nucleotide sequences [Jeff90; Silv86; Hamo85; Hamo83; Peng92]. One popular method maps the four individual bases to steps in a variant of a random walk. Unfortunately, when the number of spatial dimensions is less than four the mapping itself introduces correlations between the bases. Nevertheless, recent results on a few sequences have shown long-range fractal or scaling correlations (see Peng et al. [Peng92]). A different attempt to establish fractal correlations in DNA base sequences was sensitive primarily to short-range differences in the occurrence probabilities of the four bases (see Jeffry [Jeff90]). Here, a new method of characterizing arbitrary symbolic sequences that does not introduce correlations between symbols is described. When applied to DNA sequences it confirms the ubiquity of low frequency, $1/f^\beta$ noise and the corresponding long-range fractal correlations, as well as prominent short-range periodicities. Moreover, averages over 5×10^7 bases from more than 25,000 sequences in ten classifications (primate, invertebrate, plant, etc.) of the

GenBank data bank [Bilo88] show systematic changes in correlations and the spectral exponent, β, with evolutionary category.

Random Processes, Spectral Density and Autocorrelation

A number of standard techniques for characterizing random processes, $X(t)$, and their correlations are familiar to physicists and mathematicians [Robi74; Reif65]. The *autocorrelation* or *pair-correlation* function, $C(\tau)$, is a quantitative measure of how the fluctuations in a quantity, $X(t)$, are correlated between times t and $t + \tau$

$$C_X(\tau) = \langle X(t) \times X(t + \tau) \rangle \tag{1}$$

where the brackets $\langle \ldots \rangle$ denote sample or ensemble averages.

The spectral density, $S_X(f)$, also provides information about the time correlations of $X(t)$. If $X(f)$ is the Fourier coefficient of $X(t)$ at frequency f

$$X(f) \propto \int X(t)e^{-2\pi i f t}dt$$

then

$$S_X(f) = \frac{|X(f)|^2}{\Delta f}$$

where Δf is the effective bandwidth of the Fourier integral.

$S_X(f)$ and $C_X(\tau)$ are not independent. In most cases they are related by the Wiener-Khintchine relations [Robi74; Reif65]

$$S_X(f) \propto \int C_X(\tau) \cos 2\pi\tau \, d\tau \tag{2}$$

and

$$C_X(\tau) \propto \int S_X(f) \cos 2\pi f \, df \tag{3}$$

Fast Fourier Transform (FFT) algorithms allow efficient direct computation of $S_X(f)$ directly from sample sequences and the estimation of $C_X(\tau)$ from $S_X(f)$ using Eq. (3).

Figure 1 displays samples of typical random functions and their spectral densities. The *white noise* $w(t)$ in Figure 1a is the most random. It is characteristic of a process that has no correlations in time. Its future is completely independent of its past, and $C(\tau) \propto \delta(\tau)$. Consequently, its spectral density, $S(f)$, equals a constant with equal power at all frequencies, f, like white light.

The integral of a white noise, $w(t)$, (or the summation of random increments) produces a *Brownian motion*, $X(t) = \int w(t)\,dt$ (or random walk), as shown in Figure 1c. $X(t)$ corresponds to the random diffusion of a particle, and the average distance traveled in a time, T, obeys the usual diffusion law

$$\Delta X(T) = \left\langle \left| X(t + T) - X(t) \right|^2 \right\rangle^{1/2} \propto T^{1/2}$$

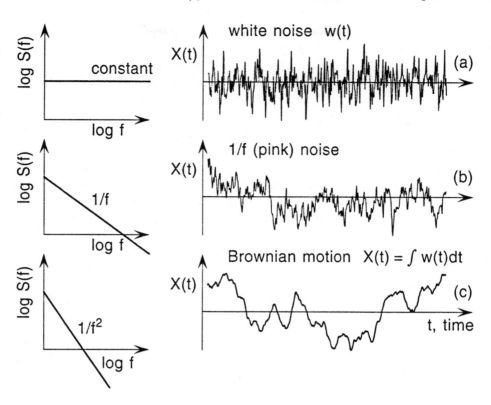

Figure 1. Typical noises and their spectral densities, $S(f)$.

Although $S(f) \propto 1/f^2$, and the appearance is much more correlated than a white noise, whether $X(t)$ increases or decreases in the future is independent of its entire past. Both the white noise, $w(t)$, and its integral, Brownian motion, are examples of true random processes with no (or trivial) dependence on the past.

$1/f$ Noise and Fractional Brownian Motion (fBm)

Although the white noise in Figure 1a and the Brownian motion in Figure 1c are well understood mathematically and physically, they are characteristic of relatively few naturally occurring fluctuation phenomena. Many natural time series look much more like the $1/f$ noise or *pink noise* in Figure 1b. A wide variety of measured quantities, from electronic voltages and time standards to meteorological, biological, traffic, economic and musical quantities, show measured $S(f)$ varying as $1/f^\beta$, with $\beta \approx 1$ over many decades (see [Voss92, 79, 78, 75] and Mandelbrot [Mand82, 69]). Such quantities represent fractal or *scaling* processes in time [Mand82]. In most cases, the physical reason for this long-range power-law behavior remains a mystery. Many physical processes and their mathematical models are characterized by a single correlation time, τ_0. In this case, $C(\tau) \approx$ constant for $\tau << \tau_0$, and $C(\tau) \approx 0$ for $\tau >> \tau_0$. $S(f)$ then takes a typical Lorentzian form that varies between white noise $S(f) \propto$ constant for $f << 1/\tau_0$, and a random walk, $S(f) \propto 1/f^2$ for $f >> 1/\tau_0$. Thus, physical processes with few characteristic times cannot generate $1/f$ noise.

As shown in earlier measurements of pitch and loudness fluctuations in music and speech [Voss88, 78, 75], $S(f) \propto 1/f$ seems to be associated with human communication. Although a white noise represents the maximum rate of information transfer, a $1/f$ noise, with its scale-independent correlations, offers much greater immunity to errors.

The most effective mathematical model for such scaling noises is *fractional Brownian motion*, or fBm, as developed by Mandelbrot and Wallis [Mand68]. fBm is a scale-independent extension to Brownian motion that allows the description and modelling of processes with infinite-range dependence on their past. Most approximations to random fractals are based on fBm [Voss85; Mand82, 68]. A fBm process, $X_h(t)$, is specified by the single parameter, h, in the range $0 < h < 1$ such that

$$\Delta X_h(T) = \left\langle \left| X_h(t+T) - X_h(t) \right|^2 \right\rangle^{1/2} \propto T^h$$

and a corresponding power law

$$S_h(f) \propto \frac{1}{f^\beta}$$

where
$$\beta = 2h + 1$$

Thus, as $h \to 0$ the fBm $X_h(t) \to 1/f$ noise. For $h = 1/2$, $X_h(t)$ becomes normal Brownian motion with the diffusive $\Delta X \propto T^{1/2}$ and $S(f) \propto 1/f^2$.

Correlations in Symbolic Sequences

The *spectral density* and autocorrelation methods described in the previous section on random processes are only applicable to numeric sequences. For non-numeric sequences, such as the four DNA bases, care must be taken to define corresponding procedures that do not make a priori assumptions about relations between the symbols. Assigning a specific number to each symbol $(A = 1, C = 2, \ldots)$ or representing each symbol as a displacement along a specific direction in a space with fewer dimensions than symbols (see Silverman and Linsker [Silv86]) introduces numeric correlations between the symbols. The following formalism allows spectral density, autocorrelation and cross-correlation measurements of symbolic sequences without introducing new correlations.

Consider a symbolic sequence $X_n, i = 1, 2, \ldots, N$ where each X_n consists of one of K allowed symbols. As a concrete example, $K = 4$ for sequences of DNA-base nucleotides (A, C, G, T). The standard definition of pair- (auto-)correlation, $C(\tau)$, in Eq. (1) requires a definition of multiplication ($\times$) for symbols. Without any assumptions about relations between different symbols, *equal-symbol multiplication* can be defined as

$$X_n \times X_m = \begin{cases} 1 & \text{if } X_n = X_m \\ 0 & \text{otherwise} \end{cases}$$

Further results can be simplified with the introduction of a binary indicator function, U_k, for each of the $k = 1, 2, \ldots, K$ allowed symbols. The U_k select the elements of X_n that are equal to symbol k

$$U_k[X_n] = \begin{cases} 1 & \text{if } X_n = k \\ 0 & \text{otherwise} \end{cases}$$

With this definition

$$X_n \times X_m = \sum_{k=1}^{K} U_k[X_n]\, U_k[X_m]$$

so $$C(\tau) = \frac{1}{N} \sum_{i=1}^{N} \sum_{k=1}^{K} U_k[X_n]\, U_k[X_{n+\tau}] = \sum_{k=1}^{K} C_k(\tau)$$

Here, $C_k(\tau)$ is the equal-symbol autocorrelation function for the individual symbol, k. $C_k(\tau)$ is the probability that $X_{n+\tau} = k$ if $X_n = k$ and is a measure of the correlations in symbol k at displacement τ. Since the spectral density, $S(f)$, is related to the pair-correlation, $C(\tau)$, by Eq. (2)

$$S(f) = \sum_{k=1}^{K} S_k(f) \tag{4}$$

where $S_k(f)$ is the equal-symbol spectral density of symbol k.

Thus, to study a symbolic sequence of N consecutive samples of the K allowed possibilities, first generate the binary sequence $U_k[X_n]$ corresponding to each of the K symbols. Each $U_k[X_n]$ identifies the position of symbol k in the sequence. A Fast Fourier Transform (FFT) routine yields the corresponding frequency components, $U_k(f)$, the individual $S_k(f) \propto |U_k(f)|^2$ and $C_k(\tau)$ from Eq. (3). Cross-correlation spectra, $S_{j,k}(f) \propto U_j(f) \times U_k(f)$ between different symbols j and k, can also be calculated.

Analysis of a Single Long DNA-base Sequence

The methods of the previous section on correlations in symbolic sequences can be illustrated with a single long sequence. This sequence has GenBank accession number X17403 [Bilo88] and consists of the 229,354 bases in the complete genome of the human Cytomegalovirus strain AD169 (see Chee et al. [Chee90]).

Figure 2 shows the corresponding four indicator functions, $U_k[X_n]$, for each of the DNA nucleotide bases ($k = A, C, G, T$) at different levels of averaging. The procedure of plotting the individual $U_k[X_n]$ next to each other graphically reveals many positive and negative correlations between different bases. At all scales the $U_k[X_n]$ are extremely irregular, and there is little change as the averaging is

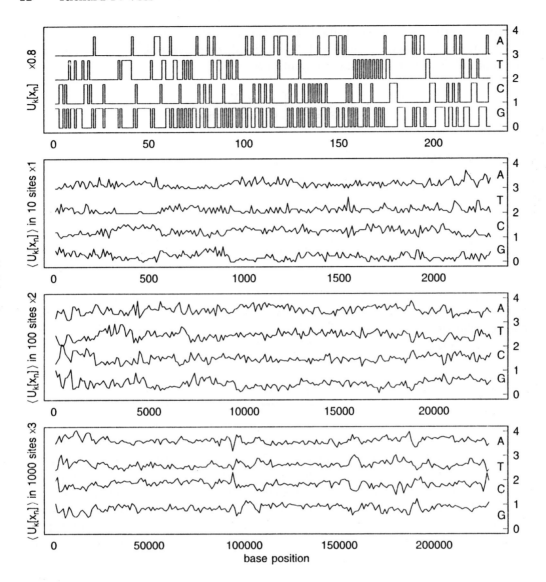

Figure 2. $U_k[X_n]$ for each of the DNA nucleotide bases ($k = A, C, G, T$). Successive curves show averages of $U_k[X_n]$ over 10, 100, and 1000 sites.

increased from 10 to 100 and 1000 sites. Moreover, the averaged $U_k[X_n]$ have a similar appearance to the $1/f$ noise of Figure 1b.

This similarity is confirmed by the measured equal-symbol, $S_k(f)$, shown in Figure 3. The entire sequence is divided into sections of size $N_{FFT} = 2^{16}$ for FFT transforms, and the results from individual transforms are averaged together. Such a log-log plot, in which the $S_k(f)$ are averaged over an effective bandwidth $\Delta f \propto f$, emphasizes the long-range scaling behavior (see Figure 3a). Although there are small differences between the different k, each of the $S_k(f)$ has the

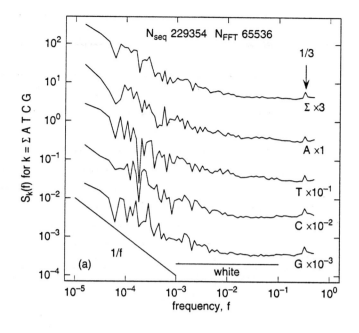

(a)

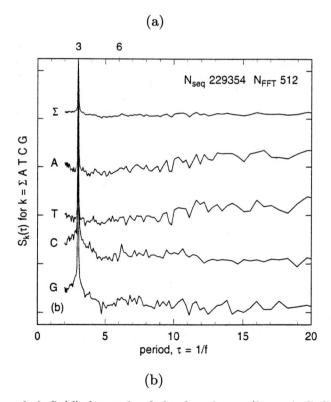

(b)

Figure 3. Equal-symbol $S_k(f)$ for each of the four bases ($k = A, C, G, T$) from the sequence in Figure 2. (a) log-log plot of $S_k(f)$ vs f; (b) linear plot of $S_k(\tau)$ vs $\tau = 1/f$. In both 3a and 3b, individual $S_k(f)$ have been offset for clarity.

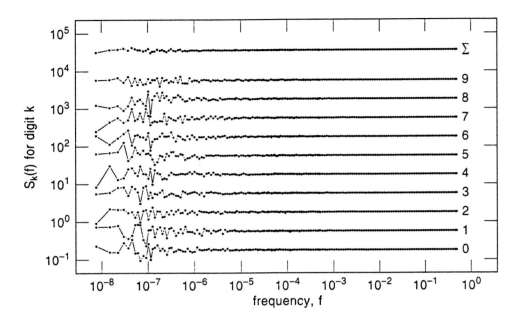

Figure 4. Equal-symbol $S_k(f)$ for the first 1.13×10^9 decimal digits of π.

same overall behavior. At large f (small displacement τ), $S_k(f)$ is dominated by the white noise characteristic of a random process. At low f (large τ), however, $S_k(f)$ shows a power-law scaling similar to $1/f$ noise. Figure 4 demonstrates that this low f $1/f^\beta$ behavior is not an artifact of the $S_k(f)$ measurements. Note that the decimal digits of π[†] form an excellent white noise source and show no evidence of correlations down to $f = 10^{-8}$.

The small averaged peak at $f = 1/3$ in Figure 3a appears in Figure 3b as an extremely large and narrow peak at period 3. This peak is probably related to the nucleotide triplet known as *codon* that codes one of 20 amino acids [Frie85]. $S_C(f)$ also shows a narrow peak at period 6. The small τ (large f) behavior is emphasized in Figure 3b, which shows linear plots of $S_k(f)$ vs period $= 1/f$, displaying short-range correlation. Some of the other peaks in Figure 3b may also be significant.

In many cases, $1/f^\beta$ noises can be studied over larger ranges by subtracting the high f white noise limit [Voss76]. This procedure assumes that the $1/f^\beta$ noise and the white noise are due to independent processes. The procedure is illustrated in Figure 5 with the $S_k(f)$ from Figure 3a. The minimum $\langle S_k(f) \rangle$, indicated by the *white noise limit* in Figure 5, is subtracted as background, $\Delta S_k(f) = S_k(f) - S_k(\infty)$ and reveals the long-range $1/f^\beta$ dependence. In all cases, the $1/f^\beta$ scaling extends over around three decades, from 100 bases to 100,000 bases. Differences in the spectral exponent, β, from least-squares fit

---

[†]First 1.13×10^9 decimal digits of π courtesy of David and Gregory Chudnovsky of Columbia University, personal communication.

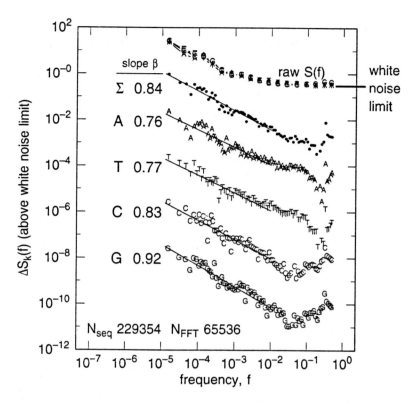

Figure 5. Equal-symbol $\Delta S_k(f)$ and $\Delta S_\Sigma(f)$ for the 229,354 bases in the complete genome of the human Cytomegalovirus strain AD169. Least-squares estimates of β are shown as solid lines.

are visible. For this sample, A is most correlated with T and C with G at low f. Similar $A - T$ and $C - G$ correlations are also found at the smallest period (highest f) in Figure 3b.

GenBank Category Averages

Although measured $S_k(f)$ from individual sequences as shown in Figure 5 demonstrate the existence of $1/f$ noise and long-range fractal correlations, there is considerable scatter about $1/f^\beta$. The large number of DNA sequences in the GenBank data bank provide an opportunity for statistical averaging. Moreover, the classification according to organism (mammal, invertebrate, plant, etc.) opens the possibility for examining changes in long-range correlation with the evolutionary category.

Figure 6 shows log-log plots of the equal-symbol $S_\Sigma(f) = \sum S_k(f)$ averaged over specific categories in the GenBank Release 68 data base. $N_{FFT} = 2048$ was used for the individual FFT's, and the average included all sequences in a given category longer than N_{FFT}. Sequences much longer than N_{FFT} contributed multiple samples to the average. As in Figure 5, the high f white noise limit to $S_\Sigma(f)$ was subtracted as background to extend the range of the least-squares estimate of β. Each $\Delta S_\Sigma(f)$ in Figure 6 was offset for clarity.

This category average significantly reduces the scatter about simple $1/f^\beta$ behavior at low f. Clear evolutionary trends in the spectral exponent, β, are visible. Both the range and accurate power-law dependence of many of the spectra in Figure 6 exceed published measurements of $1/f$ noise in physical systems (see [Voss79, 78, 76, 75; Mand82, 69]). The variations visible at high f are due to uncertainties in the white noise limit and local correlations.

The category average can also be applied to the small period (high f) variations as shown in Figure 7. Here $N_{FFT} = 512$, and again the spectra were offset for clarity. As in Figure 3b, the codon peak at period 3 is the most prominent feature, but the increased averaging allows small structures to be visible. For example, the peak at period 9 for *primates, vertebrates* and *invertebrates* is absent in the other categories.

Discussion

The individual base indicator function, $U_k[X_n]$, the corresponding individual equal-symbol spectral density, $S_k(f)$, and the sum $S_\Sigma(f) = \sum S_k(f)$ are powerful new tools for studying correlations in symbolic sequences. They have been applied here to both individual DNA-base nucleotide sequences and complete category averages from the GenBank data bank. In all cases, $S(f)$ shows a white noise limit with some sharp peaks at high f and a power-law $1/f^\beta$ dependence at low f. The most prominent peak at period 3 is believed to be related to the codon triplet for amino acids.

The $1/f^\beta$ behavior is the signature of fractal (scaling) correlations that extend to the largest sequences measured (of order 100,000 bases). Systematic changes in the spectral exponent, β, are most clearly seen in the category averages. Of the categories shown in Figure 6, the *bacteria* and *phage* categories show the smallest range of scaling behavior. For the remaining eight categories, there is a systematic increase with evolutionary status in β from the 0.64 for Eukaryotic *organelle* to the 1 (exact $1/f$ noise!) of invertebrates. This is followed by a decrease to 0.77 for primates. For β in the range 0 to 1, an increase of β increases the possibility of recovering from a DNA replication error but decreases the information content per unit length.

It is interesting to note the connection between the ubiquitous presence of $1/f$ noise in both music [Voss92, 88, 79, 78, 75] and DNA sequences. As emphasized by Gardner [Gard78], the early measurements of $1/f$ noise in pitch and loudness fluctuations in music [Voss78, 75] suggest that music is imitating the irregular but scale-independent fractal correlations of many natural processes. These new measurements lend support to a basis of music in nature.

There were previous attempts to connect genetic coding with music composition [Ohno86], but this work introduced spurious long-range correlations by

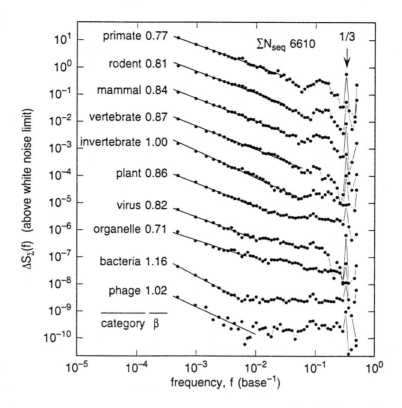

Figure 6. Equal-symbol $\Delta S_\Sigma(f) = S_\Sigma(f) - S_\Sigma(\infty)$ for categories of DNA-base sequences from the GenBank Release 68 data bank. Least-squares fits to $1/f^\beta$ and the resulting β are tabulated.

arbitrary octave shifts. Each base (A, C, G, T) was assigned some note *within an octave*. A specific music melody thus produced a unique (for this mapping) DNA sequence, but the reverse process was not unique. In mapping DNA sequences to melodies, the octaves were chosen to make the music *sound best*. As shown by Landini [Land90], this produced melodies with a $1/f$-like $S(f)$. This $1/f$ noise, however, was the result of human intervention in the choice of octave, not a property of the DNA $\to$ note mapping. In fact, for the length of sequences investigated [Land90; Ohno86] spectral analysis of an arbitrary numeric coding of the four bases (without octave shifts) yields white noise (and a disappointing composition).

Although the measurements presented here are quite striking, they represent only a beginning to the possible analysis of the expanding DNA sequence data bank. Numerous cross-spectra averages have already been measured, and graphic techniques are being developed to *highlight* specific correlations (long- or short-range) along the sequence.

Acknowledgments. The author wishes to thank Professor Avy Goldberg for posing the problem of fractal analysis of DNA sequences, for exposure to earlier

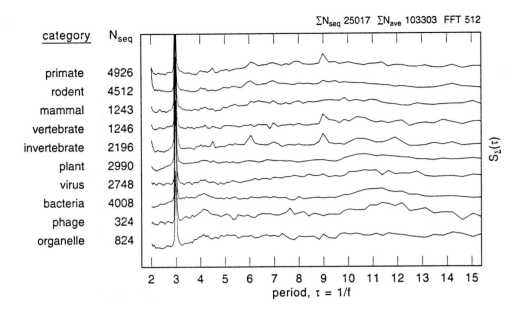

Figure 7. Equal-symbol $S_\Sigma(f) = \sum S_k(\tau)$ vs period $\tau = 1/f$ for specific categories of DNA-base sequences from the GenBank Release 68 data base.

work such as that by H.J. Jeffry [Jeff90] and for providing some initial sample DNA sequences for testing.

REFERENCES

[Bilo88]
   Bilofsky, H.S., and Burkes, C.,The GenBank (R) genetic sequence data bank, *Nucl. Acids Res.*, Vol. 16, pp. 1861–1864, 1988.

[Chee90]
   Chee, M.S., et al.,Analysis of the protein coding content of human cytomegalovirus strain AD169, *Curr. Top. Microbiol. Immunol.*, Vol. 154, pp. 125–169, 1990.

[Frie85]
   Friedland, P., and Kedes, L.H.,Discovering the secrets of DNA, *CACM*, Vol. 28, pp. 1164–1186, 1985.

[Gard78]
   Gardner, M.,White and brown music, fractal curves, and one-over-f noise, Mathematical games column in *Sci. Amer.*, Vol. 238, p. 16, 1978.

[Hamo83]
   Hamori, E., and Ruskin, J.,H curves, a novel method of representation of nucleotide series especially suited for long DNA sequences, *Jour. Biol. Chem.*, Vol. 258(2), pp. 1318–1327, 1983.

[Hamo85]
   Hamori, E.,Novel DNA sequence representations, *Nature*, Vol. 314, pp. 585–586, 1985.

[Jeff90]
Jeffry, H.J.,Chaos game representation of gene structure, *Nucl. Acids Res.*, Vol. 18, pp. 2163–2170, 1990.

[Land90]
Landini, G.,Private communication, 1990.

[Mand68]
Mandelbrot, B.B., and van Ness, J.W.,Fractional Brownian motion, fractional noises and applications, *SIAM Review*, Vol. 10, pp. 422–437, 1968.

[Mand69]
Mandelbrot, B.B., and Wallis, J.R.,Some long-run properties of geophysical records, *Water Resources Research*, Vol. 5, pp. 321–340, 1969.

[Mand82]
Mandelbrot, B.B., *The Fractal Geometry of Nature*, San Francisco: W.H. Freeman, 1982.

[Ohno86]
Ohno, S., and Ohno, M.,The all pervasive principle of repetitious recurrence governs not only coding sequence but also human endeavor in musical composition, *Immunogenetics*, Vol. 24, pp. 71–78, 1986.

[Peng92]
Peng, C.-K., Buldyrev, S.V., Goldberger, A.L., Havlin, S.,Sciortino, F., Simmons, M., and Stanley, H.E., Long-range correlations in nucleotide sequences, *Nature*, Vol. 356, pp. 168–170, 1992.

[Reif65]
Reif, F.,Irreversible processes and fluctuations, Chap. 15 in *Fundamentals of Statistical and Thermal Physics*, New York: Mc-Graw Hill, 1965.

[Robi74]
F.N.H. Robinson,*Noise and Fluctuations*, Oxford: Clarendon Press, 1974.

[Silv86]
Silverman, D.D., and Linsker, R.,A measure of DNA periodicity, *Jour. Theor. Biol.*, Vol. 118, pp. 295–300, 1986.

[Voss75]
Voss, R.F., and Clarke, J.,*1/f noise* in music and speech, *Nature*, Vol. 258, pp. 317–318, 1975.

[Voss76]
Voss, R.F., and Clarke, J.,Flicker (1/f) noise: equilibrium temperature and resistance fluctuations, *Phys. Rev. B*, Vol. 13, pp. 556–573, 1976.

[Voss78]
Voss, R.F., and Clarke, J.,*1/f noise* in music: music from 1/f noise, *Jour. Accous. Soc. Am.*, Vol. 63, pp. 258–263, 1978.

[Voss79]
Voss, R.F.,1/f noise: a brief historical review, *Proc. 33rd Frequency Control Symposium*, Atlantic City, Electronics Industries Assoc., Washington DC, 40–46, May, 1979.

[Voss85]
Voss, R.F.,Random fractal forgeries, in *Fundamental Algorithms for Computer Graphics*, Earnshaw, R.A., Ed., Berlin: Springer-Verlag, 1985.

[Voss88]

Voss, R.F.,Fractals in nature: from characterization to simulation, in *The Science of Fractal Images*, Peitgen, H.-O., and Saupe, D., Eds., New York: Springer-Verlag, 1988.

[Voss92]

Voss, R.F.,1/f noise and fractals in economic time series, to appear in *Proc. Workshop on Fractals and Computer Graphics*, Sakas, G., Ed., Darmstadt Germany, June 1991, Berlin: Springer-Verlag, 1992.

Fractal Geometry of Music:
From Bird Songs to Bach

Kenneth J. Hsü

Abstract

A parallelism of the fractal geometry of natural landscape and that of music suggests that music can be investigated through a visual representation of acoustic signals. The parallelism inspires us to make musical abstracts by scaling the original down to a half, quarter or eighth of its original length. An algorithm for music reduction has been devised. The self-similarity of Bach's music has been demonstrated by this analysis.

Bird songs, nursery rhymes and classical music are distinguished by their diatonic scale. Bird songs and nursery rhymes are not well-structured successions of tones, dominated by unison or seconds ($i = 0, 1, 2$). A proper combination of selected songs can, however, include enough variety to achieve a fractal geometry. The progress to baroque and classical composers is manifested by the approximation to fractal geometry in Bach's and Mozart's music, simulating the harmony of nature. This harmony is absent in modern music.

Physics of Music

Music is an art form, and art is, in the opinion of Frederick Schiller, an exclusive endeavour of homo sapiens. Yet birds do sing. Or do they?

Albert Einstein once commented that music consists of acoustic waves, which are definable by their frequency and amplitude. There are acoustic waves which are not music; how are such noises distinguished from music? Music is variously defined. The 'serialists', successors of Schönberg and Webern, attempted to define it as an ordered arrangement of single sounds of different frequency in succession (melody), of sounds in combination (harmony) and of sounds spaced in temporal succession (rhythm). Melodies are supposedly a series of single notes in orderly succession, deliberately rearranged according to a pattern from a preexisiting series that has been handed down by tradition and is accepted as a convention. Bird songs are composed by birds independent of human tradition. Are bird songs melodious? How do they differ from classical music? How do we describe the evolution from bird songs to nursery rhymes and from there to the fugues and sonatas of Bach and Mozart?

What are music notes? What kind of succession constitutes an orderly succession that can be described as melody? Is modern music melodious? Why do many of us get irritated by modern music? These questions my son Andrew and I have discussed at our dinner table ever since he became a music student.

Musicologists give an answer in precise language. In addition to arithmetic, geometry and astronomy, music was until the 17th century one of the four mathematical disciplines of the *quadrivium*. Music notes do not constitute a continuous spectrum of pitch or acoustic frequency; they are waves with only certain acoustic frequencies or pitches, so that the pitches of any two music notes have a ratio of two small integers. The cause of consonance, in terms of Aristotelian analysis, was stated to be *numerous sonorus*, or harmonic number. The pitch ratio of 2:1 producing an octave is one such harmonic number; this has been known since the time of Pythagoras in the 6th century B.C.

A music note has pitch, or acoustic frequency, f, defined by the relation

$$\frac{f}{f_0} = 2^{i/n} \tag{1}$$

where f_0 is the pitch of the base note and i and n are small integers. The choice of the f_0 is arbitrary; it can be chosen, for example, to represent the base-note pitch. Music notes are commonly equal geometrical divisions of an octave. In the evolution of the music of Western civilization the octave has, since 1800, been divided into 12 equal intervals. Thus, $n = 12$ and i is $1, 2, 3, \ldots, 12$. For each note which is an octave higher than a base note the value of i is 12, so that f/f_0 is 2, as observed experimentally.

In the early 18th century Johannes Sebastian Bach calibrated the intervals and produced an almost exact geometrically equal division of the octave. These 12 divisions are the frequencies produced by striking the 12 successive keys of a clavichord or harpsichord. Bach wrote *The Well-tempered Clavier* in 1722, including compositions in the 12 major and 12 minor keys to illustrate the musicality of this accurately calibrated scale.

The chromatic scale is the music of the West. Theoretically, it is not absolutely necessary to choose $n = 12$. The octave can be, and in some instances has been, subdivided by making $n = 3, 4, 5, 6, 8, 12, 16$, etc., but such tones sound strange to occidental ears.

Striking piano keys in succession produces tones or sounds with pitches in certain geometric ratios. A semitone is represented by $i = 1$, a full tone by $i = 2$, a small third by $i = 3$, a large third by $i = 4$, a fourth by $i = 5$, a diminished fifth (or enlarged fourth) by $i = 6$, a fifth by $i = 7$, etc., and an octave by $i = 12$. These note intervals, as indicated previously, have a ratio of small integers; they constitute the more sonorous tones. Others are represented by a ratio of larger integers. A diminished fifth ($j = 6$) is somewhat exceptional: it has a ratio of about 1000:705. This is not a ratio of small integers. This note interval has traditionally been considered dissonant and has rarely been used in classical compositions.

More sonorous notes are easier to produce. Vinzenzo Galilei, father of Galileo Galilei, found by experimentation that the octave can be produced through scaling the geometric dimensions of musical instruments according to a scale of 2^d:1 [Pali85]. It is 2:1 for string lengths ($d = 1$), 4:1 for weights attached to the strings, inversely related to the cross-sectional areas of strings ($d = 2$), and 8:1 in terms of volume of sound-producing bodies, such as organ pipes ($d = 3$). This experimental relation was later generalized by the French mathematician, Marin Mersenne, that the pitch for string vibrations varies directly with the square root of its tension, but inversely with its length. This law of pitch is a basic principle for making music instruments.

For the current analysis, it seems more appropriate to define melody as a succession of note intervals, e.g., C–E, E–G, etc., not as a succession of music notes, C, E, G, etc. The semitones, tones, thirds, fourths, fifths, etc. are the building blocks of music, not individual notes.

Can Birds Sing?

Biologists define bird-singing on the basis of a behavioral pattern: Birds are singing when they are perched on top of trees and make pleasant sounds [Koni85]. Songs are distinguished from calls by several criteria. In many songbirds only the sexually mature male sings during the breeding season, whereas most calls are produced by both sexes all year round. In most species song is the most elaborate vocalization. The delivery of songs is usually highly periodic and spontaneous, while calls may be produced at irregular intervals, often in response to specific stimuli such as predators. Highly stereotyped postures and movements accompany singing. Most calls are produced without such conspicuous involvement. Songs are species-specific, i.e., each species has unique songs. Playback of songs in the field shows that male birds defending their territories during the breeding season respond exclusively to the song of their own species. The study of song variations indicates that songs have characters both common and unique to different individuals. Some of the common properties are used for species recognition. Individual differences in songs vary conspicuously from one geographic area to another, while they are unusually homogeneous in each area. This phenomenon is known as 'song dialect'.

This description of bird songs is not a physical definition. Are bird songs music? After a century of investigation, and thanks particularly to the recording of bird songs, the answer is in part affirmative. Not all birds can sing; calls made by crows in response to outside stimuli do not constitute a succession of music notes arranged in intervals of the diatonic or chromatic scale. But many birds can sing; they produce sounds of definitive pitches, with the ratio of different pitches having musical intervals as defined by Eq. 1. Bird songs can be and have been transcribed by Heinz Tiesen as a series of music notes in the diatonic scale [Ties53]. Tiesen's favorite composers are blackbirds (*Turdus merula merula*). This musician and amateur ornithologist spent half a century collecting songs of blackbirds and identified more than 300 motifs. Their song vocabulary includes almost all the intervals of our diatonic scale. Another musician/ornithologist, Peter Szöke, has a partiality for great tits (*Parus major*) [Szok65]. His recording of their songs illustrates the complex motifs, including triad melodies familiar to many of us [Szok87].

What is the melodic structure of bird songs, and how is it different from folk songs, nursery rhymes and classical music?

Fractal Geometry of Music

As Freeman Dyson told us [Dyso78], "*fractal* is a word invented by Mandelbrot to bring together under one heading a large class of objects that have played an historical role in the development of pure mathematics. A great revolution of ideas separated the classical mathematics of the 19th century from the modern mathematics of the 20th century. Classical mathematics had its roots in the regular geometric structures of Euclid and the continuously evolving dynamics of Newton. A revolution was forced by the discovery of mathematical structures that did not fit the patterns of Euclid and Newton. These new structures were graded ... 'pathological', showing that the world of pure mathematics contains a richness of possibilities going far beyond the simple structures which they saw in Nature. Now ... Nature has played a joke on the mathematicians ... The same pathological structures invented to break loose from 19th century naturalism turn out to be inherent in familiar objects all around us."

Fractal geometry has been defined by the power function

$$N = \frac{c}{r^D} \tag{2}$$

where N and r are two variables related by the fractal relation, c is a constant of proportionality and D is the fractal dimension of the process [Mand77]. Mandelbrot coined fractal from the Latin adjective *fractus*, through a consideration that fractal dimension is almost always a fraction. The fractal dimension is, by definition, not a whole number, because the relation in that case would be represented by Euclidian geometry.

Equation (2) can be restated as

$$\log N = c - D \log r \tag{3}$$

This is, of course, the inversely linear log-log relationship discovered by geophysicists to relate the magnitude and frequency of earthquakes. Mandelbrot [Mand77] cited several examples to advance his postulate that fractal geometry is a manifestation of the harmony of nature. By that he meant that natural processes are not chaotic, nor are they deterministic or Gaussian. But they are statistically predictable according to the laws of fractal geometry.

Music has also been considered an expression of nature's harmony. Musical notes have been compared to elementary particles, and their relationships seem to bear a mysterious parallelism to the structure of the universe and seem to follow the same laws of thermodynamics as crystals, gases or any other measurable substance. Murchie once remarked that "a composer, then, need only to make the entropy (disorder) of his music low enough to give it some recognizable pattern, yet at the same time high enough for an element of suspense and individuality, and he may be well on his way toward a judicious compromise between the Scylla of wanton discord and the Charybdis of dull monotony" [Murc61]. This description of music was written before the publication of Mandelbrot's classic in 1977, otherwise Murchie almost certainly would have used the term fractal geometry, or $1/f$ noise, in place of the "judicious compromise between the Scylla of wanton discord and the Charybdis of dull monotony".

Voss and Clarke [Voss75] analysed acoustic signals produced by recordings of music. They found an approximate fractal distribution of loudness in Bach's first *Brandenburg Concerto*. The relative abundance, or the frequency of incidence, of notes of different pitch in music is, however, not fractal. This is not surprising, because music does not consist of notes of different pitch but of note intervals or changes in pitch. Voss and Clarke did note that pitch fluctuation is fractal, or that music has the same blend of randomness and predictability that is found in $1/f$ noise.

We undertook a preliminary study of the relative abundance of note intervals, $i = 0, 1, 2, 3, \ldots, 12$ in several musical compositions [Hsu90]. We chose for our first study a composition by Bach, the first movement of *Invention no. 1 in C Major*, BWV 772 (see Figure 1a). The percentage incidence frequency, F (%), of the note interval between successive notes was measured. To analyse the possible difference between the score for the right hand and the score for the left hand, both were analysed separately; the results show that there is no significant difference in the distribution pattern in the relation between F and i in the two-part scores [Hsu90]. This is easily understood, because Bach's music is polyphonic; each voice of the polyphone is given an equal role to express the motifs, or the musical landscape. Combining both sets of data, the F–i relation is

$$\log F = a - b \log i$$

Letting $a = \log c$ and $b = D$, we have

$$F = \frac{c}{i^D} \qquad (4)$$

This log-log inversely linear relation is an expression of fractal geometry. The relation is more or less valid for the interval $1 < i > 10$; the notable deviations from the plot are the deficiency of $i = 6$. Although the deviation is small it is nevertheless meaningful to a musician. The diminished fifth is an interval not represented by a ratio of small integers. The note is thus difficult to sing or play accurately on a string instrument. It used to be called a 'devil's note'. Composers of classical music thus consciously avoid this note.

We then analysed the first movement of Bach's *Invention no. 13 in A Minor*, BWV 784 (Figure 1b). This was chosen because Bach tried to impart to each of his 15 inventions a different character, and we wanted to explore the difference in structure underlying the different musical expressions. We again find the fractal relation given in Eq. (4). This relation is, however, only valid for the range $i > 3$ and is thus different from the pattern of the compositions which have fractal

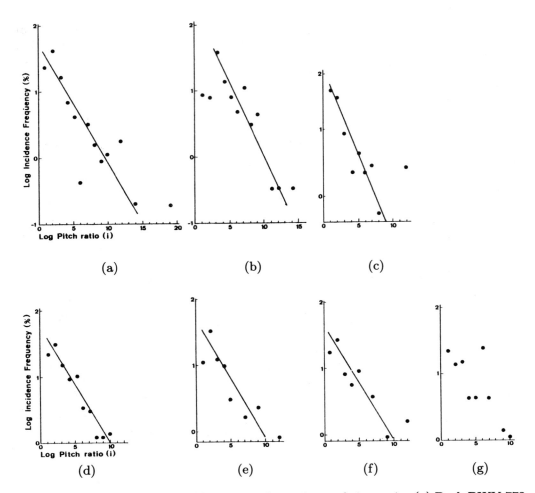

Figure 1. Fractal geometry of frequency of note intervals in music. (a) Bach BWV 772; (b) Bach BWV 784; (c) Bach BWV 910; (d) Mozart KV 533; (e) six Swiss children's songs; (f) Mozart KV 331; (g) Stockhausen's *Capricorn*.

relations valid for $i > 1$ or $i > 2$. The unusual deficiency of the full-tone interval small second ($i = 2$) is not neglected by chance but is a deliberate attempt by Bach to achieve a special effect through the establishment of the small third as the most frequent note interval. The excess of the sonorous fifth ($i = 7$), deviating significantly from the fractal relation, is also no accident.

The third composition chosen was the adagio movement of Bach's *Toccata in F-sharp Minor*, BWV 910 (Figure 1c). A log-log linear plot gives the same relation expressed above in Eq. (4) for $1 < i > 8$. The fractal relation is less perfect than that of BWV 772. The deviation from a perfect fractal can be considered a manifestation that the toccata is one of the most modern of Bach's compositions. The F/i plot has a pattern equally between classical music and modern atonal music. This adagio movement is particularly modern, in the sense that it seems to pose a question and to increase tension before the problem is resolved. This is apparently achieved through deviations from the fractal relation. There is, by the way, an unusually large amount of note repetition ($i = 0$); the excessive repetitions represent a musical technique designed to excite and to persist. There is a deficiency for $i = 4$. The intentional omission of the harmonious major third makes the toccata sound harsh and different. The structure indicates that Bach has intuitively found the right combinations of note intervals to achieve his goal.

Leaving Bach, we turn to Mozart and analyse the first movement of a sonata in F Major, KV 533; the results are shown in Figure 1d. In Figure 1, F is the percentage frequency of incidence of note interval i. The approximately linear log-log plots suggest a fractal geometry for this classical music. Significant deviations from the linearity have musicological significance. A fractal relation seems to be established for the interval $1 < i > 10$. A notable deviation is the excessive use of the note $i = 5$, the sonorous fourth, and a deficiency in the diminished fifth ($i = 6$).

To explore the structuring of simple music, we analysed six Swiss children's songs and group the results together in order to obtain significant statistics. The result is a less than perfect log-log inversely linear correlation of F and i, as shown in Figure 1e. A most notable feature is the excessive use of note repetition ($i = 0$). This seems to suggest that children's music tends to sail close to the Charybdis of monotony. Themes of folk songs often form the basis of classical compositions, such as the first movement of Mozart's *Sonata in A Major*, KV 331. We analysed the first part of this movement; the result is shown in Figure 1f. This composition is characterized by the same excessive note repetition ($i = 0$) as the children's songs, and the imperfect fractal relations of the two are amazingly similar (see Figures 1e and f). Not surprising is the total absence of the 'devil's note', namely, the diminished fifth ($i = 6$), in both compositions.

Another characteristic of Mozart's music, as distinguished from that of Bach, became very apparent when we made this analysis. Unlike Bach's compositions, where either the left-handed or right-handed piano score has a fractal geometry, the fractal geometry of Mozart depends upon a combination of both. This is a manifestation of the change of the polyphonic of the baroque period (1600–1760) to the homophonic music of the classical period (1750–1827). Motifs are carried by one of the voices in a symphonic composition, while the other(s) serve as accompaniment.

To illustrate the obvious difference between classical and modern music, we present our analysis of Stockhausen's *Capricorn* (see Figure 1g). No systematic trend in distribution of note intervals is apparent in the music by Stockhausen. Having been wrecked on the shore of Scylla of discord, there is no resemblance to fractal geometry in this work. The notable deficiency of the major third ($i = 4$) seems to continue a tradition initiated by Bach's *Toccata*. The extreme excess of the diminished fifth ($i = 6$) goes a long way towards making modern music atonal.

Voss and Clarke [Voss75] analysed the loudness of music and found an approximate fractal distribution of loudness in Bach's first *Brandenburg Concerto*.

They have, however, worked with an interpretation of Bach by a performer. Was that intended by Bach? One possiblility for evaluating the amplitude is to analyse the number of notes that are played simultaneously, because more notes sounding together should make the sound louder. We again chose Bach's *Toccata*, because four melodies are played simultaneously in that fugue. But we did not find a fractal distribution, which indicates that this is not an effective way of evaluating loudness. Recognizing, then, that the intensity of the sound is greatest when a note is first struck on a keyboard, we analysed the number of notes that are struck simultaneously and found an apparent fractal distribution of amplitude [Hsu90].

Scale Independency of Music

An anecdote has been told about the dialogue between Emperor Joseph and Mozart after the first performance of his *Abduction from the Seraglio*: The Emperor complimented the composer for the heavenly music but complained that it had too many notes. Mozart's reply was, of course, that not one note is dispensable. We agree that we cannot arbitrarily subtract a single note from the master's composition. Yet if we eliminate half the notes does the music still show some resemblance to Mozart's original composition? Can a musical composition be summarized by an abstract as is a literary composition?

Having established the fractal geometry of musical melody, is scale independency implied? In other words, can a musical composition with a fractal geometry be represented by a music score of a different scale, using a half, a quarter or twice as many notes. Emperor Joseph, if he chose, should have been able to listen to *Abduction* on a different scale based upon an abbreviated music score which contains a half or a quarter as many notes as Mozart's score.

Mandelbrot [Mand77] explained the phenomenon of scale independency by referring to map making. The outline of Spain is similar, regardless of whether it is made on a 1:1,000,000 or 1:2,000,000 scale. Yet the outline, as defined by the borders, does not have a definitive length; the length of a national boundary or a coastline is a function of the measuring unit. This now famous paradox of indeterminate length of state boundaries was first discovered by L.F. Richardson, a British physicist, who found to his astonishment that the lengths of the common frontier between Spain and Portugal, as reported in these neighbours' encyclopedias, differ by more than 20 percent (see Figure 2a). The common frontier between Spain and Portugal is 987 km according to a Spanish encyclopedia but is 1214 km according to a Portugese encyclopedia. The same boundary was surveyed. The discrepancy had resulted from the choice of the measuring unit, ϵ. In this case, this was the length of the chain link used in the surveying. Portugal, being a smaller country, chose a shorter chain to measures its border. The explanation is obvious: measurement by a shorter chain link follows zigzagging details of the border more faithfully. These details must be partly smoothed out when measuring with longer chains. The same relation holds for other linear features in nature, e.g., the length of a river or of a coastline. The relation of the measured length, $L(\epsilon)$, to that of the measuring unit, ϵ, is expressed by

$$L(\epsilon) = \frac{c}{\epsilon^D}$$

This is, of course, a manifestation of the fractal relation defined by Eq. (1).

Can we compare the fractal geometry of music to that of a coastline? If a coastline has no definite length, can we state that Mozart's music has no definite number of note intervals or tones? If the total length of a national border or a coastline, $L(\epsilon)$, is a function of the unit ϵ, is there a similar expression for music? After considerable investigation we suggest that the length of a music score, Σi, can be represented by the sum of all note intervals in a composition, i.e., all the primaries, seconds, thirds, fourths, ..., etc., with values of i equal to 1, 2, 3, 4, 5, ..., etc. The shortest beat of a composition can be considered the unit ϵ to measure the 'length' of the total intervals, i, of a music score. If the shortest 'length' is a sixteenth beat, we can measure the total interval by summing up the note intervals between successive sixteenth beats.

A comparison of the fractal geometries of landscape and of music suggests that music can be investigated through an optical representation of acoustic signals. In fact, conventional music scores are such a representation. The ups and downs of music notes can be compared to the rise and fall in topography, and the melody of a musical composition can be compared to the silhouette of a distant skyline. Now a silhouette can be represented by a scaled-down profile, while the profile, independent of its scale, portrays the original relief of the silhouette,

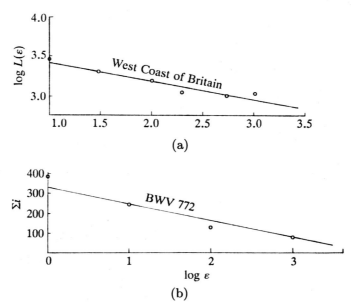

Figure 2. As a function of the 'yardstick' length we show (a) rate of decrease of coastline length $L(\epsilon)$; (b) decrease of musical note intervals.

even though much of the original detail cannot be represented by profiles on a very small scale.

This consideration of parallelism in visual and acoustic landscapes leads us to the possibility of abbreviating music. If a musical composition is an acoustic landscape, we should be able to scale the original down to a half, a quarter or an eighth of its original length and still obtain an abbreviation depicting a gross configuration of the original. An abstract of a creative literary work is, of course, never as good as the original, but the abstract serves its function. The fractal reduction of Bach or Mozart is certainly not intended to be new Bach or new Mozart, but the reduction can tell us something essential about the original which we might otherwise have overlooked.

To reduce the musical score by half we devised the following algorithm [Hsu91]:

Taking an existing music score, digitize the score with number codes, i, which represent the ratio of the pitch (f) of a note to a standard pitch (f_0) using Eq. (1)

$$\frac{f}{f_0} = 2^{i/n} \qquad (1)$$

In this case f_0 is chosen to represent the frequency of deepest C at 60 cps. The coded notes are plotted against time as expressed by successive beats. The digitized scores of Bach's *Invention no. 1* and *Invention no. 10* are shown in Figure 3.

Revise the digitized score so that each unit of the number codes represents the shortest note in that score, which can be, for example, a sixteenth note or sixteenth of a full beat. In that case a quarter note (of a minor third, $i = 3$, for example) in the music score is replaced by four successive sixteenth notes (of the minor third), etc.

After all notes are reduced to sixteenth notes, strike out every other note on the digitized score; the score is now reduced to half as many beats as in the original.

Revise the digitized score by combining the formerly divided notes. For example, the two remaining of the four successive sixteenth notes (of the minor third, for example) derived from an original quarter note are now recombined to form an eighth note (of the minor third) of the new digitized score. In other words, the original quarter note is converted into an eighth note in the reduced score.

Translate the digitized score into a conventional score. This is the half reduction.

The process is repeated to obtain quarter, eighth, sixteenth, ... reductions. The yardstick for the various reductions, ϵ, is thus expressed as a power function of 2^ϵ, with $\epsilon = 0, 1, 2, 3, \ldots$ representing zero, half, quarter, eighth, ... reductions of the beats.

Using this method and working again on Bach's music, notes are translated into visual signals (Figure 4). The 'irregularities' of the original music landscape are smoothed out through successive reductions. The total number of note intervals is correspondingly less. Take, for example, the first five notes of the BWV

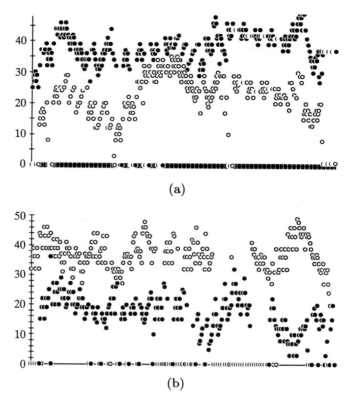

Figure 3. Digitized scores of Bach's (a) *Invention no. 1*; (b) *Invention no. 10*. ○, right hand; ●, left hand.

772 for the right hand (Figure 4a and b); the $\Sigma i_{\epsilon=0}$ value is $1 + 1 + 1 + 2 = 5$. The $\Sigma i_{\epsilon=1}$ value for the half reduction is, however, only $2 + 1 = 3$. For straight segments of the note variation, like a straight coastline, the measured length, Σi, is independent of the length of the yardstick, ϵ. For the irregular part, the measured length is smaller for larger ϵ values. The total sum of the note intervals, Σi, of Bach *Invention no. 10* is 391 intervals ($\epsilon = 0$). It is 243 intervals after a half reduction ($\epsilon = 1$), and 121 and 77 intervals for $\epsilon = 2$ and 3, respectively. The Richardson effect on BWV 772 is demonstrated by the relation

$$\Sigma i = \frac{c}{\epsilon^D} \tag{5}$$

as shown by Figure 2b, where D is a fractal dimension and c an empirical number.

Plotted in Figure 4 are the shapes of the 'reduced landscapes' of Bach's *Invention no. 1*, BWV 772, using $\epsilon = 0$ (original composition), 1, 2, 3, 4 and 5. The similarity in the landscape is shown clearly by Figures 4a–c, and broadly by Figures 4d–f. A half or quarter reduction gives an outline of the music as written by Bach. The reader can appreciate the scale independency in audio signals by playing the reduced scores on a piano. To a novice, the half or quarter

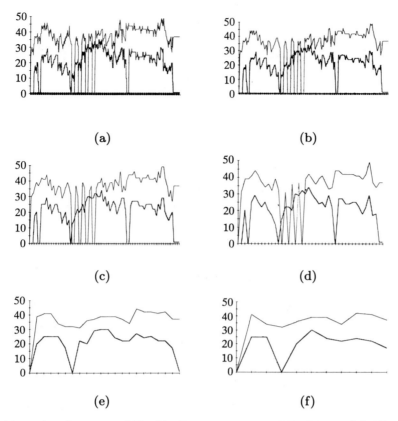

Figure 4. Fractal reductions of Bach's *Invention no. 1*, BWV 772. (a) The original; (b) 1/2 reduction; (c) 1/4 reduction; (d) 1/8 reduction; (e) 1/16 reduction; (f) 1/32 reduction of the score.

Bach sounds pretty much like Bach, although one notices that the composition has an economy of trills and ornamentations. Further reductions to an eighth, sixteenth and thirty-second tend to eliminate more and more of the "irregularity of the silhouette", yet the distinguishing broad outline of the musical landscape is preserved. A final reduction to a sixty-fourth gives only three notes; they are the three key notes, upon which the foundation of the whole composition is built.

Other aspects of fractal geometry have been called Noah's effect and Joseph's effect. Referencing the Bible, Mandelbrot used the term Noah's effect to denote that an event of great magnitude is extremely rare. The fractal geometry of the F–i relation discussed previously in Eq. (1) can be viewed as a Noah's effect. Tones of very large interval difference, such as sixth ($i = 9$) and seventh ($i = 11$), are rare compared to seconds ($i = 2$) and minor thirds ($i = 3$).

The Joseph's effect in fractal geometry refers to clustering: "There came seven years of great plenty throughout the land of Egypt. And there shall arise after them seven years of famine" (Genesis 41: 29–30). Mandelbrot [Mand77] showed on the basis of historical data that successive yearly discharges and flood levels of the Nile and many other rivers have an extraordinarily persistent pattern. The clustering of notes in music, as shown by Figure 4, can be considered a musical expression of the Joseph's effect.

We have so far chosen to make the music 'yardstick' a power of 1/2. For music such as waltzes with 3/4 rhythm, a one-third reduction is more appropriate than a half. We noticed this while experimenting with some of Chopin's études.

Self-similarity of Music

While performing a preliminary analysis we sample only one of several movements of the musical compositions selected. We recently made an in-depth study of Bach's *Invention no. 5*, BWV 776, and analysed the distribution of note intervals of the whole score. Figure 5 shows that a fractal relation between $2 < i > 8$ is more nearly perfect when more data are made available for statistical analysis. The relation is log-log inversely linear, because the interval i is a logarithmic expression of pitch. There is the usual scarcity of monotones ($i = 0$) and near-absence of the diminished fifth ($i = 6$). We have no adequate explanation for the relatively more frequent occurrence of the higher note intervals of the octave.

A most remarkable feature of the fractal geometry of nature is self-similarity. Headlands and coves are a scaled-down version of the coastline of peninsulas and bays. Branching trees find self-similarity in the veining of leaves. The self-similarity of the geometrical figures generated by the Mandelbrot set is truly amazing. The self-similarity of music is appreciated by musicians who recognize the structuring of a symphony on the basis of a few themes. The same self-similarity should be noticeable in a visual representation. In making a sixteenth reduction of BWV 776 we recognize a visual documentation of the self-similarity of music.

Using the methodology described previously, we made successive reductions of BWV 776. The digitized original score and the fourth reduction are shown in Figure 6. The general similarity of the two 'silhouettes' is self-evident, even though the sixteenth ($\epsilon = 4$) reduction seems to lose the details which are exhibited by the original. Yet the self-similarity becomes manifest when a sixteenth

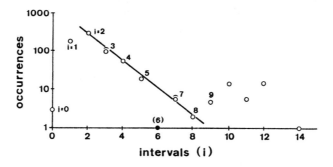

Figure 5. Frequency (F) distribution of various note intervals, Bach BWV 776.

reduction is plotted on the same time scale as that of the original. The six notes representing the last six bars of BWV 776 (see Figure 7) are the theme of this composition. In Figure 7 note that the theme of the last six bars as stated by the four black dots in the original score finds its self-similarity in the four black dots in a sixteenth reduction.

Fractal Geometry of Bird Songs

The melodious music of Bach and Mozart has a fractal distribution of tones, as indicated by the $F-i$ plots. What happens to the fractal geometry after reductions? The excellent fractal relation ($2 < i > 8$) of BWV 776 is rendered imperfect after a reduction by half. Notably there is a deficiency of major thirds and pure fourths, the components of triads, which are some of the most sonorous elements of classical music. The fractal geometry is increasingly affected by further reduction. This discovery leads us to speculate on the relation of the

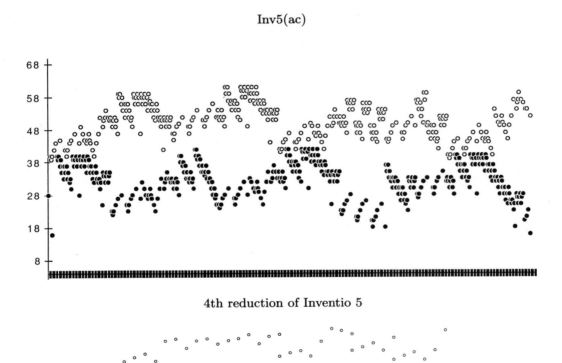

Figure 6. Digitized scores of Bach's *Invention no. 5*, BVW 776. The upper is digitized from the original score, and the lower is a fourfold (sixteenth) reduction.

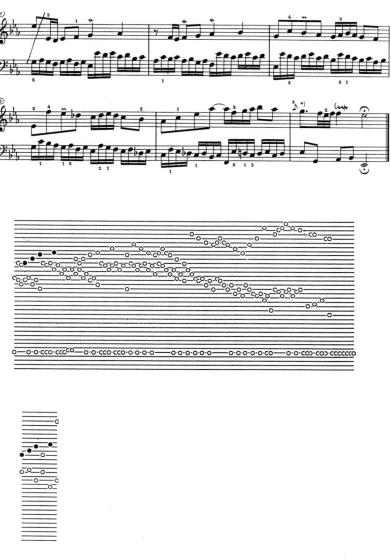

Figure 7. The last six bars of BWV 776: The music score (top) is digitized (middle) and then reduced to a sixteenth of its original length (bottom).

evolution of music to its fractal geometry. Has there been an increasing fractal geometry in the evolution of music from bird songs to nursery tunes to Bach and Mozart?

Do bird songs have a fractal geometry? We analysed the scores noted down by Tiesen and found that most bird songs are not characterized by a fractal relation. Harris's sparrow (*Zonostrichia querula*) makes sounds with unchanging steady pitch ($i = 0$). These monotones are the simplest form of music (see Szöke [Szok65]). Yellow hammers (*Emberisa citrinella citrinella*) seem to know only primary ($i = 0, 1$) and seconds ($i = 2$), and Cuckoos (*Cuculus canorus*

canorus) prefer minor thirds ($i = 3$) [Ties53]. Nightingales (*Luscinia megarhyn-chos megarhychos*) like to sing in unchanging pitch ($i = 0$) in especially regular rhythmic succession, and they often make pure semitones ($i = 1$) and major seconds ($i = 2$), and occasionally other intervals ($i = 3, 4, 5, 7, 9, 11, \ldots$). The precision of their pitch led some to consider them the greatest singers among birds [Ties53]. The predominance of sounds of unchanging pitch ($i = 0$) or seconds ($i = 1$, $i = 2$) is reminiscent of some children's nursery rhymes, but the melodic structuring is certainly not fractal, tending toward the Charybdis of monotony.

The veeries of North America (*Hylocichla fuscenscens*) seem to grope their way between discord and monotony, and their tones begin to approximate a fractal distribution. But the deficiency in the minor thirds is unmistakable. Yet the minor thirds, which are oddly missing in these good composers of bird songs, are the most common tones sung by cuckoos and some varieties of great tits. Black birds are Tiesen's favorite composers. Some have their songs dominated by intervals ($i = 0, 1$ and 2) interspersed with rare major thirds and pure fourths, the building blocks of triads, as well as minor and major sixths. The notable rarity of minor thirds ($i = 3$) and pure fourths render their compositions far from being fractal. Yet other blackbirds almost exclusively sing songs composed of major thirds, pure fourths and major sixths. A symphony of two varieties of blackbirds, accompanied by cuckoos or great tits, can have enough combination of tones to make a music of fractal geometry.

Self-affinity of Bird Songs

Birds sing very fast and at very high pitch, but their songs can be recorded, slowed down mechanically and transposed to a lower octave. Peter Szöke [Szok87] slowed down, or stretched, bird songs in tape recordings to 2, 4, 8, 16, 32, 64 or even 128 times the original duration. The tones are thus lower by 1, 2, 3, 4, 5, 6 and 7 octaves, respectively. The pitch of bird songs ranges from 2 to 6 kHz. A 4-octave reduction reduces the range of the pitch to about the 125 to 750 Hz range, well within the range sung by human voices. At the same time, a speed of 50–150 pitch modulations per second is reduced to 3 to 10 beats per second, about within the range of the fingering technique of a pianist. Using this technique, indistinguishable melodies can be transformed from their natural hidden form into folksong-like melodies. Their melodic structure bears considerable similarity to anthropomorphous music.

Our reductions of Bach have not changed the musical essence of Bach; Bach reduced in half still sounds like Bach. The slow down of bird songs has, however, changed them from harsh squawks to melodious music. This transformation is thus not self-similar but is a self-affine transformation. In this case, the scaling factors for different coordinates are not the same. We use this technique, for example, to construct three-dimensional topographical models of land in low relief. Often the hills and valleys of land in low relief are not obvious unless we have a 2x, 4x, 8x, ... vertical exaggeration. In the self-affine transformation of bird songs by Szöke [Szok87], the music landscape is changed from rugged Alpine topography to the rolling hills of Kansas. Through a vertical distortion of the scale, homo sapiens can see the music landscape of the birds.

Birds sing with different pitch and different speed of pitch modulation, probably because their life is much shorter than ours. If we use, for example, a 32-scaling factor for speed, a 10-second bird song sounds like a 5-minute first movement of a Bach concerto. Birds seem thus to have developed different 'hardware' than we have. While our neurophysiological system is tuned to pitches of hundreds of hertz, a bird's sensitivity to pitch is in the kilohertz range.

This leads us to a philosophical question posed by a Chinese philosopher, Zhuanzi, of the 5th century B.C. Is a daily lifespan of an insect comparable to that of an octagenarian? If birds have adopted a different time scale for their musical life, what is so absolute about the time scale adopted by homo sapiens, one of the millions of species of the organic world? Is this not an essence of the fractal geometry of time?

Inheritability of Musicality and Evolution of Music

Bird songs serve as a window to the auditory perceptual world. Species specificity and individual and populational difference in bird song development suggests an intricate relationship between genetic and environmental determinants. Bird songs, nursery rhymes and classical music are distinguished by their diatonic scale. Bird songs and nursery rhymes are not well structured; they are successions of tones, dominated either by unison or seconds ($i = 0, 1, 2$), or by note intervals of higher pitch. A proper combination of selected songs can, however, combine enough data to demonstrate a fractal geometry. The achievement of baroque and classical composers is manifested by the approximate fractal geometry of their music, simulating the harmony of nature. Or, as Voss said, "music is imitating the characteristic way our world changes in time".

A very significant discovery is the total lack or extreme rarity of the diminished fifth ($i = 6$) in bird songs, in nursery rhymes and in baroque and classical compositions; the 'devil's tone' did not become a favorite until the 20th century. Does not this suggest that the abhorrence of a frequency ratio not involving small integers goes back to the common ancestors of birds and mammals? Is our musicality not a product of cultural evolution but an inheritance from the far distant geologic time? Or is that a convergence in the evolution? Is the evolution of musicality a progress? Are we more musical than the birds?

The ability of songbirds to hear and learn new songs is amazing. Szöke [Szok87] illustrated with his recordings the songbirds' extraordinary speed of perception and their learning capacity. A hybrid young of a goldfinch and a canary was taught from a tape recording and quickly learned three different songs of a chaffinch in all their microacoustic detail. There is a trilling sound near the end of one song, for example, the natural speed of which is 150 pitch per second.

Szöke counted the pitch modulations of the original and the copy by slowing down the trill to 64 times its natural duration. It was a noteworthy achievement that the bird's ear and memory managed to faithfully acquire and reproduce the speed and shape of such a microacoustic trill. The feat is comparable to that told about Mozart, that when young he could memorize and write down the notes of an oratorio after first hearing it in a concert. If we define innate musicality as the ability to distinguish sounds of different acoustic frequency and to reproduce these sounds faithfully or in varied forms of pitch modulation, is homo sapiens, i.e., most of us who are not Mozart, more musical than finches?

If musicality has evolved in biologic evolution, what is its value in the struggle for existence? Bird songs play an important role in the scheme of Darwinian natural selection. Birds which can sing well should mate and multiply, and birds which cannot sing should leave no progenies. But what is the definition of a bird which can sing well? What is a definition of fitness in this survival of the fittest?

Tiesen [Ties53] considered interspecific comparisons meaningless. Nightingales are Carusos, known for their voice virtuosity; blackbirds are Strausses, famed for their compositions. Intraspecific comparisons have not been made. Species-specific songs throw a doubt on the assumption that one species of bird can be better composers than another. The comparative singing ability of nightingales has not been documented, although birds developed in acoustic isolation seem to have abnormal vocal development [Koni85]. But what is the survival value of musicality? If tone-deaf birds have the same genetic pool as the musical, their elimination from the general population should not influence the evolutionary drift.

What indeed is the survival value of musicality? I was told only dolphins and bats, in addition to birds and homo sapiens, can sing. Why can our nearest kin, the monkey, not sing? Why should the genes, the DNA sequencings, giving an organism the ability to discriminate musical pitches, remain dormant for so many generations of cladistic development until they resurface again with the rise of man?

Acknowledgments. This work is a summary of the cooperation by two amateurs in an interdisciplinary area neglected by the musicology establishment. We have been encouraged by discussions and correspondence with numerous friends and colleagues: Benoit Mandelbrot, Dieter Imboden, Erwin Engeler, Don Turcotte, Barclay Kamb, Kurt Schillenghuber, Georg Ligeti and others. They are expert mathematicians or accomplished musicians, but all disclaim an expertise in the fractal geometry of music. We are indebted to Christine Hsü for her help in analysing the fractal geometry of bird songs, and to Mark Konishi, Professor of Behavior Biology at Cal Tech, Pasadena, CA, for his enlightening information on songbirds.

References

[Dyso78]
Dyson, F., Characterizing irregularity, *Science*, Vol. 200, pp. 677–678, 1978.

[Hsu90]
Hsü, K.J., and Hsü, A.J., Fractal geometry of music, *Proc. Natl. Acad. Sci. (USA)*, Vol. 87, p. 938, 1990.

[Hsu91]
Hsü, K.J., and Hsü, A.J., Self-similarity of the $1/f$ noise called music, *Proc. Natl. Acad. Sci. (USA)*, Vol. 88, p. 3507, 1991.

[Koni85]
Konishi, M., Birdsong: From Behavior to neuron, *Ann. Rev. Neurosci.*, Vol. 8, p.125, 1985.

[Mand77]
Mandlebrot, B.B., *The Fractal Geometry of Nature*, New York: W.H. Freeman, 1977.

[Murc61]
Murchie, G., *Music of the Spheres*, Vol. II, *The Microcosm*, New York: Dover, p. 397, 1961.

[Pali85]
Palisca, C.V., *Humanism in Italian Renaissance Musical Thought*, New Haven, CT: Yale Univ. Press, p. 276, 1985.

[Rich61]
Richardson, L.F., The problem of contiguity: An appendix to 'The statistics of deadly quarrels', *General Systems Yearbook*, Vol. 6, pp. 139–187, 1961.

[Szok65]
Szöke, P., A madárhang mikrovilága éo biomuzikális természete, Elövilág (Budapest, Hungary) Vol. 10, p. 205, 1965.

[Szok87]
Szöke, P., The Unknown Music of Birds, an ornithomusicological record, made by HUNGAROTON MHV, RΘvai Nyomda, Budapest, Hungary, 1987.

[Ties53]
Tiesen, H., *Musik der Natur*, Zurich: Atlantic Musikbuch, 1953.

[Voss75]
Voss, R.F., and Clarke, J., '$1/f$ noise' in music and speech, *Nature (London)*, Vol. 258, pp. 317–318, 1975.

2D and 3D Modelling of Marine Sessile Organisms

Jaap A. Kaandorp

Abstract

In this paper the development of a model for simulating radiate accretive growth in 3D is discussed. This growth process is widely found among members of various classes of marine sessile organisms. The model is developed using an existing 2D model for radiate accretive growth by extending a subset of the rules to 3D. The 2D as well as the 3D model are based on an iterative geometric construction. The final 3D model is suitable for the simulation of the emergence of branching growth forms.

Introduction

Radiate accretive growth is defined as an iterative growth process in which layers of material are added externally to the tip of a preceding growth step, which remains unchanged in the next growth steps. In this process the thickness of the layers is highest at a minimal angle between a tangential element and an axis of growth (see Figure 1) and decreases towards the sides of the tip. In this way a typical radiate architecture is formed, where the longitudinal elements (the ascending lines in Figure 1) are set perpendicular to the preceding tangential elements (the growth lines in Figure 1). This type of growth is found among members of various groups of modular [Harp86] and sessile marine organisms, e.g., stony-corals [Grau82] and sponges [Kaan91b].

A typical characteristic of many modular organisms is that they often exhibit a wide range of growth forms, caused by differences in the physical environment. It is often possible to arrange the growth forms along a physical gradient; the forms gradually transform into each other with the changing environmental parameter. An example of such a range, of a modular organism with radiate accretive growth, is shown in Figure 2. Basically, the growth forms of the displayed species, the sponge *Haliclona oculata*, range from quite regular, thin-branching to irregular plate-like forms. The thin-branching form is typical for sheltered conditions, while the plate-like form is found under conditions with more exposure to water movement [Kaan91b].

The growth process of an organism with radiate accretive growth can be simulated with a 2D model in which the structure formation as seen in a longitudinal

Figure 1. Longitudinal section through a branching organism with radiate accretive growth. The layers of material added in the growth process are visible as growth lines.

section (see Figure 1) is modelled. In this paper only a brief outline of the 2D model is given; a more detailed description of the 2D model is found in [Kaan92b, 91a], while a more extensive biological discussion of the model is presented in [Kaan92a, 91b]. The biological significance of all steps and assumptions in the model is only indicated briefly. The outline of the 2D model is restricted by rules which are extended in the 3D model, where the complete formation of a radiate accretive architecture is simulated. Some aspects of the growth process are simulated with a 2D model; a more realistic simulation is only adequately done with a 3D model.

The tangential and longitudinal elements in an organism with radiate accretive growth are consolidated in a 3D network with a layered structure. The 3D mesh in a tip of such an organism possesses a radial symmetry; a longitudinal section (as in Figure 1), parallel to the axis of the tip, always shows about the same structure. The tips, however, may only be somewhat flattened (Figure 2c). Although this structure emerges in taxonomically very different organisms and consists of chemically very different materials, there is another essential correspondence.

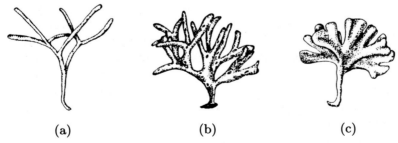

(a)   (b)   (c)

Figure 2. Range of growth forms of the sponge *Haliclona oculata*, found along an environmental gradient. In the range A–C the exposure to water movement increases.

The surfaces of the growth layers are often simplified as a regular tessellation using pentagons and hexagons. Examples of tangential views of organisms with radiate accretive growth are depicted in Figure 3. In Figure 3a the surface of the sponge *Haliclona simulans* is shown, the surface of this species is tessellated with triangles, which again can be considered organized in pentagons and hexagons. In Figure 3b such a penta-hexagonal organization for the stony-coral *Montastrea annularis* is shown, the same tangential structure is found in many other organisms with radiate accretive growth (e.g. *Haliclona oculata*, see [Kaan92a]). The formation of this generic structure, found in very different taxonomically groups, is the principle of the 2D and 3D model discussed in this paper.

A 2D Model for Radiate Accretive Growth

The growth process of an organism with radiate accretive growth, in two dimensions, can be modelled as an iteration process (see Figure 4) in which the formation of the skeleton, as seen in a longitudinal section, is simulated. The growth lines, the tangential elements of the object, correspond to the projections of the tangential tracts in Figure 1 on the plane of the longitudinal section. In the 2D simulation, the tangential elements are situated on growth lines of the object. The longitudinal elements correspond to the ascending lines in Figure 1. In each iteration step a layer consisting of new longitudinal elements (perpendicular to the preceding layer of tangential elements) and new tangential elements (the new surface of the object) is constructed.

The length, l, of new longitudinal elements is calculated in Eq. (1) and consists of the product of four functions

$$
l = \begin{cases} sf(\alpha)\, h(rad\_curv)\, l(\theta)\, k(c) & \text{for} \quad f(\alpha)\, h(rad\_curv)\, l(\theta)\, k(c) > \\ & \qquad\qquad\qquad\quad inhibition\_level \\ 0 & \text{for} \quad f(\alpha)\, h(rad\_curv)\, l(\theta)\, k(c) \leq \\ & \qquad\qquad\qquad\quad inhibition\_level \end{cases} \tag{1}
$$

All functions return values in the range 0–1.

The argument α in function f represents the angle between an axis of growth (see dotted lines in Figure 4) and a tangential element

$$
f(\alpha) = \begin{cases} 1 & \text{for } \frac{\pi}{2} \leq \alpha \leq \left(\frac{\pi}{2} + \frac{\pi}{n} \right) \\ sin\left(\dfrac{\frac{\pi}{2}}{\frac{\pi}{2} - \frac{\pi}{n}} \right)(\pi - \alpha) & \text{for } \left(\frac{\pi}{2} + \frac{\pi}{n} < \alpha \leq \pi \right) \end{cases}
$$
$$
n > 2 \tag{2}
$$

When α is $\pi/2$ or slightly higher (as determined by the constant n in Eq. 2), l attains its maximum value. The constant, n, represents a widening factor in the function f, without which a column-like object is generated by the iteration

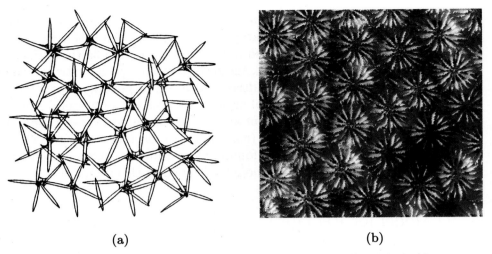

(a)   (b)

Figure 3. Tangential views of (a) the arrangement of skeleton elements in the sponge *Haliclona simulans* ([deWe86]); (b) the stony-coral *Montastrea annularis*, depicted showing a penta-hexagonal organization of the basic building elements (the corallites).

process. Tangential sides towards the sides of the branches of the object have a larger value for α, and thus l decreases.

The argument *rad_curv* in the function h represents the radius of curvature formed by points situated on neighbouring tangential elements. This parameter expresses the amount of contact of the elements with the environment. When *rad_curv* exceeds a certain maximum value, *max_curv*, the value of l decreases and two local maxima values for l emerge. In the simulations, various values for

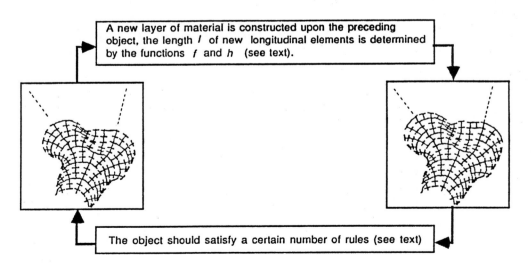

Figure 4. Iteration process in which the growth of an organism with radiate accretive growth is modelled.

max_curv and a single constant value for *min_curv* are used, e.g.

$$h(rad\_curv) = 1 - \frac{(rad\_curv - min\_curv)}{(max\_curv - min\_curv)} \quad \text{for } min\_curv \le$$
$$rad\_curv \le max\_curv$$
$$h(rad\_curv) = 1 \qquad\qquad\qquad \text{for } rad\_curv < min\_curv$$
$$h(rad\_curv) = 0 \qquad\qquad\qquad \text{for } rad\_curv > max\_curv$$

$$(3)$$

The functions $l(\theta)$ and $k(c)$ represent the influence of the physical environment on the growth process. In the function $l(\theta)$ the influence of the light intensity is modelled, while in $k(c)$ the influence of the local nutrient distribution is simulated. In the 2D and 3D models presented in this paper the influence of the physical environment is not discussed. A more detailed discussion of the introduction of the functions $l(\theta)$ and $k(c)$ in the two-dimensional model is found in [Kaan92b]. These functions remain constant and are set to the value 1 in the simulated 2D and 3D forms. The values s and *inhibition_level* in Eq. (1) are constants. s is the size of a tangential element, and *inhibition_level* is the minimal length of a longitudinal element.

In the iteration process four rules are applied. The first states that the tangential elements should be interconnected (continuity rule). The second states that as soon as the distance between neighbouring tangential elements becomes too large, new elements are inserted (insertion rule). Without these two rules, the coherence between the elements in the objects is soon lost in subsequent iteration steps. In the third rule, the most protruding points of the object develop new growth axes (association rule). Protrusions arise when *rad_curv* exceeds the maximum value *max_curv*, as mentioned previously. The result is that, in the examples shown in this paper, an old axis is replaced by two new axes (see Figure 5). The last rule states that branches may not intersect each other (non-intersection rule). Two more evolved examples of the iterative construction from Figure 4 are shown in Figure 6. In Eq. 3, a larger value for *max_curv* is applied for the object in Figure 6b than for that in Figure 6a.

A 3D Model for Radiate Accretive Growth

The triangles in the tangential view in Figure 3a can be thought to be arranged in, predominantly, pentagons and hexagons. In some cases, seven or eight spicules meet in one point, and septagons and octagons are formed. In an idealized version of the triangular network, it is transformed into a network of five- or six-sided polygons by removing some of the skeleton elements which meet at one point. The result of this transformation is a *Haliclona oculata*-like network (see [Kaan91b]).

As becomes clear in the next sections, *Haliclona simulans* is a good case study for a model where the objects are represented in the iteration process by layers of

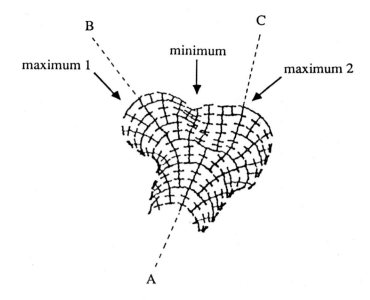

Figure 5. Development of new growth axes in the model.

triangular tessellations. The layered triangular tessellation is a suitable subject to mimic in a simulation model. This layered structure is used as a basis to model a layered penta-hexagon tessellation, which serves as a general model for organisms with radiate accretive growth.

REPRESENTATION OF A MULTILAYER TRIANGULAR TESSELLATION

An example of a layered system, where a triangular tessellation is constructed upon another triangular tessellation, is shown in Figure 7. The edges of the triangles are situated at the surface of the layers. These edges are indicated as

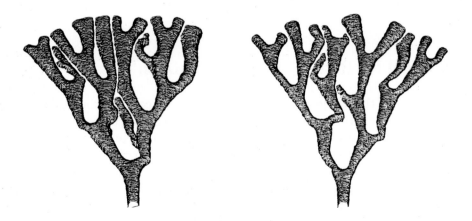

Figure 6. Two more evolved examples of the iterative construction from Figure 4.

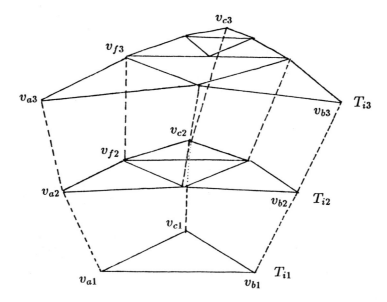

Figure 7. A layered system, where a triangular tessellation is constructed upon another triangular tessellation.

the tangential elements of the layered structure. The indices of the vertices are represented as a list of vertex index lists

$$
V = \begin{cases}
v_{11}, v_{21}, \ldots \\
v_{12}, v_{22}, \ldots \\
. \\
. \\
. \\
v_{1m}, v_{2m}, \ldots
\end{cases}
\tag{4}
$$

where each index refers to a corresponding list of coordinate lists. The tessellated layers are represented in a list of triangle lists

$$
T = \begin{cases}
T_{11}, T_{21}, \ldots \\
T_{12}, T_{22}, \ldots \\
. \\
. \\
. \\
T_{1m}, T_{2m}, \ldots
\end{cases}
\tag{5}
$$

Each triangle, T_{ij}, from T is represented in the form of Eq. (6). In this representation the indices of the neighbouring triangles are also included. Its neighbours are identified by

$$
T_{ij} = \left((v_{aj}, v_{bj}, v_{cj}), (T_{aj}, T_{bj}, T_{cj}), (parent1, parent2, level) \right)
$$
$$
v_{aj}, v_{bj}, v_{cj} \in V
$$

triangle T_{aj} borders at edge (v_a, v_b)

triangle T_{bj} borders at edge (v_b, v_c)

triangle T_{cj} borders at edge (v_c, v_a)

$$T_{aj}, T_{bj}, T_{cj}, parent1, parent2 \in T \tag{6}$$

Triangle T_{ij} is described in Figure 8. The indices of the surfaces are underlined, and the indices of the vertices of triangle T_{aj} bordering on T_{ij} are arranged opposite to the vertices in T_{ij}. There are three possible arrangements for the vertices in T_{aj}: v_{bj}, v_{aj}, v_{dj}; v_{aj}, v_{dj}, v_{bj} and v_{dj}, v_{bj}, v_{aj}. The arrangement of the vertices is indicated in the diagram with an arrow. The first edge of a triangle is displayed with an arrow and a line. By consistently ordering the vertices in the triangles, we define the normal vector of each triangle unambiguously. When T_{aj}, T_{bj} or T_{cj} equals *null* in Eq. (6), the edge (v_{aj}, v_{bj}), (v_{bj}, v_{cj}) or (v_{cj}, v_{aj}) does not border on another triangle. In the representation of Eq. (6) we easily identify the neighbours of triangle T_{ij} in a mesh of triangles and determine the set of triangles surrounding a vertex of triangle T_{ij}. The set of triangles surrounding

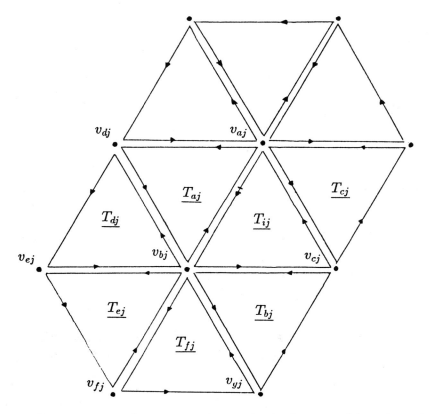

Figure 8. Diagrammatic description of triangle T_{ij} from Eq. (6). The indices of the surfaces are underlined.

the vertex v_{bj} is denoted as $st(T_{ij}, v_{bj})$, the set of vertices surrounding the vertex v_{bj} as $sv(T_{ij}, v_{bj})$, i.e.

$$st(T_{ij}, v_{bj}) = \{T_{ij}, T_{aj}, T_{dj}, T_{ej}, T_{fj}, T_{bj}\}$$
$$sv(T_{ij}, v_{bj}) = \{v_{bj}, v_{aj}, v_{cj}, v_{dj}, v_{ej}, v_{fj}, v_{gj}\} \qquad (7)$$

In the representation of Eq. (6) it is possible to subdivide the triangle into new triangles while leaving the neighbours unchanged. The necessity to create a mesh in which triangle T_{ij} is subdivided in smaller triangles while one or more neighbours remain(s) unchanged occurs when an additional condition is applied which states that the edges of T_{ij} can only vary between two limits, i.e.,

$$0.5s \leq d(v_{aj}, v_{bj}) \leq 1.5s$$
$$0.5s \leq d(v_{bj}, v_{cj}) \leq 1.5s$$
$$0.5s \leq d(v_{cj}, v_{aj}) \leq 1.5s \qquad (8)$$

When T_{ij} is enlarged and all edges exceed $1.5s$, it is necessary to subdivide T_{ij} into four new triangles; a situation as described in Figure 9 might then occur.

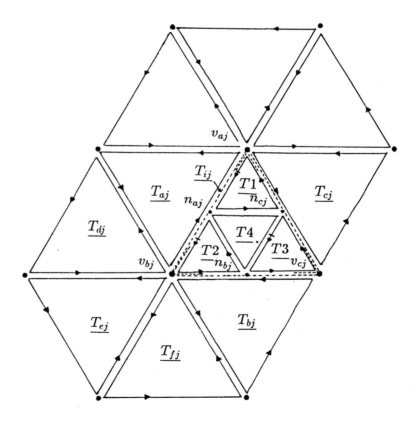

Figure 9. Diagrammatic description of triangle T_{ij} after subdivision into four children, $T1_{kj} \ldots T4_{k+3,j}$. The representation of the parent and children triangles are given in Eqs. (10) and (9).

The parent triangle, T_{ij}, is split up into four children, $T1_{kj} \ldots T4_{k+3,j}$. Three new points, n_{aj}, n_{bj}, n_{cj}, are added to vertex indices lists, V.

A representation of a child, $T1_{kj}$, is

$$T1_{kj} = \big((v_{aj}, n_{aj}, n_{cj}), (null, T4_{k+3,j}, null), (T_{ij}, T_{k+4,j}, 0)\big) \quad v_{aj}, n_{aj}, n_{cj} \in V$$
$$\text{triangle } T4_{k+3,j} \text{ borders at edge } (n_{aj}, n_{cj}) \quad T4_{k+3,j}, T_{ij}, T_{k+4,j} \in T$$

$$(9)$$

Triangle $T1_{kj}$ shares an edge with triangle $T4_{k,j+3}$; the other edges are shared with no other triangles. The nonexisting neighbours are indicated with the value null in the second triplet. In the description of $T1_{kj}$, a reference to its parent, T_{ij}, is included. The last number indicates that $T1_{kj}$ is a zero-level triangle which is not further subdivided.

A representation of the parent, T_{ij}, is

$$T_{ij} = \big((T1_{kj}, T2_{k+1,j}, null), (T_{aj}, null, null), (null, null, 1)\big)$$
$$\text{triangle } T_{aj} \text{ borders at edge } (v_{aj}, v_{cj}) \quad T1_{kj}, T2_{k+1,j}, T_{aj} \in T \quad (10)$$

The indices in the first triplet indicate that T_{ij} is composed of two triangles, $T1_{kj}$ and $T2_{k+1,j}$. The second triplet shows that the parent triangle T_{ij} borders on triangle T_{aj}. The last triplet indicates that the parent T_{ij} is not enclosed in any other parent triangle, and that T_{ij} is only subdivided one time (level 1). In the representation of the child triangle (Eq. 9) we see that the zero-level triangle, $T1_{kj}$, is enclosed in two level-1 parent triangles, T_{ij} and $T_{k+4,j}$.

With the representation

$$T_{ij} = \begin{cases} \text{for } level = 0 \\ (\{set\ of\ 3\ vertex\ indices\}, \{set\ of\ 1-3\ neighbours\}, \\ \quad \{set\ of\ 0-2\ parents\}, level) \\ \text{for } level > 0 \\ (\{set\ of\ 2\ children\ and\ 1\ null\}, \{set\ of\ 1\ neighbour\ and\ 2\ nulls\}, \\ \quad \{set\ of\ 0-2\ parents\}, level) \end{cases}$$

$$(11)$$

it is possible to create a hierarchical description of a triangular mesh, where a triangle can be subdivided n times (see also [DeFl89]). The vertex and triangle indices of the parent, T_{ij}, can be arranged in a hierarchical structure.

In Figure 7 the layer T_{i3} is constructed upon T_{i2} and T_{i2} upon T_{i1}. In the same sequence, the total number of vertex indices for each layer increases. Between some of the vertices there is a straight correspondence. For example, the vertices v_{a3}, v_{b3} and v_{c3} in layer T_{i3} seem to be derived from v_{a2}, v_{b2} and v_{c2} during the construction of T_{i3} upon T_{i2}. The vertices of triangle T_{a3} emerge in the construction, with no straight correspondence with vertices in layer T_{i2}. The connections between corresponding vertices are visualized in Figure 7 as dotted lines. These connections are indicated as the longitudinal elements.

In the representation of Eq. (11) one can find the neighbours of a given triangle in the multilayered structure. The (possibly existing) corresponding triangle in the succeeding and preceding layer can be detected without traversing all vertex index lists.

AN ITERATIVE GEOMETRIC CONSTRUCTION SIMULATING THE RADIATE ACCRETIVE GROWTH PROCESS IN 3D

In 3D models for radiate accretive growth the method for multilayered triangular tessellations discussed previously is used to represent the objects in the iteration process. In the model a skeleton structure, such as found in *Haliclona simulans* (see Figure 3a), is simulated. A layer consisting of a triangular tessellation is constructed upon a preceding layer. In this simulation model the tangential elements of *Haliclona simulans* are represented as tangential edges with an approximately constant size, while the longitudinal elements are mimicked as edges with a variable length (see Figure 4). The multilayered structure is an imitation of the structure of *Haliclona simulans*. It can be transformed into a multilayered structure of pentagons and hexagons. This structure serves as a more general model for organisms with radiate accretive growth.

The Initiator

A triangulated sphere is used as initiator for the iterative geometric constructions shown here. The triangulated sphere can be derived from the icosahedron, in which all vertices are situated on the surface of a sphere. When the triangles of the icosahedron are subdivided into four new triangles (as in Figure 9) and the resulting new vertices projected onto the sphere, exactly enclosing the original icosahedron, a series of triangulated spheres is obtained. In this series (see Figure 10) the triangles of a triangulated sphere are subdivided further. These subsequent subdivisions of the icosahedron serve as initial polyhedrons for the iteration process. The original icosahedron is shown at the left side of the picture. The series of triangulated spheres is also known as a series of icosahedral geodesic domes with different frequencies (see [Wenn79]). The spheres are tiled with triangles which are not completely equilateral, since the spheres are tiled with triangles which can be organized into pentagons and hexagons. A convex object cannot be tiled with only pentagons or hexagons (see [Lord84; Wenn71]). The centres of the pentagonal and hexagonal groups of triangles are called the pentavalent and hexavalent vertices of the triangulated spheres. The frequency of such a sphere is determined by counting the number of edges between the pentavalent vertices, using the shortest path. The frequency of the spheres depicted in Figure 10 is 1, 2, 6, from left to right, respectively. The pentavalent vertices in this figure are the original vertices of the icosahedron.

Members of this series of icosahedral domes are often found in nature. An example of this is the spherical radiolarian, *Aulonia*, shown in Figure 11. Another famous example of spheres tiled with pentagons and hexagons, which is derived from the series of icosahedral domes for given frequencies, is the fullerenes (see [Carl91]). In these C molecules, of which the "Bucky ball" is the most famous example, the C atoms are organized in a sphere tiled with pentagons and hexagons.

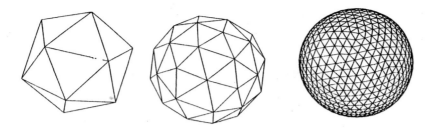

Figure 10. A series of triangulated spheres derived from an icosahedron (displayed on left of figure), by subdivision of a triangle of a preceding sphere into four new ones.

The biological relevance of the spherical initiator for objects with radiate accretive growth is that in many of these organisms the growth process starts from hemispherical protrusions which develop in an encrusting layer. The arrangement of the tangential elements in the triangulated spheres corresponds with the penta-hexagonal arrangements which can be observed in tangential views of organisms with radiate accretive growth (see Figure 3).

The 3D model for radiate accretive growth is developed stepwise; this development is shown in Figure 12. The initiators used in the constructions discussed in this section are all n-frequency derivatives from the icosahedron.

The Basic Construction: the Generator

The basic construction of 3D models for radiate accretive growth is depicted in Figure 13. In this figure a new longitudinal element with length l is constructed upon a preceding layer. The longitudinal element is constructed perpendicular to the preceding layer by determining the mean value of the direction of the normal vectors in $st(T_{ij}, v_{ij})$, the set of triangles surrounding the vertex, v_{ij} (see also Eq. 7). The length, l, is determined by the function given in Eq. (2). The angle α between the longitudinal element and the vertical is used as the argument in this function. The construction generates a new vertex, v_{ij+1}, and the newly generated vertices together define new triangles, T_{ij+1}. The construction is basically similar to that used in Figure 4. But in Figure 4 a new 'fertile' tangential side and a 'nonfertile' longitudinal one are added to the originally

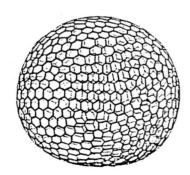

Figure 11. Example of a spherical radiolarian, *Aulonia hexagona* (after Haeckel [Haec1987]).

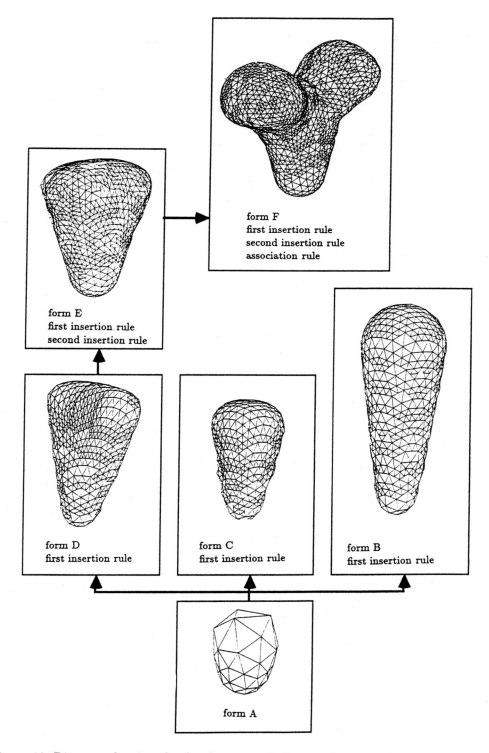

Figure 12. Diagram showing the development of 3D growth models for organisms with radiate accretive growth.

'fertile' tangent sides, while in Figure 13 originally 'fertile' vertices generate new 'fertile' vertices. The new vertices define new longitudinal and tangential elements. The tangential elements are, by definition, connected. This makes the continuity rule as applied in the 2D construction superfluous. The result of the construction after a few iteration steps is displayed at the bottom of the diagram in Figure 12, form A.

Modelling a Skeleton with Nearly Equal-sized Tangential Elements

After each iteration step in Figure 12, form A the tangential elements dilate further. To obtain an object where the surface is tessellated with triangles with nearly equal-sized tangential elements, an additional rule is necessary. In the most simple case this problem is solved by subdividing a triangle in which all three edges exceed the maximum value $1.5s$ allowed for a tangential element (Eq. 8) into four triangles. Similar subdivisions are shown in Figures 7 and 9. The result of applying a maximum size for a tangential element is depicted in Figure 12, form B. The subdivision of too-large triangles corresponds with the insertion rule used to preserve the coherence in the 2D skeleton.

The consequence of the 3D insertion rule is that new triangles and longitudinal elements are generated. In Figure 14 a few column-like objects are displayed, emerging subsequently in the iteration steps. Each time a new vertex is generated in the iteration process the beginning point of a corresponding new longitudinal

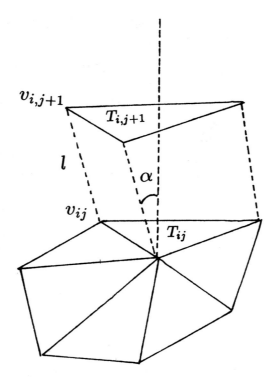

Figure 13. The basic construction applied in the 3D models for radiate accretive growth.

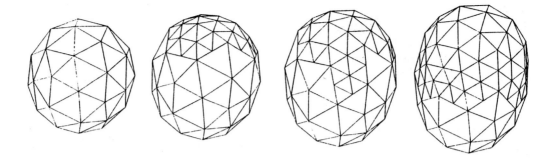

Figure 14. Objects emerging subsequently in the iteration process by applying the model of Figure 12, form B.

element is defined on the growth layer. The biological relation of this 3D insertion rule is obvious. In reality, the surface of the organism is tessellated with discrete skeleton elements which vary only in size (see Figure 3).

In order to avoid the generation of a multilayered structure with arbitrarily short longitudinal elements, a threshold value (*inhibition_level* in Eq. 2) is used. The biological interpretation of this rule is: in organisms with radiate accretive growth where the skeleton elements are secreted internally (as in the *Haliclona* species), the longitudinal lines cannot become too short, since these are built from discrete skeleton elements.

Modelling the Formation of a Widening Column

In Figure 12, form B the curvature of the top of the object remains unchanged in the iteration process. In order to obtain objects which flatten slightly at the top, a function such as the one from Eq. (2) can be used to determine the length, l, of new longitudinal elements. The result is a club-shaped, or clavate, object such as is seen in Figure 12, form C. In this object the degree of widening is controlled by the parameter, n.

A variation on the function with a widening effect is one in which the widening is not equal in all directions, e.g.

$$d = \frac{n}{\cos \beta} \qquad \text{for} \quad 0 \leq \beta \leq \frac{\pi}{2}$$

$$f(\alpha, \beta) = \begin{cases} 1 & \text{for} \quad 0 \leq \alpha \leq \frac{\pi}{d} \\ \cos\left(\dfrac{\frac{\pi}{2}}{\frac{\pi}{2} - \frac{\pi}{d}\left(\alpha - \frac{\pi}{d}\right)}\right) & \text{for} \quad \left(\frac{\pi}{2} + \frac{\pi}{d}\right) < \alpha \leq \pi \end{cases}$$

$$l = \begin{cases} sf(\alpha, \beta) & \text{for} \quad f(\alpha, \beta) > inhibition\_level \\ 0 & \text{for} \quad f(\alpha, \beta) \leq inhibition\_level \end{cases}$$

$$n > 2 \tag{12}$$

In this function the degree of widening, d, depends on the angle β (see Figure 15), the angle between the projection of the mean normal vector in vertex v_{ij} on the xz plane and the horizontal (indicated as the x-axis). When $\beta = 0$ the widening effect, which is controlled by the parameter, n, is maximal; for $\beta = \pi/2$ the widening effect is minimal. Applying this function results in a flattened clavate or planar object (see Figure 12, form D).

The relation between the widening effect in the model and the actual objects is seen in Figure 1, where the branch widens before branching. Without widening the organism splits up into continually smaller branches. In the longitudinal section the organism widens slightly because there is a small area of equal longitudinal elements at the tip of the branch. The widening effect can work equally in all directions, causing a club-shaped organism.

In most cases, for example in both *Haliclona* species, observe that branches do not widen equally in all directions. Especially in *Haliclona oculata* (see Figure 2) the sponge widens more in one direction than in the other, causing a flattened

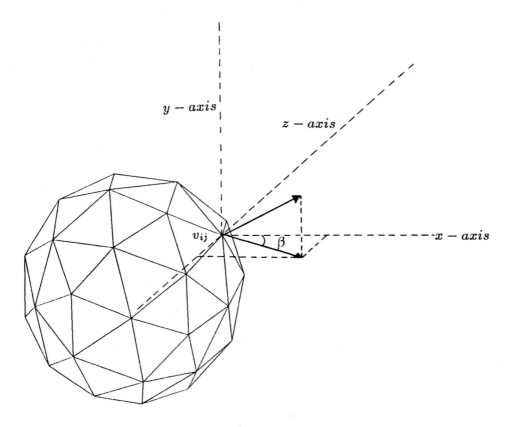

Figure 15. Determination of the angle β between the projection of the mean normal vector in a vertex, v_{ij}, on the xz plane and the horizontal (indicated as the x-axis).

growth form. For many marine organisms the growth process takes place in an environment with tidal flows. The pattern for a laminar flow might occur as depicted in Figure 16 (see [Voge83; Koeh82,76; Wain76]. The flow pattern reverses direction two times a day because of the tidal movement. The flow velocities around the object are zero at point A (flow perpendicular to the object), increase towards the sides and have a maximum at point B. The flow velocities are highest at the sides of the organism parallel to the flow, together with the supply of suspended material. The consequence is a relatively stronger growth process towards the side parallel to the flow. The growth velocity at a point in the organism depends on the angle β, which is the angle between the projection of the mean normal vector in a point on the xz plane and the x-axis (when the organism is using the y-axis as the growth axis and the flow is in the z direction). The dependency of the position of the object with respect to a laminar flow is modelled in the function $f(\alpha, \beta)$ (see Eq. 12). In many marine sessile organisms flattened growth forms emerge in which the organism is positioned perpendicular to the governing flow direction (see [Jack79]). This emergence is explained by assuming that the growth velocities are not equal in all directions but depend on the position of the object with respect to this flow direction.

Conservation of a Tessellation of Almost Equilateral Triangles

A side-effect which occurs in the generation of a planar object (Figure 12, form D) is that the triangles on the surface are not enlarged equally in all directions, as in the clavate object (Figure 12, form C). The result is an object in which one or two edges exceed $1.5s$ in Eq. (8); when the construction is continued, a tessellation emerges where the triangles are no longer almost equilateral. The problem

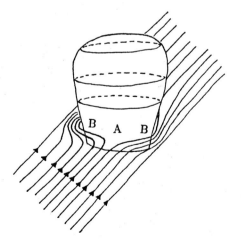

Figure 16. Flow pattern around an organism growing in a laminar flow.

cannot simply be solved (first 3D insertion rule) by subdivision of the triangle with one or two too-large edges into four smaller daughter triangles. This operation yields triangles with one or more too-small (smaller than $0.5s$) edges. A solution to this problem is depicted in Figure 17. In this solution two triangles, both with two edges which exceed $1.5s$ in Eq. (8), are subdivided into four daughter triangles. This subdivision method (second 3D insertion rule) does not disturb the penta-hexagonal organization of the tessellation by introducing, for example, an octovalent vertex; all vertices remain quadri-, penta- or hexavalent. The result of using both 3D insertion rules is shown in Figure 12, form E. The biological interpretation of the second 3D insertion rule corresponds with the one for the first 3D insertion rule. The preservation of the penta-hexagonal organization is based on observations of tangential views of the biological objects (see Figure 3), where generally only quadri-, penta- and hexavalent vertices are observed.

Formation of Branches

Branches are formed by analogy with the 2D model. For this purpose a series of estimations are done for the local radius of curvature at a vertex, v_{bj}. The first step is to collect a set of vertices, $sv2$, surrounding the vertices in the set $sv(T_{ij}, v_{bj})$ (see Eq. 7). The set sv is then deleted from $sv2$, leaving a set of vertices which is situated approximately in a circle around the vertex v_{bj} (see Figure 18). From these vertices three pairs of vertices (indicated with black dots) are selected which are situated at a maximum distance from each other. The vertices in a pair are situated approximately diametral on the circle. In the second step, for the vertex v_{bj} and each pair the radius of curvature is estimated. In the third step these radii of curvature are normalized (see function $h(rad\_curv)$ in Eq. 3). The maximum allowed radius of curvature (max_curv^*) now depends on the angle β (see Figure 15), i.e.

$$max\_curv^* = \sqrt{[(w \cos \beta)^2 + sin^2\beta] \, max\_curv^2} \qquad (13)$$

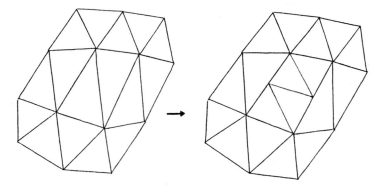

Figure 17. Subdivision of two triangles, both with two edges which exceed $1.5s$ in Eq. (8), into four daughter triangles.

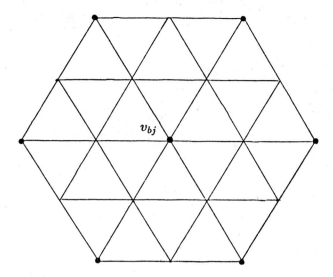

Figure 18. Determination of a set of vertices situated approximately in a circle around the vertex v_{bj}.

By selecting a value for w larger than 1 (see the widening factor in Eq. 2), the maximum allowed radius of curvature in the xy plane becomes larger than that in the xz plane. After the determination of max_curv^* the normalized value for the radius of curvature is calculated with $h(rad\_curv)$. In step four the mean value of the three normalized values of the radius of curvature is calculated and used as an estimation of the overall radius of curvature at a vertex, v_{bj}.

In Figure 12, form F this estimation of the (normalized and mean) radius of curvature is used to determine the length, l, of new longitudinal elements (see Eq. 1). In this construction a planar object is used which widens more in the xy plane than in the xz plane. As soon as the radius of curvature exceeds the maximum allowed value, two local maxima are formed in the xy plane (see Figure 5). In the 3D model the longitudinal elements with a local maximum value are surrounded by smaller ones. In correspondence with the 2D model, these local maxima are associated with new growth axes (association rule). In Figure 12, form F the old growth axis (the y-axis) is replaced by two new axes (both situated in the xy plane). Some more evolved objects, generated with the same construction, are shown in Figure 19 and Plate 1.

Conclusions

With the present 3D model we can simulate branching growth forms of organisms with radiate accretive growth. Introducing the influence of the environment on the growth process is a major improvement (compare the functions $l(\theta)$ and $k(c)$ in the 2D model), thus making the model more suitable for ecological research.

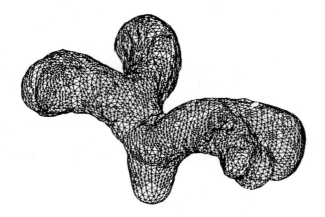

Figure 19. A more evolved object generated with the construction from Figure 12, form F.

REFERENCES

[Carl91]
Carl, R.F., and Smalley, R.E., Fullerenes, *Sci. Amer.*, Vol. 265(4), pp. 32–41, 1991.

[DeFl89]
De Floriani, L., A pyramidal data structure for triangle based surface description, *IEEE Comput. Graph. and Appl.*, Vol. 9, No. 2, pp. 67–78, 1989.

[Grau82]
Graus, R.R., and Macintyre, I.G., Variation in growth forms of the reef coral *montastrea annularis* (Ellis and Solander): a quantitative evaluation of growth response to light distribution using computer simulation, *Smithson. Contr. Mar. Sci.*, Vol. 12, pp. 441–464, 1982.

[Haec1887]
Haeckel, E., Challenger monograph on Radiolaria, Rep. H.M.S. Challenger Scient. Results, 1887.

[Harp86]
Harper, J.L., Rosen, B.R., and White, J., *The Growth and Form of Modular Organisms*, London: The Royal Society, 1986.

[Jack79]
Jackson, J.B.C., Morphological strategies of sessile animals, in *Biology and Systematics of Colonial Organisms Volume II*, Larwood, C., and Rosen, B.R., Eds., London, New York: Systematics Assoc., Academic Press, 1979, pp. 499–555, Proc. of Internat. Symposium at Univ. Durham.

[Kaan92a]
Kaandorp, J.A., and de Kluijver, M.J., Verification of fractal growth models of the sponge *haliclona oculata* (Porifera; class Demospongiae) with transplantation experiments, *Mar. Biol.*, Vol. 113, pp. 133–143, 1992.

[Kaan92b]
Kaandorp, J.A., Modelling radiate accretive growth with iterative geometric constructions and a concentration gradient model, in *Growth Patterns in Physical*

Sciences and Biology, Louis, E., Sander, L.M., Meakin, P., and Garcia-Ruiz, J.M., Eds., NATO ASI Series, to be published.

[Kaan91a]

Kaandorp, J.A., Modelling growth forms of sponges with fractal techniques, *Fractals and Chaos*, Crilly, A.J., Earnshaw, R.A., and Jones, H., Eds., New York: Springer-Verlag, 1991., pp. 71–88.

[Kaan91b]

Kaandorp, J.A., Modelling growth forms of the sponge *haliclona oculata* (Porifera; Demospongiae) using fractal techniques, *Mar. Biol.*, Vol. 110, pp. 203–215, 1991.

[Koeh82]

Koehl, M.A.R., The interaction of moving water and sessile organisms, *Sci. Amer.*, Vol. 247, No. 6, pp. 110–120, 1982.

[Koeh76]

Koehl, M.A.R., Mechanical design in sea anemones, in *Coelenterate Ecology and Behaviour*, Mackie, G.O., Ed., New York: Plenum Press, 1976, pp 23–31.

[Lord84]

Lord, E.A., and Wilson, C.B., *The Mathematical Description of Shape and Form*, New York: Ellis Horwood Ltd., 1984.

[Voge83]

Vogel, S., *Life in Moving Fluids*, Princeton, NJ: Princeton Univ. Press, 1983.

[Wain76]

Wainwright, S.A., and Koehl, M.A.R., The nature of flow and the reaction of benthic cnidaria to it, in *Coelenterate Ecology and Behaviour*, Mackie, G.O., Ed., New York: Plenum Press, 1976, pp. 5–21.

[deWe86]

de Weerdt, W.H., A systematic revision of the northeastern Atlantic shallow-water Haplosclerida (Porifera, Demospongiae), part II: Chalinidae, *Beaufortia*, Vol. 36(6), pp. 81–165, 1986.

[Wenn79]

Wenninger, M.J., *Spherical Models*, Cambridge, UK: Cambridge Univ. Press, 1979.

[Wenn71]

Wenninger, M.J., *Polyhedron models*, Cambridge, UK: Cambridge Univ. Press, 1971.

The Prediction of Ship Capsize:
Not All Fractals Are Environment Friendly

Steven R. Bishop and Mohamed S. Soliman

Abstract

An approach towards the classification of the stability of a ship is presented. This concept is based on the evaluation of the basin of transient attraction of the response of a ship in roll. The determination of these basins allows us to summarise the global transient behaviour of the ship. A sudden erosion of these basins implies a loss of engineering integrity of the system, which can often happen at a wave height that is considerably smaller than that predicted by a steady state analysis. The analysis can be used to investigate the transient behaviour of a ship and can lead to guidelines which can be incorporated in ship hull design.

Introduction

Recent developments have shown that chaos and fractals are typical of many natural systems. We now know that chaos is a typical ingredient of engineering dynamics which has been observed in mechanical and structural systems governed by Newton's laws of motion applicable to machine operations, vibration of structures and the response of marine vehicles and other compliant structures. Newtonian dynamics is not only applicable to solid bodies but also to fluid systems, thus the umbrella of problems which can experience chaotic behaviour is much widened. The associated motions of a chaotic system are irregular, with a broad band power spectrum; but more importantly, they are unpredictable and can lead to unexpected failure of what was thought to otherwise be a safe and deterministic system. Steady state chaos, chaotic transients and chaotic modes of instability all add a very real element of indeterminacy into the response, and hence safety, of engineering systems. Following the early work of Ruelle and Takens [Ruel71], much work still continues to identify aspects of chaotic dynamics which are significant in fluid mechanics as well as celestial mechanics. Early examples of where these new discoveries are being applied in traditional structural and civil engineering are in the design of offshore facilities [Virg88; Bish87], the prevention of ship capsize [Thom91; McRo90], the failure of beams, as well as the implications for design of the prediction of flashover in building fires, to name but a few with which the authors are associated.

Rather than focusing on the long-term, chaotic steady state solutions which produce chaotic attractors from which the dimensionality and the state of the system can be deduced, engineers must quantify the integrity of a system through the transient motions from short bursts of excitation. In many engineering dynamical problems the regularity of forcing does not remain constant for any length of time; thus the system model must be constantly updated. Earthquake engineers take a slightly different approach and calculate response spectra of the transient. But in order to tackle complex and difficult problems, engineers often avoid transients, and indeed even dynamics, by only considering a static formulation. Typically, the changes in the system caused by an alteration in forcing are severe and cannot be written as a simple perturbation of a deterministic model. The importance should thus be shifted from the attractors to the transient dynamics displayed by the system.

Thus, at first it would appear that the new theories of chaos have little to offer the engineer in developing a new design. Yet the topological methods of geometric nonlinear dynamics can still be applied, and the organisation of the bifurcational behaviour can be established, for instance through the use of symbolic and lobe dynamics, offering fresh insight for engineers. New methods can be developed which allow us to view the evolutionary dynamics of a particular system, giving us a better understanding of the physical problem.

The behaviour of a small vessel in ocean waves can seldom be described as a steady state. Invariably a ship is moving in some irregular fashion, including heave and roll. Therefore it seems unlikely that new theories based on the long term attractors of a model of dynamical system can lead to any positive conclusions. Yet much effort is placed on establishing the stability of such a ship in still water. Stability is still often calculated in the static sense, with little attention paid to the transient behaviour of the vessel as a result of a never ending sequence of irregular waves. Can it be that traditional methods for establishing the stability, and hence safety, of small ships are not always trustworthy? After all, capsize is a transient event!

Despite the apparent unpredictability of capsize, it is still possible to ascertain the global stability of vessel response by examining the basins of attraction in a transient sense. These basins become fractal as a result of a homoclinic tangle of the manifolds of an unstable saddle solution heralding the onset of a loss of engineering integrity. This fractal nature of the basins, leading to a loss of engineering integrity of the system, can be brought on by a changing environmental sea state, such as an increase in the wave height or perhaps frequency, hence the title of this paper.

Applications of New Theories to Ship Stability

Ship stability analysis is a subject that has been studied for many years. When designing a new hull form the stability of the ship is usually treated as a static problem, and the characteristics of the new design are compared with those of ships with proven stability [Gilf91; Pric74]. In an upright position the weight of the vessel acts through the centre of gravity, G, and is opposed by an in-line buoyancy force acting through the centre of buoyancy, Z. If the prevailing wind or wave action causes the ship to heel, then the centres of gravity and buoyancy no longer act through the same line and a restoring moment is generated. Still water tests are typically performed to establish the restoring moment which opposes a heeling force. The righting lever is usually denoted by GZ, and the restoring moment at a given angle is equal to the displacement times GZ. For small angles of heel a measure of the ship's stability is the position of the metacentric height, GM, which is the distance above G of the metacentre, M (the point of intersection between the ship's centre line and the line of buoyancy; see Figure 1). Note that if G lies above M the ship has negative stability and hence will capsize. The metacentric height can also be calculated experimentally using weights to incline the ship, but for large angles of displacement the only direct measure of the ship's stability is by using the GZ curve. A typical form of the righting lever, together with the damping moment, is shown in Figure 2, obtained from data relating to a well-documented hull form belonging to a trawling vessel called the *Gaul*. In order to use these characteristics as part of a numerical simulation, the form of the forces is approximated by mathematical functions. These models can be complex (see [Virg87] and Wright and Marshfield [Wrig80], who used a polynomial of order 14, for further analysis), though for small angles of displacement this form can be assumed linear. For larger angles nonlinearity cannot be avoided, and the question of stability can no longer be answered in terms of closed-form analysis. Despite this, ships are still classified in terms of this static approach which specifies the relative areas under particular portions of the righting and heeling moment graphs. Classifications based on these graphs were developed over many years with, it must be said, considerable insight and

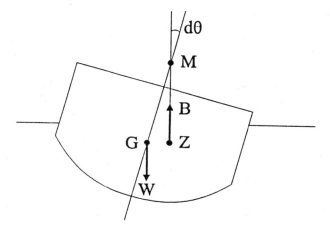

Figure 1. The righting lever, GZ, due to out-of-line action between the weight and buoyancy of a vessel which act through the centre of gravity, G, and the centre of buoyancy, Z, respectively.

success. The problem is how to develop new techniques which quantify stability and which encapsulate traditional as well as modern concepts.

A full dynamic analysis of the ship's motion is an extremely complicated task, involving the solution of the ship as a rigid body with its full six degrees of freedom (the analysis of vessels that in addition are allowed some flexibility provides yet further complication; see the work of Pegg et al. [Pegg91]). The surface of the vessel is usually defined by several hundreds of elements, and by using wave diffraction theory the fluid forces on the vessel are laboriously calculated. Once the analysis and program have been set up, the motion of the ship and hence its stability are monitored for specific wave parameters. This is a step forward in hull design, yet the systems so derived are so complex that it is often possible to perform only selected runs of the simulation. What is really required is a systematic study of the parameters which govern the stability in terms of the ship's characteristics, etc., and the environmental forcing, e.g., wave height or frequency, or a given distribution for random forcing environments. Perhaps as computer technology advances such studies will be possible, but for the moment we consider the use of modern geometrical methods developed for

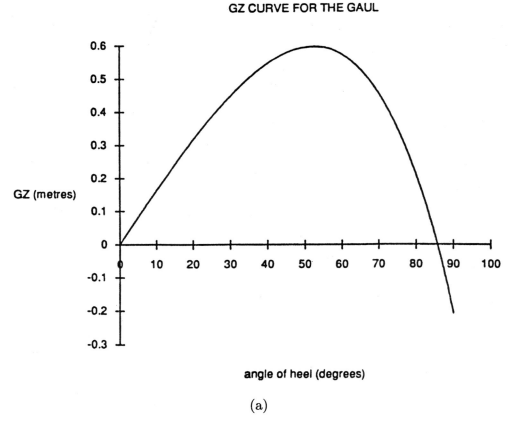

(a)

Figure 2. From data relating to a well-documented hull form belonging to a trawling vessel called the *Gaul*. (a) *GZ* righting lever; (b) damping moment.

DAMPING FOR THE GAUL

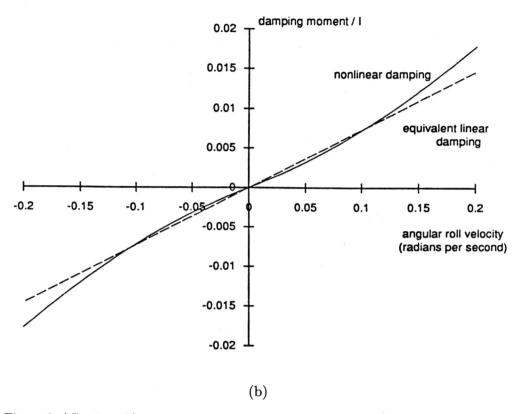

(b)

Figure 2. (*Continued.*)

dynamical systems theory to view the global behaviour of the vessel in global phase space (see [Soli91; Rain90]). The analysis has been extended to study of ship motions under combined external and parametric excitations in [Thom92].

Despite the apparent and real complexity of ship motions, there are certain types of motion which lead to considerable simplification of the differential equations that are used to describe these motions. During an investigation of the capsizing of several fishing vessels off Canada's west coast, Miller et al. [Mill86] highlighted three separate mechanisms of capsize corresponding to resonant and subharmonic rolling in beam seas and loss of stability at a wave crest. The latter of these mechanisms is particularly disturbing, since there is little or no warning of the impending capsize. Further mechanisms for capsize have been established, one of which is due to a rolling motion induced by a parametric resonance in head waves studied by Nayfeh [Nayf88] and de Kat and Paulling [deKa89]. Of course, new insights are constantly being offered into the complex way in which ship motions can be modelled (see for instance [Thom92]), but for the moment we restrict our attention to those situations in which the vessels' motions can adequately be described by a differential equation with a single degree of freedom.

Basins of Attraction Corresponding to Ship Roll and Capsize

The rolling motion of a ship can be described using Newton's laws, incorporating information obtained by experimental results or calculations based on the hull shape. The subsequent equation of motion, though simplified, contains nonlinear terms associated with the restoring moment, as described above, namely

$$\ddot{\theta} + g(\dot{\theta}) + GZ(\theta) = F(t) \tag{1}$$

where θ is a measure of the angle of roll, $g(\dot{\theta})$ is a damping function, $GZ(\theta)$ is the restoring force and $F(t)$ is a term which represents the wave forcing. For a wide range of roll excitation the damping is assumed to be linear, corresponding to viscous damping, and a first approximation to the forcing term is to assume that the ship is being driven by a regular wave.

For vessels of a similar nature these restoring curves have similar shape. A useful approach in order to consider a class of problems is to approximate these curves by the simplest form available to allow fast numerical solutions which can be investigated interactively. This approach was followed by Thompson [Thom89a], resulting in studies of the canonical form

$$\ddot{x} + \beta\dot{x} + x - x^2 = F\sin\omega t \tag{2}$$

This equation closely matches the behaviour of other systems described by Eq. (1) [Lans90] and can also be thought of as representing the motion of a particle of unit mass in a potential well of the form

$$V(x) = \frac{1}{2}x^2 - \frac{1}{3}x^3 \tag{3}$$

which is the universal form encountered in a mechanical system as it approaches a fold catastrophe (see [Thom82,88b]). This model corresponds to oscillations of a ship in roll which is biased to capsize in a favoured direction of roll due to wave or wind action, or possibly an uneven or shifted cargo. Having chosen a model for capsize, these equations can now be numerically integrated for a range of sea states to determine whether the transient motion from a particular starting condition is stable, resulting in a steady state oscillation, or whether capsize occurs. In the analogy with the canonical form of the escape equation, capsize of the vessel corresponds to the particle escaping from the potential well. This scenario is best visualised in the first instance by considering the phase portrait of the global dynamics of the system in the displacement/velocity, or *phase plane* with zero forcing. This is shown in Figure 3, where initial conditions in the blank region decay onto the attracting stable solution, while points initiated in the shaded area lead to capsize. The unstable saddle solution at $x = 1$ plays an important part in the dynamics of the system, since it delineates those trajectories that lead to a stable solution from those which lead to capsize [Virg90]. The set of trajectories that lead to this saddle, more generally termed

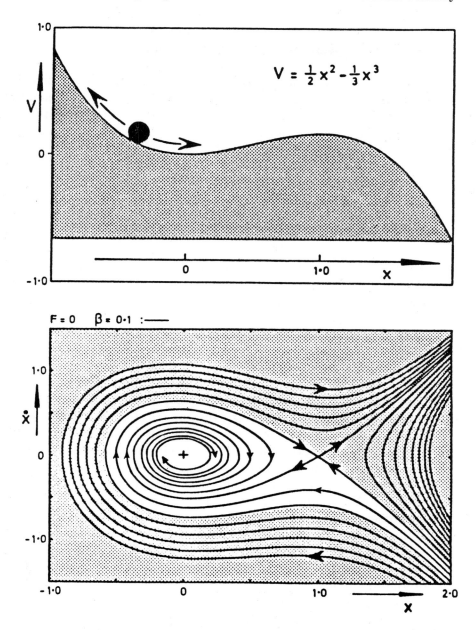

Figure 3. Phase portrait of the dynamics of an archetypal ship roll equation.

manifolds, are called the *separatrix*, since they separate the motions which result in attraction to the different solutions (here at $x = 0$ and infinity).

In the presence of forcing, the phase space is now three-dimensional. We must view the dynamics by considering the projection of this space onto the two-dimensional displacement/velocity plane, $(x, \dot{x})$. However, if we neglect information between cycles of the excitation we can project the sampled trajectory in the same manner and still reveal much of the dynamics [Thom86]. Considering systems of the type mentioned in Eq. (1), the manifolds which lead towards the unstable solution (now an unstable saddle cycle) still separate the trajectories which lead to a steady state periodic oscillation from those which diverge to infinity and capsize. The only difference here is that points no longer smoothly move along the lines, as was the case for the flow when $F = 0$, but rather step along as each trajectory is discretely sampled.

Fractal Basin Erosion and Unpredictable Capsize

When attempting to solve a problem such as ship motions, the sea environment is such that it is not possible to say with any accuracy the conditions of the vessel at any one point in time. Thus, the starting conditions for a simulation are not always known, and instead of focusing attention on a single trajectory (as described above for the full six degrees of freedom case taking into account wave diffraction theory, etc.) stability can be assessed by examining the basins of attraction which define an ensemble of solutions leading towards a common attracting solution. For nonzero values of F corresponding to waves of differing wave height but constant frequency, the path of the stable harmonic oscillation can be followed [Alex89; Park89], and a variety of steady state attractors within the potential well can appear, typically as a result of a bifurcation of the fundamental path or instantaneously at a global bifurcation. At each of these events the basin of attraction changes in shape and disappears altogether if the solution loses its stability. However, if for the moment we again consider a single trajectory then it is possible to locate that solution which initiates very close to the saddle, falls off and moves directly, i.e., asymptotically, towards the attractor.

For obvious reasons this trajectory is sometimes termed the *outset*, while the trajectory leading to the saddle is called the *inset*. For low values of the forcing amplitude the outset and the inset do not intersect, but as F is used as a control parameter and wound up these two manifolds alter so that they approach one another. Once these manifolds intersect they must do so an infinite number of times; the subsequent phenomenon, called a homoclinic tangle, is schematically illustrated in Figure 4 [Guck83]. The upper diagram shows the inset and outset of the hill top saddle of a driven oscillator. The middle diagram is just prior to the homoclinic tangle, immediately after which the tongues, or fingers, of the inset come sweeping into the basin of attraction. The consequences of this global event are dramatic, even if not immediately so. Points which used to lie within the basin of attraction immediately before the tangle, which lead to a steady, safe solution, find themselves within one of the fractal fingers and now lead to capsize. The basin of attraction, for further increases in wave height, undergoes complicated changes in its shape; and the boundary, once smooth, now has finer and finer detail at small scale. The boundary is now said to be fractal [Thom87].

Before discussing the engineering significance of these fractal basin boundaries, we first see how these fractal tongues develop for increased wave height and sweep in to erode the basin of attraction for that of the steady state harmonic solution.

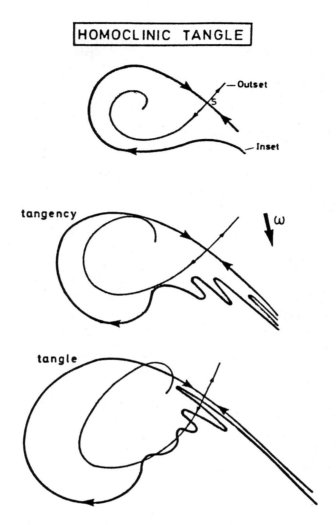

Figure 4. Schematic diagrams of events leading towards a homoclinic tangle.

Figure 5 shows the space of initial conditions $(x, y = \dot{x})$ for the system (2) for four different values of the forcing amplitude (also see [Thom89b]). The position of the harmonic attractor is denoted by a white circle with a plus sign inside, while a subharmonic solution has a star inside (bottom right). Unexplored portions are denoted by a question mark (?), though it is now known that these areas will contain finer and finer detail. At $F = 0.0725$ (top left) the basin boundary, though fractal, does not severely impinge on the overall area of the basin of attraction, here shown in black. As F increases (0.0750 and 0.0775) we see that the basin becomes eroded; in the last diagram ($F = 0.0872$) the basin is considerably diminished. This last picture also includes the added complication of the appearance of a coexisting subharmonic solution of order 3. In this final picture the harmonic solution is still stable in the classical sense of Lyapunov

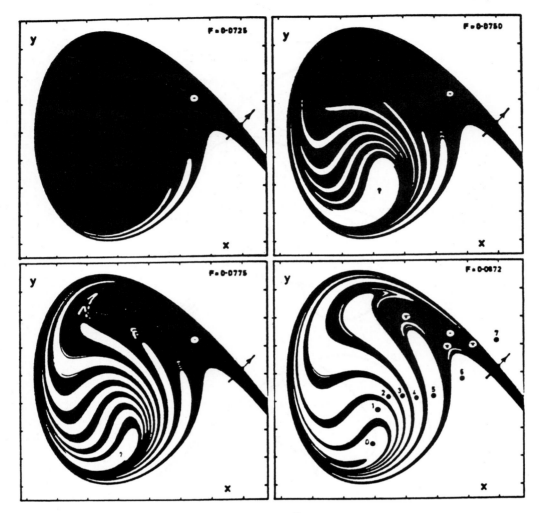

Figure 5. Erosion of the basin of attraction following a homoclinic tangle of the escape equation modelling ship capsize. Courtesy of Nick Alexander [Alex89].

against infinitesimal disturbances. However, note that the solution has lost its engineering integrity, i.e., points can lie within a finite n-sphere around the attractor which lead to escape. We also note on this figure that the escape sequence for a single trajectory is marked, which leads to escape within eight cycles of the forcing. Not only have we thus shifted our attention away from statical analysis and Lyapunov stability to dynamics and engineering integrity, but it is now clear that we can also formulate design criteria based on transient dynamics.

Efficient algorithms now exist which are based on a cell-to-cell mapping technique described by Hsu [Hsu87] (also see [Foal91]) to evaluate basins of attraction which minimise the amount of calculations performed by allowing a screen pixel to represent a 'cell' of the phase space. These are particularly suited to the microcomputing environment. A cell is integrated forward in time and labelled with a colour depending on whether it decays onto an attractor or escapes to infinity. We see this in Figure 6, in which the black points correspond to initial conditions (x, y) which decay in time onto the attractor marked with a circle. The apparent jagged nature of the basin boundaries is caused by the discretization of the cells and can be improved if finer scale is used. As before, the integrity of the system as a result of the fractal basin erosion is much decreased. Also, the fractal nature of the boundary, and hence the basin, adds a new element of indeterminacy to the system. Given an arbitrary initial condition within the basin, without infinite precision it is not clear whether the subsequent transient trajectory will result in a safe solution or will capsize. All this is without the

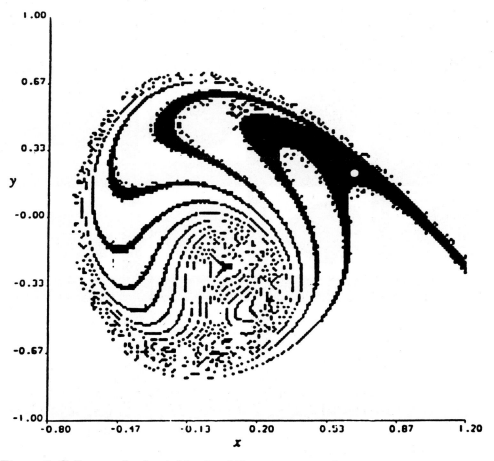

Figure 6. Cell map of a fractal basin of the escape equation.

strict presence of chaos, though fractal basins do imply the presence of long chaotic transients.

To establish the sequence of events which lead to the loss of the system's integrity as a result of a fractal incursion, a series of cell maps is shown in Figure 7 for the system (2). Note that the basins of attraction are shown black and that the main attractor is denoted by a triangle. White represents escape within 16 cycles of the forcing. The appearance of a fractal basin is visible at $F = 0.07$, but note that at least immediately after the basin has become fractal the integrity of the system remains, since the basin itself is not eroded. A dramatic change, however, occurs at $F = 0.08$, after which the integrity of the system must be questionable even though in the classical sense a stable solution still remains. This dramatic erosion of the area is seen more clearly when the integrity (suitably scaled by the window size) is plotted against the wave height, as in Figure 8. Here we consider that failure occurred if the trajectory has diverged sufficiently within only 16 waves. The dramatic loss of engineering integrity highlights the undesirable character of the fractal basins. A further point to note is that the corresponding curve for infinite time matches the $m = 16$ curve very closely. In other words, the integrity of the system is accurately estimated by only considering the response of the system to 16 waves [Soli89].

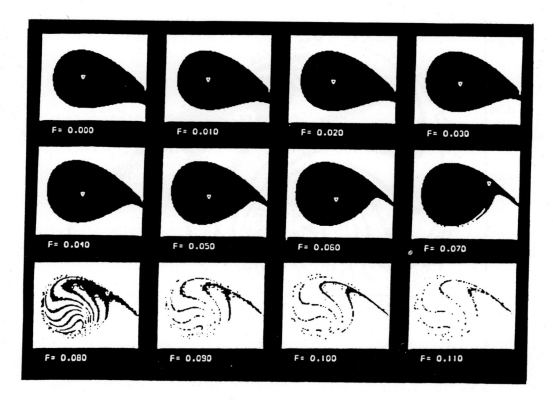

Figure 7. A sequence of cell maps showing the basins of attraction of the main attractor for the escape equation with parameters as before, i.e., $\omega = 0.85$, $\beta = 0.1$.

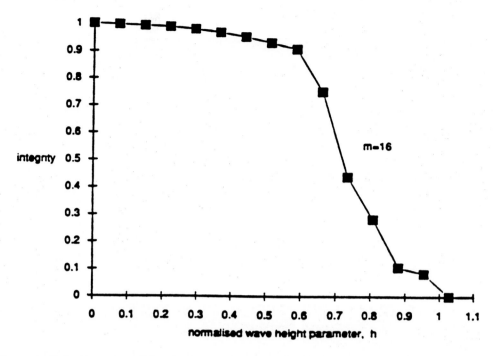

Figure 8. Integrity curve for capsize within 16 waves from cell maps obtained from the escape equation, as displayed in Figure 7.

Design criteria based on this transient technique thus provide speedy results and meaningful estimates of the overall safety of the ship's design.

A further illustration of the appearance of fractal boundaries, included here as Figure 9, is a sequence of basins relating to the *Gaul*, using the restoring moment data shown earlier in Figure 2; the control parameter which is varied here is the normalised wave height, h (for further details see [Soli91]). The basin of attraction of the fundamental solution, shown as white, has a different shape due to the symmetric nature of the restoring force allowing capsize in both directions of roll. We note that although the detail is different, the rapid erosion of the basin still occurs with the subsequent loss in integrity. The *Gaul* conformed to all the required safety standards, with nothing wrong with its design; yet in February 1974 it capsized with the loss of 36 lives.

Conclusions

The appearance of fractal basins as a result of a homoclinic tangle of the invariant manifolds of a saddle point have been shown to dramatically decrease the integrity of a system modelling the dynamic motions of a ship. The continuing loss of life due to the capsize of small vessels implies that attention must be paid to dynamic effects rather than relying on static formulations of stability. Furthermore, simple methods developed for evaluation of the engineering integrity

Gaul, $-1.74 < \theta < 1.74$ $-1.05 < \dot{\theta} < 1.05$:

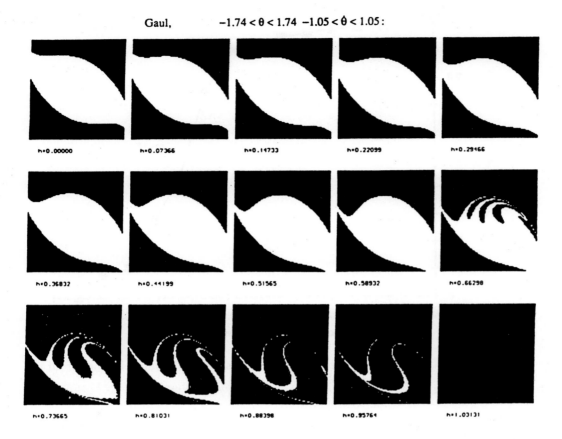

Figure 9. Safe basins (shown white) of initial conditions for the *Gaul* which do not capsize within 16 cycles.

can be based on transient dynamics. The incorporation of these new ideas into the established field of ship hull design has still to be completed, with much research to be performed.

Acknowledgments. The lead author is an Advanced Research Fellow of the Science and Engineering Research Council and he acknowledges their support. Both authors also thank the Marine Technology Directorate, who fund a research project which covers the work described in this paper (GR/F86786), and Stephen Foale for his help with the manuscript.

REFERENCES

[Alex89]
Alexander, N.A., Computational algorithms for the global stability analysis of driven oscillators, Ph.D. Thesis, Univ. London, 1989.

[Bish87]
Bishop, S.R., and Virgin, L.N., The onset of chaotic motions of a moored semi-submersible, *Proc. Sixth Int. Offshore Mech. and Arctic Engng. Symp.*, Vol. II, pp. 319–323, 1987.

[deKa89]
de Kat, J.O., and Paulling, J.R., The simulation of ship motions and capsizing in severe seas, *Trans. SNAME*, Vol. 97, pp. 139–168, 989.

[Foal91]
Foale, S., and Thompson, J.M.T., Geometrical concepts and computational techniques of nonlinear dynamics, *Comp. Meth. in Applied Mech. and Engng.*, Vol. 89, pp. 381–394, 1991.

[Gilf91]
Gilfillan, A., Ship stability — Statical approach, Notes for Scottish Hydraulics Study Group, 1991.

[Guck83]
Guckenheimer, J., and Holmes, P., *Nonlinear Oscillations, Dynamical Systems, and Bifurcations of Vector Fields*, New York: Springer-Verlag, 1983.

[Hsu87]
Hsu, C.S., *Cell to Cell Mapping: A Method of Global Analysis for Nonlinear Systems*, Heidelberg: Springer-Verlag, 1987.

[Lans90]
Lansbury, A.N., and Thompson, J.M.T., Incursive fractals: a robust mechanism of basin erosion preceding the optimal escape from a potential well, *Phys. Lett. A*, Vol. 150, Nos. 8, 9, pp. 355–361, 1990.

[McRo90]
McRobie, F.A., and Thompson, J.M.T., Chaos, catastrophes and engineering, *New Scient.*, Vol. 126, pp. 41–46, 9 June 1990.

[Mill86]
Miller, D.R., Tam, G., Rainey, R.C.T., and Ritch, R., Investigation of the use of modern ship motions prediction models in identifying ships with a larger than acceptable risk of dynamic capsize, Arctec Canada Ltd. Report No. TP7407E, for the Transportation Development Centre of the Canadian Government, 1986.

[Nayf88]
Nayfeh, A.H., On the undesirable roll characteristics of ships in regular seas, *Jour. Ship Res.*, Vol. 3, pp. 36–46, 1988.

[Park89]
Parker, T.S., and Chua, L.O., *Practical Numerical Algorithms for Chaotic Systems*, Heidelberg: Springer-Verlag, 1989.

[Pegg91]
Pegg, N.G., Gilroy, L.E., and Cumming, D.W., Load, motions and structural response trials of the SWATH vessel *Frederick G. Creed*, in *Dynamics of Marine Vehicles and Structures in Waves*, Price, W.G., Temarel, P., and Keane, A.J., Amsterdam: Elsevier, pp. 81–91, 1991.

[Pric74]
Price, W.G., and Bishop, R.E.D., *Probabilistic Theory of Ship Dynamics*, London: Chapman and Hall, 1974.

78   Steven R. Bishop and Mohamed S. Soliman

[Rain90]
Rainey, R.C.T., Thompson, J.M.T., Tam, G.W., and Noble, P.G., The transient capsize diagrams — a route to soundly based new stability regulations, 4th Int. Conf. on Stability of Ships and Ocean Vehicles, Naples, 24–28 September 1990.

[Ruel71]
Ruelle, D., and Takens, F., On the nature of turbulence, *Comm. Math. Phys.*, Vol. 20, pp. 167–192; Vol. 23, pp. 343–344, 1971.

[Soli89]
Soliman, M.S., and Thompson, J.M.T., Integrity measures quantifying the erosion of smooth and fractal basins of attraction, *Jour. Sound and Vibration*, Vol. 135, pp. 453–475, 1989.

[Soli91]
Soliman, M.S., and Thompson, J.M.T., Transient and steady state analysis of capsize phenomena, *Appl. Ocean Res.*, Vol. 13, pp. 82–92, 1991.

[Thom82]
Thompson, J.M.T., *Instabilities and Catastrophes in Science and Engineering*, Chichester, UK: Wiley, 1982.

[Thom86]
Thompson, J.M.T., and Stewart, H.B., *Nonlinear Dynamics and Chaos*, Chichester, UK: Wiley, 1986.

[Thom87]
Thompson, J.M.T., Bishop, S.R., and Leung, L.M., Fractal basins and chaotic bifurcations prior to escape from a potential well, *Phys. Lett. A*, Vol. 121, No. 3, pp. 116–120, 1987.

[Thom88]
Thompson, J.M.T., and Bishop, S.R., From Newton to chaos, *Phys. Bull.*, Vol. 39, pp. 232–234, 1988.

[Thom89a]
Thompson, J.M.T., Chaotic phenomena triggering escape from a potential well, *Proc. Roy. Soc. London Ser. A*, Vol. 421, pp. 195-225, 1989.

[Thom89b]
Thompson, J.M.T., New frontiers in nonlinear dynamics and chaos, *Proc. Second Nat. Congr. on Mech.*, Athens: Hellenic Soc. for Theoretical and Appl. Mech., pp. 19–28, June 1989.

[Thom91]
Thompson, J.M.T., Rainey, R.C.T., and Soliman, M.S., Ship stability criteria based on chaotic transients from incursive fractals, *Phil. Trans. Roy. Soc. London A*, Vol. 332, pp. 149–167, 1991.

[Thom92]
Thompson, J.M.T., Rainey, R.C.T., and Soliman, M.S., Mechanics of ship capsize under direct and parametric wave excitation, *Phil. Trans. Roy. Soc. London A*, Vol. 436, pp. 427–448, 1992.

[Virg87]
Virgin, L.N., The nonlinear rolling response of a vessel including chaotic motions leading to capsize in regular seas, *Appl. Ocean Res.*, Vol. 9, No. 2, pp. 89–95, 1987.

[Virg88]

Virgin, L.N. and Bishop, S.R., Complex dynamics and chaotic responses in the time domain simulations of a floating structure, *Ocean Engng.*, Vol. 15, No. 1, pp. 71–90, 1988.

[Virg90]

Virgin, L.N. and Bishop, S.R., Catchment regions of multiple dynamic responses in nonlinear problems in offshore mechanics, *Jour. Offshore Mech. and Arctic Engng.*, Vol. 112, pp. 127–133, 1990.

[Wrig80]

Wright, J.H.G., and Marshfield, W.B., Ship roll response and capsize behaviour in beam seas, *Trans. R. Instit. Nav. Archit.*, Vol. 122, pp. 129–148, 1980.

On the Synthesis and Processing of Fractal Signals and Images

Jonathan M. Blackledge

Abstract

This paper discusses some of the techniques available for synthesizing and process-ing random fractal signals and images. The methods presented are derived from a Fourier-based description of a random scaling fractal and are therefore able to utilize a Fast Fourier Transform. This provides the potential for constructing a real time facility by implementing available DSP hardware, the principal criterion for developing the techniques presented in this paper.

Introduction — Fractals and Image Processing

Fractal geometry is rapidly being assimilated into many diverse areas of physics and mathematics. The application of such geometry to imaging science is now receiving serious attention; a number of articles have recently been published on this subject (see [Knil90; Peli90; Funa89; Bram89; Peit88]). In many applications of fractal geometry to digital image processing, one of the primary interests is image simulation and segmentation. In both simulation and segmentation, a feature which is of particular interest is image 'texture' [Denn89; Kell89; Pele84].

It is worth stating at the outset that there is no universally accepted mathe-matical definition of texture — "texture is an elusive notion which mathemati-cians and scientists tend to avoid because they cannot grasp it" and "much of fractal geometry could pass as an implicit study of texture", according to B. Mandelbrot [Mand83]. However, textural analysis, under the guise of some useful mathematical definition of the term, is important for the field of computer vision. In particular, the segmentation of digital images based on some measure of image texture is essential for generating an unsupervised, automatic means of extracting textural features that agrees with human sensory perception.

In general, images convey information which relates to two broad categories:

deterministic information;

textural information.

Deterministic information includes features whose recognition is related to the surface topology of an imaged object, which in turn is determined or inferred from a boundary representation of the object, i.e., from its edges. As a consequence, computer recognition of man-made objects, using primarily optical imaging systems, is invariably concerned with the process of edge detection, e.g., the boundary representation of objects and image scenes at different frequency bands [Marr80]. In other imaging systems, in particular coherent imaging systems, deterministic features may not be easily decernable, and image interpretation is governed more by the ability (or inability) to delineate between regions which appear to exhibit different textures. One way of doing this is to examine the grey level histogram of an image at different spatial locations and study the deviation of the distribution obtained, or changes in the distribution itself. Another way is to study the power spectrum of the data at different spatial locations of an image. This provides information on the spatial variations of the frequency content of the data. Either way, image understanding, and in particular the comprehension and interpretation of coherent images, is invariably concerned with an analysis of image texture in the context of some useful and manageable mathematical definition of the term. It is this aspect of digital image processing that is discussed in this paper.

The Similarity (Fractal) Dimension

Central to fractal geometry is the concept of self-similarity, which means that some types of mainly naturally occurring objects look similar at different scales. The degree of self-similarity is determined by a parameter called the 'similarity dimension' or the 'fractal dimension', D, which is defined as (see [Peit88])

$$Nr^D = 1 \qquad D = -\frac{\ln N}{\ln r} \tag{1}$$

where N is the number of distinct copies of an object which has been scaled down by a ratio $r < 1$ in all coordinates. There are two distinct types of fractals which exhibit this property:

deterministic fractals;

random fractals.

Deterministic fractals are objects which look identical at all scales. Each magnification reveals an ever finer structure which is an exact replication of the whole, i.e., they are exactly self-similar. Random fractals do not, in general, possess such deterministic self-similarity; such fractal sets are composed of N distinct subsets, each of which is scaled down by a ratio $r < 1$ from the original and is identical in all statistical respects to the scaled original — they are statistically self-similar. The scaling ratios need not be the same for all the scaled down copies. Certain fractal sets are composed of the union of N distinct subsets, each of which is scaled down by a ratio $r_i < 1$, $1 \leq i \leq N$ from the original in all coordinates. The similarity dimension is given by the generalization of Eq. (1), namely

$$\sum_{i=1}^{N} r_i^D = 1$$

A further generalization leads to self-affine fractal sets which are scaled by different ratios in different coordinates. The equation

$$f(\lambda x) = \lambda^H f(x) \quad \forall \lambda > 0 \tag{2}$$

where λ is a scaling factor and H is the scaling exponent implies that a scaling in the x coordinate by λ gives a scaling of the f coordinate by a factor λ^H. A special case of Eq. (2) occurs when $H = 1$; in this case we have a scaling of x by λ producing a scaling of f by λ, which yields self-similarity.

Naturally occurring fractals differ from strictly mathematically defined fractals in that they do not display statistical or exact self-similarity over all scales but exhibit fractal properties over a limited range of scales. Methods exist for computing the upper and lower scale limits [Yoko89].

Random Scaling Fractal Signals and Images

A random scaling fractal signal is defined as a signal, $f(x)$, whose power spectrum, $P(k)$, is characterized by [Peit88]

$$P(k) \propto \frac{1}{|k|^\beta} \qquad \beta = 5 - 2D \quad 1 < D < 2 \tag{3}$$

where k is the spatial frequency in cycles per metre. This important and fundamental result is a consequence of the scaling relationship

$$g(x) = \frac{1}{\lambda^H} f(\lambda x) \qquad \forall \lambda > 1 \quad \text{and} \quad 0 < H < 1 \tag{4}$$

in which the statistical properties of g and f are identical.

A random scaling fractal image is defined as an image, $f(\mathbf{r})$, whose power spectrum, $P(\mathbf{k})$, is characterized by [Peit88]

$$P(\mathbf{k}) \propto \frac{1}{|\mathbf{k}|^\beta} \qquad \beta = 8 - 2D \quad 2 < D < 3 \tag{5}$$

where $\mathbf{r} = \hat{\mathbf{x}}x + \hat{\mathbf{y}}y$ and $\mathbf{k} = \hat{\mathbf{x}}k_x + \hat{\mathbf{y}}k_y$. Here, k_x and k_y are the spatial frequencies and $\hat{\mathbf{x}}$ and $\hat{\mathbf{y}}$ are unit vectors in the x and y directions, respectively. This is a consequence of the generalization of Eq. (4) to 2D (random fractal images, or 'Mandelbrot surfaces') [Fede88], i.e.

$$g(x,y) = \frac{1}{\lambda^H} f(\lambda x, \lambda y) \qquad \forall \lambda > 1 \quad \text{and} \quad 0 < H < 1$$

These (spectral) definitions, i.e., Eqs. 3 and 5, respectively, for random fractal signals and images are well known and are used to compute the fractal dimension, D, of a given (random fractal) signal or image. This is discussed further in the section on computing the fractal dimension.

Fractional Differential Equations

We now examine the relationship between random scaling fractals and certain types of fractional differential equations. In particular, we show that a random scaling fractal can be the solution to certain classes of fractional differential equations.

Fractional calculus is nonstandard but has been studied in some detail [Dold74; Oldh74]. In simple terms, fractional calculus is concerned with the analysis of derivatives of the type $d^q f/dx^q$, where q is noninteger and the corresponding fractional integration, which is formally defined using the notation $d^{-q} f/dx^{-q}$. Fractional differential (or differintegrable) equations contain terms of this type and are used for modelling a variety of stochastic processes (self-similar or otherwise) [Tato89].

FRACTAL SIGNALS

Consider the fractional differential equation

$$\frac{d^q}{dx^q}\, f(x) = n(x) \tag{6}$$

where n is a stochastic function characterized by white Gaussian noise, i.e., noise with a uniformly distributed, or 'white', spectrum and a Gaussian probability distribution function. A solution to this equation is obtained by generalizing the well-known result

$$\frac{d^n}{dx^n}\, f(x) = \frac{1}{2\pi} \int_{-\infty}^{\infty} (ik)^n F(k) \exp(ikx)\, dk \qquad \text{for integer } n$$

to $\qquad \dfrac{d^q}{dx^q}\, f(x) = \dfrac{1}{2\pi} \displaystyle\int_{-\infty}^{\infty} (ik)^q F(k) \exp(ikx)\, dk \qquad \text{for noninteger } q$

where F is the Fourier transform of f given by

$$F(k) = \int_{-\infty}^{\infty} f(x) \exp(-ikx)\, dx$$

This definition is just one of a number of 'generalizations' used over the last 300 years, i.e., from the time of Leibnitz onwards, to address the 'meaning of' a fractional differential and to derive a consistent formulation for the fractional calculus [Oldh74]. However, this definition is of particular value for studying the spectral properties of f.

Using the previous definition for a fractional derivative, Eq. (6) is written as

$$(ik)^q F(k) = N(k) \qquad F(k) = \frac{1}{(ik)^q} N(k)$$

where

$$N(k) = \int_{-\infty}^{\infty} n(x) \exp(-ikx) \, dx$$

Hence, taking the inverse Fourier transform, we obtain a solution of the form

$$f(x) = \frac{1}{2\pi} \int_{-\infty}^{\infty} \frac{1}{(ik)^q} N(k) \exp(ikx) \, dk \qquad (7)$$

This form of analysis is the same as that used to solve conventional linear differential equations using the Fourier transform. This solution to Eq. (6) shows that the function f is constructed by filtering the complex spectrum of the stochastic function, n, with a special type of lowpass filter, i.e., $1/(ik)^q$. If n is a noise function with a uniformly distributed complex spectrum, N, then (see Eq. 3)

$$\text{Power Spectrum:} \qquad |F(k)|^2 \propto \frac{1}{|k|^{2q}} \qquad (8)$$

Another way of analysing the solution in Eq. (7) is to evaluate the integral explicitly. Since f is given by the inverse Fourier transform of the product of two spectra, $1/(ik)^q$ and N, using the convolution theorem we write f in the form

$$f(x) = \int h(x - x') n(x') \, dx' \qquad (9)$$

where

$$h(x) = \frac{1}{2\pi} \int_{-\infty}^{\infty} \frac{1}{(ik)^q} \exp(ikx) \, dk$$

A simple method of evaluating h is obtained by first constructing the Bromwich integral by replacing ik with p, giving

$$h(x) = \frac{1}{2\pi i} \int_{c-i\infty}^{c+i\infty} \frac{1}{p^q} \exp(px) \, dp$$

Formally, this is the inverse Laplace transform of $1/p^q$. Now the Laplace transform of x^n, where n is a positive integer, is easily evaluated to give

$$I_n = \int_0^{\infty} x^n \exp(-px) \, dx = -\frac{1}{p} \left[x^n \exp(-px) \right]_0^{\infty} + \frac{n}{p} \int_0^{\infty} x^{n-1} \exp(-px) \, dx$$

$$= \frac{n}{p} I_{n-1} = \frac{n}{p} \frac{(n-1)}{p} I_{n-2} = \frac{n}{p} \frac{(n-1)}{p} \frac{(n-2)}{p} I_{n-3} = \ldots = \frac{n!}{p^{n+1}}$$

Generalizing this result for noninteger values of q we write [Jone66]

$$\int_0^\infty x^q \exp(-px)\,dx = \frac{q!}{p^{q+1}} \qquad \text{for} \quad q > -1$$

or

$$\frac{1}{(q-1)!} \int_0^\infty x^{q-1} \exp(-px)\,dx = \frac{1}{p^q} \qquad \text{for} \quad q > 0$$

The last equation provides us with the result

$$h(x) = \frac{1}{(q-1)!}\, x^{q-1}$$

or using the 'Gamma function' notation

$$h(x) = \frac{1}{\Gamma(q)}\, x^{q-1}$$

where

$$\Gamma(q) = \int_0^\infty x^{q-1} \exp(-x)\,dx = (q-1)!$$

This allows us to write Eq. (9) in the form

$$f(x) = \frac{1}{\Gamma(q)} \int \frac{1}{(x-x')^{1-q}}\, n(x')\,dx' \tag{10}$$

Expressed in this form, the solution to Eq. (6) is simply a convolution of $n(x)$ with a special type of Kernel, i.e.

$$\frac{1}{\Gamma(q)\, x^{1-q}}$$

The limits of integration for f in Eq. (10) are deliberately omitted for generality. Formally, if this solution for f is to be considered a convolution then the range of integration is $[-\infty, \infty]$. However, in general the limits of integration depend on additional criteria that need to be satisfied. For example, if Eq. (10) is to produce the same result as ordinary differentiation when q is a positive integer, then the range of integration should be $[a, x]$ where a is some constant. Then, when $q = 1$

$$f(x) = \int_a^x n(x')\,dx'$$

which is a solution to

$$\frac{d}{dx} f(x) = n(x)$$

This expression for f, i.e. Eq. (10), for $x' \in [a, x])$ is known as the Riemann-Liouville (fractional) integral [Bate54]. When $a = 0$ we have Riemann's definition, and when $a = -\infty$ it is equivalent to Liouville's definition [Dold74]. Other 'variations on a theme' also satisfy Eq. (6), such as the Weyl (fractional) integral where the range of integration is $[x, \infty]$. However, all these fractional integral transforms have a common scaling property, i.e.

$$g(x) = \frac{1}{\Gamma(q)} \int \frac{n(\lambda x')}{(x - x')^{1-q}}\, dx' = \frac{1}{\lambda^q}\, \frac{1}{\Gamma(q)} \int \frac{n(y)}{(\lambda x - y)^{1-q}} dy = \frac{1}{\lambda^q}\, f(\lambda x)$$

where $y = \lambda x'$ (see Eq. 4). In this sense we define a random scaling fractal as the solution to Eq. (6). Moreover, a relationship between q and D is established by comparing Eq. (8) with Eq. (3), yielding

$$q = \frac{5 - 2D}{2}$$

and since $1 < D < 2$, then $1/2 < q < 3/2$.

FRACTAL IMAGES

Consider the partial fractional differential equation

$$\nabla^q f(\mathbf{r}) = n(\mathbf{r}) \qquad \mathbf{r} = \hat{\mathbf{x}}x + \hat{\mathbf{y}}y \tag{11}$$

In common with the basic definition used to construct a solution to Eq. (6), consider the expression

$$\nabla^q f(\mathbf{r}) = \frac{1}{(2\pi)^2} \int_{-\infty}^{\infty} F(\mathbf{k})|\mathbf{k}|^q \exp(i\mathbf{k}\cdot\mathbf{r})\, d^2\mathbf{k}$$

for noninteger q. This generalization immediately provides us with a solution to Eq. (11) of the form

$$f(\mathbf{r}) = \frac{1}{(2\pi)^2} \int_{-\infty}^{\infty} \frac{1}{|\mathbf{k}|^q}\, N(\mathbf{k}) \exp(i\mathbf{k}\cdot\mathbf{r})\, d^2\mathbf{k} \tag{12}$$

where

$$N(\mathbf{k}) = \int_{-\infty}^{\infty} n(\mathbf{r}) \exp(-i\mathbf{k}\cdot\mathbf{r})\, d^2\mathbf{r}$$

Here, the complex spectrum of a 2D white Gaussian noise function is filtered with a lowpass filter of the form $1/|\mathbf{k}|^q$; hence, $f(\mathbf{r})$ has a characteristic power spectrum

$$|F(\mathbf{k})|^2 \propto \frac{1}{|\mathbf{k}|^{2q}} \tag{13}$$

This solution is written in terms of a 2D convolution integral using the convolution theorem. The result [Jone66] is

$$\int_{-\infty}^{\infty} |\mathbf{r}|^{q-2} \exp(-i\mathbf{k}\cdot\mathbf{r})\, d^2\mathbf{r} = \frac{\alpha}{|\mathbf{k}|^q}$$

where

$$\alpha = \frac{\left(\frac{q-2}{2}\right)!}{\left(-\frac{q}{2}\right)!} \, 2^q \pi$$

giving

$$f(\mathbf{r}) = \frac{1}{\alpha} \int \frac{N(\mathbf{r}')}{|\mathbf{r}-\mathbf{r}'|^{2-q}} \, d^2\mathbf{r}$$

This equation has the characteristic scaling property

$$g(\mathbf{r}) = \frac{1}{\alpha} \int \frac{N(\lambda\mathbf{r}')}{|\mathbf{r}-\mathbf{r}'|^{2-q}} \, d^2\mathbf{r}' = \frac{1}{\lambda^q} \frac{1}{\alpha} \int \frac{N(\mathbf{y})}{|\lambda\mathbf{r}-\mathbf{y}|^{2-q}} \, d^2\mathbf{y} = \frac{1}{\lambda^q} \, f(\lambda\mathbf{r})$$

where $\mathbf{y} = \lambda\mathbf{r}'$. The relationship between q and the fractal dimension, D, in this case is obtained by comparing Eq. (13) with Eq. (5), giving $q = 4 - D$.

Tailoring Fractal Signal and Images

From the results discussed in the earlier section on fractional differential equations, it is clear that a random fractal signal or image can be synthesized using Eqs. (7) and (12), respectively. These equations are the basis for a well-known algorithm commonly referred to as the 'Fourier filtering method' [Peit88]. For Eq. (12) in particular it is based on the following computational procedure:

compute the complex spectrum N;

filter N using a filter of the form $1/|\mathbf{k}|^q$;

inverse Fourier transform.

In practice N is computed directly, using random number generators to provide random amplitude, A, and phase ϕ values, in which case $N = A\cos\phi + iA\sin\phi$. Alternatively, N can be generated indirectly using a random number generator to provide the function n in 'real space' and then computing its Fourier transform. Of course, in either case discrete functions are used, and both the forward and inverse Fourier transform can be computed using a Fast Fourier Transform [Pres87]. In computing the quotient $N/|\mathbf{k}|^q$, the singularity of the filter, $1/|\mathbf{k}|^q$ (which occurs when $|\mathbf{k}| = 0$), must be avoided by setting a suitable DC level. The value of this DC level only affects the scale of the fractal, $f(\mathbf{r})$, and has no influence on its 'roughness'. In some algorithms the DC level is given a random value [Peit88], or it might be set to the value of its nearest offset. However, depending on the actual value assigned, the fractal does or does not possess negative values. This is important if, for example, the fractal is to be rectified, i.e., if $f < 0$ then set $f = 0$, in order to simulate certain types of sea- or landscapes where, for example, the parts of the fractal with negative height are assumed to be submerged under water and are therefore not displayed. Ultimately, in practical algorithms, like the value of the fractal dimension, the DC level can be a user-dependent parameter. Another user-dependent parameter is concerned with the generation of the stochastic function, n. This parameter — the so called 'seed' — affects the sequence of numbers that a random number generator actually outputs [Pres87]. Typically, the seed is some positive integer which alters the 'shape' of the fractal — its functional form. Hence, in practice random fractal algorithms are usually designed around two user input parameters:

the seed;

the fractal dimension.

Changing the fractal dimension changes the roughness of the image. The larger the value of D the rougher the fractal is. By implementing algorithms based on Eq. (7) or Eq. (12) on a digital computer and applying suitable graphics to the output for different values of the fractal dimension, it is easy to acquire a perspective on the 'realism' of the signal or image with respect to a given value of the fractal dimension. This allows a user to acquire a degree of prior knowledge about the roughness of the fractal signal or image before it is generated by inputting a given value of the fractal dimension.

Although the roughness or texture of a fractal is determined by the value of D, the shape or form of a fractal, i.e., its amplitude variations as a function of space, is governed by the amplitude variations of the stochastic function, n, which in turn are controlled by the value of the seed. It is, therefore, possible to 'document' the form of a fractal for different values of the seed. However, suppose a fractal is required with a predetermined form in which certain features, for example large scale amplitude variations, dominate/influence the fractal at a given locality. Clearly, some form of deterministic information on the form of the fractal must be included in the algorithms compounded in Eqs. (7) and (12). The problem is how to introduce this deterministic information in such a way that the final output is still a random scaling fractal, in the strict mathematical sense of the word. Since the form of the fractal is determined by the functional behaviour of n, prior information of the form required and compounded in the functional characteristics of a deterministic function, p for example, can be introduced by perturbing n with p. In order to have some control over the amount by which p perturbs n we introduce a control parameter, t, the transmission coefficient, such that as $t \rightarrow 1$ the effect of n on the fractal is negligible, and as $t \rightarrow 0$ the effect of p on the fractal is negligible. For applications to fractal signals and images, this idea is compounded by generalizing Eqs. (7) and (12) to the following forms, respectively

$$\frac{d^q}{dx^q} f(x) = (1-t)n(x) + tp(x) \tag{14}$$

and
$$\nabla^q f(\mathbf{r}) = (1-t)n(\mathbf{r}) + tp(\mathbf{r}) \tag{15}$$

where
$$0 \leq t \leq 1$$

Following the analysis provided in the earlier section on fractional differential equations, the solution to these equations is written in the form

$$f(x) = \frac{1}{2\pi} \int_{-\infty}^{\infty} \frac{1}{(ik)^q} \left[(1-t)N(k) + tP(k)\right] \exp(ikx)\,dk$$

and

$$f(\mathbf{r}) = \frac{1}{(2\pi)^2} \int_{-\infty}^{\infty} \frac{1}{|k|^q} \left[(1-t)N(\mathbf{k}) + tP(\mathbf{k})\right] \exp(i\mathbf{k}\cdot\mathbf{r})\,d^2\mathbf{k} \qquad (16)$$

respectively, where P is the Fourier transform of p.

The above results, in particular Eq. (16), were derived with the specific aim of 'tailoring' fractal landscapes for the synthesis of realistic terrain data whose applications, to date, include the computer generation of Radar 'ground truth' models. These landscapes, or Mandelbrot surfaces, are designed by constructing a function, $p(\mathbf{r})$, which contains the forms and features required in the fractal landscape, e.g., hills, valleys, ridges, etc. The functional characteristics of these forms and features is arbitrary and can be designed in a variety of ways, depending on the application and the deterministic information available. A variety of primitives have been considered, including circularly symmetric features such as Gaussians, cones and cylinders, and nonsymmetric features, such as rectangular blocks and pyramids. The amplitude, spatial extent and spatial location of each of the primitives used to construct p can be varied. Constructing p using mixtures of different features is also possible. In each case, by adjusting the value of t a Mandelbrot surface is generated whose global topological form is controlled by the forms and features incorporated in p, e.g., the number of hills, mountains and valleys, etc., and where they are placed in the image scene, but whose detailed structure is still seed dependent. In this way random fractals can be tailored to derive landscapes with a predetermined form. Note that in practice p and n may need to be rescaled so that $|p|_{\max} = 1$ and $|n|_{\max} = 1$. This ensures that the dynamic range of the functions used to generate the tailored fractal depends on the value of t alone and not on the original scales of n and p. Some examples of the results obtained using this approach are shown in Plates 2 and 3, which were computed on a 486 microprocessor with purpose-built graphics using Microsoft C. In each case the function, p, is displayed at the top left corner of the plate, below which is a display of the tailored fractal image. The associated surface plots are also provided. The displays were coded using a 4-bit topographic colour code. The numbers given in the plates refer (from left to right) to: picture number, seed, fractal dimension D, grid size, transmission coefficient t, graphics mode. The two displays at the bottom left corner of these plates are for diagnostic purposes only.

The influence of the deterministic information on tailoring the form of the fractal is self-evident. The global topology of the surfaces shown in Plates 2 and 3 reflects the functional form of p introduced by Eq. (16), but the detailed surface features are governed by the noise function, n, and the roughness of the model by the fractal dimension, D. In terms of the analysis provided in the earlier section on fractional differential equations, images of this type can be considered graphical representations of the solution to Eq. (15). A special case of this equation occurs when $t = 1$ and $q = 2$, yielding

$$\nabla^2 f(\mathbf{r}) = p(\mathbf{r})$$

This is Poisson's equation for a deterministic potential, p, which has the Green's function solution

$$f(\mathbf{r}) = \int \frac{p(\mathbf{r}')}{|\mathbf{r} - \mathbf{r}'|} \, d^2\mathbf{r}'$$

Computing the Fractal Dimension

Algorithms for computing fractal signals and images are well known and are used to synthesize a variety of complex images [Peit88]. The extension of the Fourier filtering method discussed in the previous section provides a solution to controlling the large scale forms and features of a random fractal. The roughness or texture of the fractal signal or image is determined by the fractional differential exponent, q, which in turn is related to the fractal dimension, D. Hence, the fractal dimension provides a measure of the roughness of a signal or the texture of an image. An interesting way to quantify the texture of an image, therefore, is to compute its fractal dimension. If the textural characteristics of an image appear to vary as a function of position then the fractal dimension can be computed as a function of position using a standard moving window technique which is discussed further in the section on fractal dimension segmentation. Either way, an efficient algorithm for computing the fractal dimension of a signal (1D data) or an image (2D data) is required. This is an inverse problem. In terms of Eqs. (14) and (15) it can be stated as: Given f, find q. In this section an algorithm for computing D is derived which provides a solution to this inverse problem.

By generating the power spectrum of a digital signal, the problem of computing the fractal dimension is reduced to that of finding a 'best fit' of the data to the curve $|k|^{-\beta}$, where $\beta = 2q$. This fit depends on the value of β and hence the fractal dimension. The analysis that follows yields an algorithm for computing β that is based on a least-squares approach to finding this best fit. It is presented in terms of discrete functions, which is consistent with the form of the data used, i.e., a digital signal or image.

FRACTAL SIGNALS

Consider a digital function, P_i, $0 \leq i \leq n$, which is composed of $n + 1$ elements and denotes the positive half of a discrete power spectrum where P_0 is the DC component squared. Let $\hat{P}_i$ be the expected form of the power spectrum of a fractal signal, i.e.

$$\hat{P}_i = \frac{c}{|k_i|^\beta}$$

where $k_i \equiv i$ and c is a constant of proportionality. Taking the natural logarithm of this equation yields

$$\ln \hat{P}_i = C - \beta \ln |k_i| \qquad C = \ln c$$

Suppose we construct a norm in the form of a least-squares error

$$e = \left\| \ln P_i - \ln \hat{P}_i \right\|_2^2$$

which from the preceding equation is written as

$$e = \sum_{i=0}^{n} \left[\ln P_i - (C - \beta \ln |k_i|) \right]^2$$

The error, e, is a function of both C and β. The values of C and β which minimize e are therefore the values for which the estimated curve, $\hat{P}_i$, provides a best fit (in a least-squares sense) to the data P_i. This occurs when

$$\frac{\partial e}{\partial \beta} = 2 \left(-C \sum_{i=0}^{n} \ln |k_i| + \beta \sum_{i=0}^{n} \left(\ln |k_i| \right)^2 + \sum_{i=0}^{n} (\ln P_i) \ln |k_i| \right) = 0$$

and

$$\frac{\partial e}{\partial C} = 2 \left(C \sum_{i=0}^{n} 1 - \beta \sum_{i=0}^{n} \ln |k_i| - \sum_{i=0}^{n} \ln P_i \right) = 0$$

Solving for β and C, we get

$$\beta = \frac{(n+1) \sum_{i=0}^{n} (\ln P_i) \ln |k_i| - \sum_{i=0}^{n} \ln |k_i| \sum_{i=0}^{n} \ln P_i}{\left(\sum_{i=0}^{n} \ln |k_i| \right)^2 - (n+1) \sum_{i=0}^{n} (\ln |k_i|)^2} \tag{17}$$

and

$$C = \frac{\sum_{i=0}^{n} \ln P_i + \beta \sum_{i=0}^{n} \ln |k_i|}{n+1}$$

Using the relationship $\beta = 5 - 2D$, Eq. (17) provides a noniterative formula for computing the fractal dimension from the power spectrum of a signal.

FRACTAL IMAGES

This previous algorithm is easily extended to 2D so that the fractal dimension of a random fractal image can be computed. In this case, the expected form of the fractal power spectrum, $\hat{P}_{ij}$, is

$$\hat{P}_{ij} = c|\mathbf{k}_{ij}|^{-\beta} |\mathbf{k}_{ij}| = \left(k_i^2 + k_j^2 \right)^{1/2}$$

where $k_i \equiv i$ and $k_j = j$. A similar calculation shows that the values of β and $C = \ln c$ which minimize the error function defined by

$$e = \sum_{i=0}^{n} \sum_{j=0}^{n} \left(\ln P_{ij} - \ln \hat{P}_{ij} \right)^2$$

are given by

$$\beta = \frac{(n+1)^2 \sum_{i=0}^{n} \sum_{j=0}^{n} \ln P_{ij} \, \ln |\mathbf{k}_{ij}| - \sum_{i=0}^{n} \sum_{j=0}^{n} \ln |\mathbf{k}_{ij}| \sum_{i=0}^{n} \sum_{j=0}^{n} \ln P_{ij}}{\left(\sum_{i=0}^{n} \sum_{j=0}^{n} \ln |\mathbf{k}_{ij}| \right)^2 - (n+1)^2 \sum_{i=0}^{n} \sum_{j=0}^{n} (\ln |\mathbf{k}_{ij}|)^2} \qquad (18)$$

and

$$C = \frac{\sum_{i=0}^{n} \sum_{j=0}^{n} \ln P_{ij} + \beta \sum_{i=0}^{n} \sum_{j=0}^{n} \ln |\mathbf{k}_{ij}|}{(n+1)^2}$$

In this case the fractal dimension is obtained from the equation $\beta = 8 - 2D$.

In each case, the value of D can be taken to provide a measure of the texture or roughness of the signal/image. In addition, C provides a measure of the 'energy' of the data, i.e., for continuous 1D functions the value of $\int |f(x)|^2 \, dx$, since from Rayleigh's theorem

$$\int |f(x)|^2 \, dx = \int |F(k)|^2 \, dk = c \int \frac{1}{|k|^\beta} \, dk$$

These formulae can be implemented using a 1D or 2D Fast Fourier Transform (FFT) to compute the discrete power spectrum of a signal or image, respectively [Pres87]. This requires data of size 2^k where $k = 1, 2, 3, \ldots$

Fractal Dimension Segmentation

By applying the algorithm described in the previous section for data within a predetermined window and then moving this window one element at a time over the signal or image, a set of values for D is obtained as a function of the window position. This is the 'moving window' principle which is used extensively for digital signal and image processing, examples of which include the finite impulse response filter, the moving average filter and the median filter. The values of D provide a characteristic profile of the fractal dimension, which in theory should vary between 1 and 2 for signal processing and 2 and 3 for image processing. In regions where the data is rough the value of D is large, and in regions where the data is smooth the value of D is small. Hence, the data can be segmented into regions of similarity which depend on the fractal dimension. This is known as Fractal Dimension Segmentation (FDS) and ultimately depends on how close the data being analysed is to a true random fractal, i.e., how close the power spectrum is to being of the form $1/|k|^\beta$ with β in the appropriate range.

In order to apply this algorithm to different signals and images, and in particular to investigate its practical implementation, software has been developed which includes the following options representing a collection of standard 'numerical recipes' for the application of FFT-based digital filters):

use of either the positive or negative half of the power spectrum;

inclusion or omission of the DC level;

specification of the size of the window used to sample a section of the signal or image; the choice is restricted to windows of size 2^k, where k is an integer, so that the FFT can be used;

a choice of data windows to be applied prior to taking the FFT (including the Square, Parzen, Welch, Hanning and Hamming windows);

padding the input data, e.g. zero padding, to ensure output of the same size.

This software has been implemented on a Silicon Graphics (IRIX) workstation using FORTRAN-77 and packaged together using a simple FORTRAN-based I/O interface. A procedure to test the accuracy of the algorithm has been used by synthesizing a fractal with a known value of D and then using the algorithm to compute D from the fractal. The techniques discussed in the earlier section on tailoring fractal signals and images have been used for this purpose. Experiments were conducted to assess the numerical accuracy of D using this algorithm and its relationship to the application of the numerical recipes given above. The two most important options are the number of samples used to compute the fractal dimension and the inclusion or omission of the DC level. In general, greater accuracy is achieved if the DC level is omitted from the data using 32 or more samples (typically with a Parzen window). In this case, the value of D computed is accurate to at least two decimal places. This accuracy is sufficient for segmenting 8-bit images. Note, as mentioned in the earlier section on tailoring fractal signals and images, although in a different context, the DC level only affects the scale of the data and has no influence on its roughness.

Application to Synthetic Aperture Radar Imagery

The algorithm discussed in the previous section has been applied to a variety of coherent and incoherent images, including optical and infrared images. However, a much closer and detailed investigation was conducted on the application of this algorithm to the segmentation of Synthetic Aperture Radar (SAR) images. Hence, the opportunity is taken to give a brief background of SAR and provide an example of the application of FDS to an SAR image.

When a pulse of microwave radiation is emitted from an airborne or satellite-borne antenna, a return signal can be recorded which is the result of this pulse interacting with structures on the ground or sea surface. This signal represents the time history of the back-scattered electric field due to the inhomogeneous nature of the earth's surface. Its character depends on both the radar cross-section and dielectric properties of this surface. By processing (matched filtering), a collection of these signals obtained by moving the antenna over a distance laterally, i.e., the tracking distance, known as the 'azimuth' direction, it is possible to generate an image of the ground or sea surface. This type of imagery is known as Synthetic Aperture Radar, because the size of the aperture and hence the resolution of the image is synthesized by processing the data [Blac89].

A SAR image is obtained by computing the amplitude modulations of the processed data. It is a fully coherent image, i.e., coherent in both range and azimuth, and, like other coherent images, contains 'speckle'. The frequency content and statistical characteristics of the speckle are a measure of the surface characteristics and composition of the ground. A wide range of textures is observed in a SAR image. SAR image understanding is almost exclusively concerned with analysis and segmentation of these textures, particularly for discrimination between man-made objects and natural ground clutter [Burl89]. Exactly how the dielectric and surface topology of the ground is related to the observed characteristics of a SAR image is extremely difficult to compute, since exact solutions to the scattering problem are only available for the simplest of objects [Mitc85].

SAR images are separable to a good approximation (the point spread function is a separable 'sinc' function). Algorithms can therefore be applied which work by processing the data in range and azimuth separately, on a signal-by-signal basis. A similar approach is adopted for the application of FDS using the algorithm discussed in the earlier section on computing the fractal dimension. The fractal dimension of all the rows and then all the columns of the data within a given window is computed using Eq. (17). The fractal dimension associated with the data defined by this window is then taken to be the average of all the D values obtained. An example of this is shown in Figures 1 and 2. Figure 1 is a 128×128 section of a SAR image of a ship (central feature) obtained with the SEASAT satellite, launched in June 1978 to carry out studies of the ocean surface using a range of microwave sensors. This image was histogram-equalized to enhance the

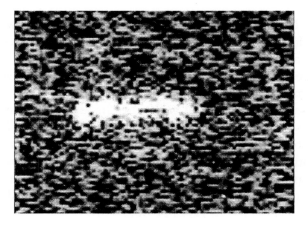

Figure 1. SAR image of a ship.

Figure 2. SAR image of a ship after Fractal Dimension Segmentation.

speckle or Radar 'clutter' caused by back-scatter from the sea surface. Figure 2 shows an image of the fractal dimension after applying FDS to the amplitude modulated signals using a 32×32 window, with the DC level omitted and a Parzen window applied. No padding was used in this example, so the output is reduced from 128×128 to 96×96. The result is a map of the fractal dimension — a floating point number between 1 and 2 — which has a very low dynamic range. In order to enhance this range, histogram equalization was applied, providing the result given in Figure 2. It is of particular interest that in tests conducted to date using SAR imagery the values of D computed using this algorithm are consistently within the theoretically valid range, i.e., between 1 and 2. In the example given in Figure 2, the minimum value of D is 1.64, the maximum value is 1.98 and the average value is 1.86. Only 0.02 percent of the total number of D values computed were outside this range.

Conclusions

Techniques have been presented for tailoring a random fractal with a given fractal dimension, and for computing the fractal dimension for a given random fractal. These methods are based on the spectral characteristics of a random fractal, and in this sense they fall into the 'Fourier-based methods' category for image analysis and segmentation [Stro86].

The use of fractional differential equations for analysing random scaling fractals provides a succinct statement of this field of study. There is clearly an unlimited class of fractional differential equations which can be considered as the basis for modelling a variety of stochastic processes, self-similar or otherwise [Tato89]. An important component of such models is the incorporation of deterministic information which can be encoded into a fractional differential equation in the manner compounded in Eqs. (14) and (15).

The algorithm for computing the fractal dimension is based on the definition of a fractal signal/image given by Eqs. (3) and (5) and, under the guise of this definition, seems the most natural technique for computing D. Extension of the algorithm to include fractal volumes, e.g., fractal clouds, involves a similar calculation. Initial work on the comparison of this algorithm with other published techniques such as the 'box counting method' [Kell89] for computing the fractal dimension indicates that it is possibly more 'robust', i.e., less sensitive to the initial characteristics of the data, and certainly less CPU intensive.

Although this paper focuses attention on the application of Fractal Dimension Segmentation to SAR images, the algorithm is not specific to any type of imagery or data. However, SAR images are a special case in that they allow the algorithm to be applied on a signal processing basis, i.e., repeated application of Eq. 17 rather than Eq. 18, which considerably reduces the CPU time involved. Also, from an examination and comparison of Figures 1 and 2 it is clear that the method might be of value in target detection as it provides an image (see Figure 2) which delineates the target (a ship in this case) from the surrounding clutter. Suitable targeting coordinates can easily be determined using the data shown in Figure 2 by, for example, computing the 'centre of gravity' of this image [Fair88].

The principal assumption required for the useful application of this algorithm is that the power spectrum of the data can, to a good approximation, be modelled according to Eq. (3) or Eq. (5). In some applications it may be necessary to consider a specific portion of the power spectrum which exhibits the proportionality compounded in these expressions [Gada91]. Finally, the algorithm has an added attraction in that because it is FFT-based it may at least be partially implemented in hardware using available real time signal and image processing technology. It should also be possible to implement Eqs. (17) and (18) in hardware.

Acknowledgments. This work is supported by the UK Science and Engineering Research Council, Reference Number GR/F 75209.

REFERENCES

[Bate54]
Bateman, H., *Tables of Integral Transforms*, Volume II, New York: McGraw-Hill, 1954.

[Blac89]
Blackledge, J.M., *Quantitative Coherent Imaging*, London: Academic Press, 1989.

[Bram89]
Brammer, R.F., Unified image computing based on fractals and chaos models, *Optical Engng.*, Vol. 28, No. 7, pp. 726–734.

[Burl89]
Burl, M.C., Owirka, G.J., and Novak, L.M., Texture discrimination in SAR imagery, 23rd Asilomar Conf. on Signals, Systems and Computers, Vol. 1, pp. 399–404, 1989.

[Denn89]
Dennis, T.J., and Dessipris. N.G., Fractal modelling in image texture and analysis, IEEE Proc., Vol. 136, F(5), pp. 227–235, 1989.

[Dold74]
Dold, A., and Eckmann. B., *Fractional Calculus and its Applications*, Lecture Notes in Mathematics, 457, Heidelberg: Springer-Verlag, 1974.

[Fair88]
Fairhurst, M.C., *Computer Vision for Robotic Systems*, Englewood Cliffs, NJ: Prentice-Hall, 1988.

[Fede88]
Feder, J., *Fractals*, New York: Plenum Press, 1988.

[Funa89]
Funakubo, N., Fractal based analysis and interpolation of 3D natural shapes, *Comput. Vision, Graph. and Image Process.*, Vol. 46, pp. 284–302, 1989.

[Gada91]
Gadallah, M.E., "Data Compression Techniques for Isolated and Connected Word Recognition", Ph.D. dissertation, Cranfield Institute of Technology, UK, 1991.

[Jone66]
Jones, D.S., *Generalized Functions*, New York: McGraw-Hill, 1966.

[Kell89]
Keller, J.M., and Chen, S., Texture description and segmentation through fractal geometry, *Comput. Vision, Graph. and Image Process.*, Vol. 45, pp. 150–166, 1989.

[Knil90]
Knill, D.C., Field, D., and Kersten, D., Human discrimination of fractal images, *Jour. Optical Soc. of America*, Vol. 7, No. 6, pp. 1113–1123, 1990.

[Mand83]
Mandelbrot, B.B., *The Fractal Geometry of Nature*, New York: W.H. Freeman, p. 310, 1983.

[Marr80]
Marr, D., and Hildreth, E., On the theory of edge detection, *Proc. Roy. Soc. London Ser. B*, Vol. 207, pp. 127–217, 1980.

[Mitc85]
Mitchell, R.L., *Radar Signal Simulation*, MARK Resources, 1985.

[Oldh74]
Oldham, K.B., and Spanier, J., The fractional calculus, *Mathematics in Science and Engineering*, Volume III, New York: Academic Press, 1974.

[Peit88]
Peitgen, H.-O., and Saupe, D., Eds., *The Science of Fractal Images*, New York: Springer-Verlag, 1988.

[Pele84]
Peleg, S., Naor, J., Hartley, R., and Avnir, D., Multiple resolution texture analysis and classification, *IEEE Trans. Patt. Anal. Mach. Intell.*, Vol. 6, No. 4, pp. 518–523, 1984.

[Peli90]

Peli, T., Multiscale fractal theory and object characterization, *Jour. Optical Soc. of America*, Vol. 7, No. 6, pp. 1101–1112, 1990.

[Pres87]

Press, W.H., Flannery, B.P., Teukolsky, S.A., and Vetterling, W.T., *Numerical Recipes*, Cambridge, UK: Cambridge Univ. Press, 1987.

[Stro86]

Stromberg, W.D., and Farr, T.G., A Fourier-based textural feature extraction procedure, *IEEE Trans. on Geoscience and Remote Sensing*, Vol. 24, No. 5, pp. 722–731, 1986.

[Tato89]

Tatom, F.B., The application of fractional calculus to the simulation of stochastic processes, *AIAA Jour.*, Vol. 89, pp. 1–7, 1989.

[Yoko89]

Yokoya, N., and Yamamoto, K., Fractal based analysis and interpolation of 3D natural surface shapes, *Comput. Vision, Graph. and Image Process.*, Vol. 46, pp. 284–302, 1989.

Fractal-based Analysis and Synthesis of Multispectral Visual Texture for Camouflage

Lewis F. Jardine

Abstract

The fractal model forms the basis of a texture analysis and synthesis technique for use on perceived visual texture in natural scenes of vegetation. Preliminary studies found that the perceived visual textures of natural scenes depart noticeably from the fractal model.[†]

The model is adapted to allow for deviation between perceived natural visual texture and true fractals. A texture generator is used to synthesize natural visual texture. Principal component analysis is used to extend the technique to multispectral images. Colour images of natural scenes are analyzed and texture inserts prepared. A subjective trial is used in order to evaluate the effectiveness of the technique for generating camouflage.

Introduction

The objective of this work was to synthesize the perceived visual texture of natural images of vegetation for the purpose of camouflage. Visual texture is a fundamental property of images which plays a key role in the description of images. Texture is an innate property of all surfaces and contains important information about the surface. Perhaps due to the abundance of texture in our everyday lives, human observers find it quite easy to recognize and describe texture in relative terms. Attempts at the mathematical description of texture have produced a wide variety of statistical and primitive based descriptions, some of which are extremely complex.

FRACTALS

Mandelbrot [Mand82, 77] developed the *fractal* concept, which describes textures very economically. The second-order statistics of a fractal texture are defined by one number, its fractional (or fractal) dimension. This real number was found

---

[†]The human eye's sensitivity to fractal dimension is already determined.

to be directly related to the perceived graininess or roughness of the texture by Pentland [Pent84].

Mandelbrot previously used the fractal model to synthesize images which imitated natural scenes well. Others, such as Peleg et al. [Pele84] and Pentland, investigated and developed these ideas and used the fractal model for analysis of visual texture. One method (documented by Pentland) for finding the fractal dimension, D, of a visual texture is to plot the $\log_{10}$ of the standard deviation of the differences in intensities between pairs of pixels against the $\log_{10}$ of their separation. The gradient of this graph is a straight line if the texture is fractal (because of self-similarity at all scales) with a gradient, g. The self-similarity factor, H, often used to describe fractals, is expressed as $H = 1 - g$. The fractal dimension is expressed in Eq. 1, where D_T is the topological dimension

$$D = D_T + 1 - H \qquad (1)$$

TEXTURE ANALYSIS

Preliminary work on the analysis of natural visual texture [Jard89] found that the visual texture of natural scenes is not truly fractal and produces curves rather than straight lines on the $\log - \log$ graph (see Figure 1). This departure from the fractal model is caused by changes in the structural generation mechanism of the vegetation model at differing scales (for example, branches and leaves). Also, natural visual texture can be anisotropic. Despite these departures from the fractal model, using the difference in intensity versus separation is still an efficient and effective method for categorizing the texture. The computed points on the graph are used instead of the gradient-related fractal dimension, and care must be taken to analyse the image in different directions to check for anisotropy.

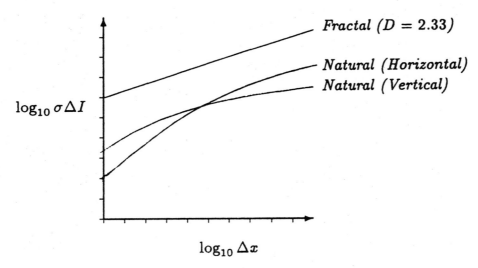

Figure 1. Graphs for true fractals and typical natural textures.

In practice only the horizontal and vertical directions were analysed, because nature grows with gravity and light rather than at random angles. Early work reported by Dodd [Dodd87] also analysed the positive diagonal direction, but this was typically found to be the mean of the vertical and horizontal directions.

Texture Synthesis

The texture synthesis algorithm used in this work has similarities with a stochastic pseudofractal texture generator proposed by Fournier, Fussell and Carpenter [Four82]. The generator is based on an algorithm for interpolating the values in a square region from those at its corners.

Interpolation Algorithm

The two corner values are averaged to find the values at the midpoints of the sides, and all the corner values are averaged to find the value of the centre point of the square. Then the algorithm is recursively repeated on the four subsquares formed from the four original corner points, the four midpoints of the sides and the centre point of the original square. These four subsquares can be thought of as the next generation, or scale. This process continues until every pixel in the square area is interpolated (see Figure 2). To achieve this the side length of the original square must be of the form $2^n + 1$, where n is an integer.

Centre Point Perturbation Algorithm

The interpolation algorithm is converted into a texture generator by perturbing the centre points of the squares at each generation by a Gaussian pseudorandom variable with a deviation specified for each generation or scale. Pseudofractal texture with $D = 2.5$ is generated by halving the deviation at successive generations to preserve self-similarity.

To prepare texture inserts, the algorithm is modified so that a border from the original image is left; only pixels not previously specified are calculated by the algorithm. This is implemented by checking to see whether the pixel to be calculated has a nonzero value; if so it is left unaltered. The area to be calculated is set to zero before the texture generation algorithm is run.

Multispectral Textures

In order to extend the texture generation techniques to cover multispectral images the eigenvector principal component transformation is used. This transforms the image onto new axes which are uncorrelated, unlike the original RGB axes; this also serves to reduce the redundancy in the image which leads to data compression [Lowi76]. The new axes are the eigenvectors of the original RGB image, and the significance of each axis is directly proportional to its eigenvalue. The eigenvectors and eigenvalues are calculated from the covariance matrix of

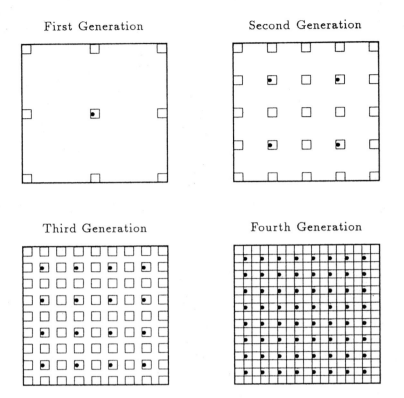

Figure 2. Points calculated in successive generations.

the image. There are various numerical techniques for doing this. (see [Prat78; Gonz77; Wata65]).

The technique works by placing the first principal component axis along the direction of maximum variance in the original image (see Figure 3). The second axis is placed on the direction of maximum variance orthogonal to the first axis, and the third axis is placed orthogonal to the other two.

For the rowan tree test image (see Plate 4) the first principal component contains *green-blue* foliage information and accounts for approximately 93% of the information in the image. The second component contains *reddish* information and accounts for approximately 5% of the information in the image. The final 2% of the information is held in the third principal component (see Plate 5).

FOUR OR MORE SPECTRAL COMPONENTS

The eigenvector approach to multispectral images is not limited to three component images (Lowitz used seven band visual images [Lowi76]), and other nonvisible spectral bands can be used as well. Four-band Landsat images have been used to test the extension of this technique. The four bands used in Landsat are red, green, 0.7 to 0.8 and 0.8 to 1.1 micron near infrared. The technique can be extended to include 2 to 5 micron infrared, 8 to 14 micron thermal-band and even

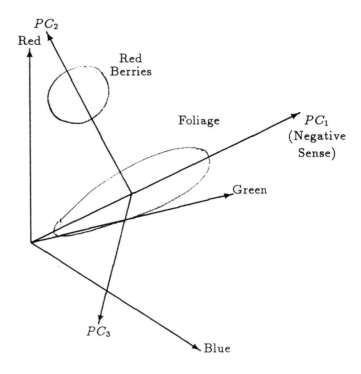

Figure 3. Principal component axes for the rowan tree picture.

ultra-violet data. One of the main practical problems in obtaining multispectral images is aligning and registering the image data from the various imagers.

Trials

HUMAN VISUAL SYSTEM

Schneider and Shiffrin [Schn77] proposed a two-process theory for the human visual system with two quite different visual search and detection processes, automatic detection and controlled search. Automatic detection is an unconscious, fast (≤ 200 ms), parallel process which operates simultaneously over the entire field of view and detects previously well-known features. Controlled search is a slower serial search process which requires the attention of the observer. Each portion of the image is analysed in turn, limited by the processing capacity of the visual system, but it is used to pick out less well-known and more difficult targets.

Biederman et al. [Bied81] found that automatic detection is unreliable for detecting targets that are small, camouflaged or violating normal relational constraints, even when they are only 3° or 4° from the centre of vision. Clearly, if the target is found by automatic detection then the camouflage is ineffective. King, Stanley and Burrows [King84] found that if automatic detection processes occur then constant detection times under 500 ms are expected. If controlled search is required for target detection then a range of longer reaction times should occur. Thus, if camouflage is effective then a range of detection times longer than 500 ms is expected, indicating that automatic detection is not occurring.

In the above experiments it was found, not surprisingly, that if the subjects were asked to search for a target in a scene which had none then relatively constant long search times could be expected. This indicates exhaustive search of the entire image. It follows that during controlled search the detection time is merely an indication of what percentage of the image has been scanned before the target is detected. Thus, detection time is a poor measure of camouflage. One solution is to allow enough search time to completely scan the image and to vary the range (and thus the visual angle the target subtends) in order to measure the maximum range at which the target is detected.

PREPARATION OF TEXTURE INSERTS

A 35mm camera was used to capture a variety of scenes containing natural vegetation on slide film. The slides were digitized using a light desk and gelatine filters to separate the red, green and blue components prior to capture. These images were to be used as the backgrounds for the subjective trials.

For each background image the covariance matrix was calculated for the area of vegetation, taking care to keep to a homogeneous region. The eigenvector matrix and eigenvalues were then calculated from the covariance matrix. The original RGB image was multiplied by the eigenvector matrix in order to transform it into principal component space. The texture of each principal component was analysed for later use in generating the artificial texture insert.

Each insert is placed in a 128×128 pixel area, with typically eight insert positions for each background image. The shape of the insert was cut out of the insert area in each of the principal components by setting the pixels that fell within the shape to zero. All shapes used in the trials had the same area in pixels. Sawtooth edges were used to avoid straight edges, which the human eye–brain system is especially good at detecting. The objective of the trials was to test the textural properties of the inserts.

A texture insert was generated for each principal component using the centre point perturbation algorithm. The coefficients at each generation were chosen to match the generated texture to the texture of the principal components of the vegetation in the background scene. First-order statistics were found by the interpolation from the surrounding region of the original image. This was necessary because any attempt to alter the first-order statistics of the texture insert after generation would have resulted in continuity breaks in grey level around the edges of the insert. These would have highlighted the inserts and invalidated trials of the texture properties.

TRIALS DESIGN

As with previous work described by Kelly and Savoie [Kell73] a forced-choice method was used to avoid error associated with individuals' differing criteria for certainty. Subjects were instructed to respond to all images at all ranges and to give their best guess if they were unsure. Untrained observers were used for the trials due to their availability.

The trial was designed to link with the Johnson Criteria, which were formulated after trials on various military targets under a wide range of conditions. The trial aimed to use the detection and recognition criteria, but identification, by its very specific definition, was unsuitable.

Subjects were shown slides of natural backgrounds with artificial texture inserts. They were asked to identify the position and shape of the insert. This was repeated at ranges of 1.6, 3, 4, 6, 8 and 11 metres. In terms of visual angle this translates to a large vehicle at ranges of 50 to 400 metres, although the reduced contrast, field of view, lack of target edges and shadows all serve to make this comparison only an approximation. The range was successively decreased for some subjects and increased for others in order to identify any learning curves. As the subjects were trained on a number of slides before the trial began there was very little learning exhibited by the subjects during the trial. Ten slides were displayed at each of the six ranges, and subjects were asked to complete a multiple choice questionnaire indicating the position and shape of the artificial insert.

The slides were projected to form an image about 90 cm by 75 cm. Analysis of previous trials information [King84] indicated that an exposure time of fifteen to twenty seconds was quite adequate for the subject to search an image subtending this visual angle. A pretrial run showed that an eighteen second exposure (with two seconds to change the slide) was sufficient. It was thought inadvisable to lengthen the exposure period beyond what was necessary, because of the risk of losing the subjects' attention.

Detection

The subjects were asked to choose which one of eight possible locations (see Figure 4) contained the artificial texture insert. Thus, a guess would be correct one in eight times; therefore, if the trial mean for an insert is less than or equal to 12.5% it indicates that the subjects are unable to detect it at that specific range.

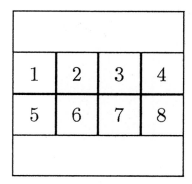

Figure 4. Eight possible insert positions.

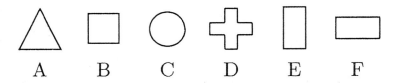

Figure 5. Six possible insert shapes.

Recognition

The second level of complexity of the trial attempted to determine at what range the subjects recognized the shape of the insert. Again a forced-choice trial was used, with the subjects being asked to pick out one of six possible shapes (see Figure 5); this gave a $1/6$ chance of a guess being correct. This part of the trial did not affect the results of the first part (detection) but was dependent on it. If the subjects looked in the wrong place for the insert then they could not possibly recognize its shape. Thus, results for the second half of the trial were valid only if the subject responded correctly to the first half. This caused some problems with low sample sizes in the trials. Backgrounds used in the trials are shown with artificial inserts in all eight possible locations in Figures 6 and 7 and in Plates 6–9. These illustrate the effectiveness of the technique. The artificial inserts are numbered to aid readers in detecting them.

Figure 6. Corn field background with inserts.

Figure 7. Woodland background with inserts.

Results

Forty-seven subjects were used in the trials. The results are presented in Table 1 with the visual angle, subtended by the entire image, used instead of range. Data is included for both position and shape of the inserts. The background type is also given to allow comparisons between background types.

One factor that makes comparison of the detectabilities of inserts difficult is that the detectabilities are measured over different visual angles. A simple solution can be found if the detectabilities of all the inserts are calculated for a specific visual angle. Analysis of the data shows an approximately linear relationship between visual angle and detectability. Linear interpolation can be used to calculate the detectability of inserts for a given background at a specific visual angle (or range). Both the detection and recognition results have been calculated in a similar manner for all seven trials backgrounds (see Figure 8). These clearly indicate that the algorithm was more successful on some backgrounds than others.

A more formal analysis of the trials data using analysis of variance (ANOVA) is presented in Appendix A. The results from the ANOVA confirm those presented above.

Conclusion

Multispectral visual texture of natural scenes of vegetation has been analyzed and synthesized. While moderately successful for all background types, the technique was especially successful for those types with a uniform isotropic texture

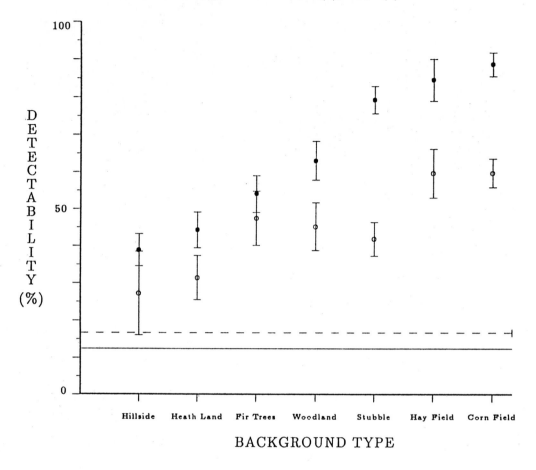

Mean Detection and Recognition by Background
With 95% Confidence Limits of Estimate of Mean
Visual Angle = 1.6° Position (•), Shape (o)

Figure 8. Relative detectabilities for backgrounds.

with no shape elements. These obviously suit the isotropic texture generator used here as well as the fact that the texture analysis is not shape-oriented. An anisotropic texture generator can be used to improve the performance of the technique on directional textures.

Acknowledgments. This work was carried out with the support of the Stores and Clothing Research and Development Establishment, Ministry of Defence. I am most grateful to Dr. Nigel Dodd and Dr. Chris Woodruff for initiating this research and for support during the early stages. I am also grateful to Dr. Alan Vickers and SCRDE for seeing its potential and supporting it financially. Many

Table 1. Table of raw trials data.

No.	Picture Background Type	Forwards Vis Ang θ	Sample n	Detect x_D	Recog x_R	Backwards Vis Ang θ	Sample n	Detect x_D	Recog x_R
1	Woodland	0.73	25	14	9	5.00	22	22	21
2	Stubble	0.73	25	15	2	5.00	22	20	12
3	Hillside	0.73	25	7	1	5.00	22	12	1
4	Corn field	0.73	25	14	0	5.00	22	19	4
5	Hayfield	0.73	25	18	18	5.00	22	22	22
6	Stubble	0.73	25	14	6	5.00	22	18	8
7	Heath land	0.73	25	2	0	5.00	22	15	6
8	Fir trees	0.73	25	7	2	5.00	21	12	7
9	Corn field	0.73	25	22	17	5.00	21	21	20
10	Fir trees	0.73	25	19	8	5.00	21	21	19
11	Corn field	1.00	25	21	9	2.70	22	22	14
12	Hayfield	1.00	25	19	10	2.70	22	21	15
13	Heath land	1.00	25	8	1	2.70	22	15	8
14	Stubble	1.00	25	18	5	2.70	22	19	8
15	Hillside	1.00	25	6	3	2.70	22	17	7
16	Stubble	1.00	25	17	3	2.70	22	20	7
17	Corn field	1.00	25	20	12	2.70	22	20	17
18	Hayfield	1.00	25	20	8	2.70	22	19	12
19	Fir trees	1.00	25	4	0	2.70	22	14	9
20	Hillside	1.00	25	10	1	2.70	22	18	3
21	Corn field	1.30	25	23	20	2.00	22	22	20
22	Woodland	1.30	25	15	11	2.00	22	19	15
23	Hillside	1.30	25	14	8	2.00	22	15	11
24	Heath land	1.30	25	13	2	2.00	22	18	4
25	Stubble	1.30	25	17	3	2.00	22	19	3
26	Corn field	1.30	25	22	19	2.00	22	22	20
27	Woodland	1.30	25	8	2	2.00	22	14	6
28	Stubble	1.30	25	23	13	2.00	22	22	16
29	Hillside	1.30	25	2	0	2.00	22	3	0
30	Heath land	1.30	25	2	0	2.00	22	12	0
31	Stubble	2.00	25	24	24	1.30	22	20	19
32	Fir trees	2.00	25	16	8	1.30	22	10	2
33	Heath land	2.00	25	8	3	1.30	22	9	3
34	Woodland	2.00	25	14	8	1.30	22	18	9
35	Hillside	2.00	25	18	2	1.30	22	7	0
36	Fir trees	2.00	25	20	12	1.30	22	20	14
37	Woodland	2.00	25	9	1	1.30	22	10	2
38	Stubble	2.00	25	17	8	1.30	22	16	8
39	Corn field	2.00	25	23	19	1.30	22	21	19
40	Heath land	2.00	25	14	1	1.30	22	10	1
41	Heath land	2.70	25	18	17	1.00	22	10	7
42	Stubble	2.70	25	21	5	1.00	22	19	1
43	Hillside	2.70	25	5	0	1.00	22	1	0
44	Stubble	2.70	25	24	11	1.00	22	17	7
45	Corn field	2.70	25	22	18	1.00	22	21	18

Table 1. Continued.

No.	Picture Background Type	Forwards Vis Ang θ	Sample n	Detect x_D	Recog x_R	Backwards Vis Ang θ	Sample n	Detect x_D	Recog x_R
46	Hayfield	2.70	25	21	13	1.00	22	22	3
47	Hillside	2.70	25	16	8	1.00	22	6	3
48	Fir trees	2.70	25	18	17	1.00	22	7	6
49	Woodland	2.70	25	19	7	1.00	22	16	1
50	Fir trees	2.70	25	20	8	1.00	22	6	1
51	Corn field	5.00	25	24	12	0.73	22	21	4
52	Hillside	5.00	25	19	11	0.73	22	8	4
53	Stubble	5.00	25	23	13	0.73	22	16	9
54	Woodland	5.00	25	20	14	0.73	22	14	3
55	Heath land	5.00	25	23	23	0.73	22	10	7
56	Hillside	5.00	25	18	9	0.73	22	8	2
57	Woodland	5.00	25	22	21	0.73	22	14	8
58	Corn field	5.00	25	22	10	0.73	22	19	2
59	Fir trees	5.00	25	21	19	0.73	22	10	5
60	Stubble	5.00	25	23	14	0.73	22	19	7

thanks to Ian Whitworth for continuing support and encouragement, and to Dr. Ed Adams for help with the statistics.

REFERENCES

[Bied81]
Biederman, I., Mezzanotte, R.J., Rabinowitz, J.C., Francolini, C.M., and Plude, D., Detecting the unexpected in photointerpretation, *Human Factors*, Vol. 23, No. 2, pp. 153–164, 1981.

[Dodd87]
Dodd, N.A., Multispectral texture synthesis using fractal concepts, *IEEE Trans. Patt. Anal. Mach. Intell.*, Vol. 9, No. 5, pp. 703–707, September 1987.

[Four82]
Fournier, A., Fussell, D., and Carpenter, L., Computer rendering of stochastic models, *CACM*, Vol. 25, No. 6, pp. 371–384, 1982.

[Gonz77]
Gonzalez, R.C., and Wintz, P., *Digital Image Processing*, Reading, MA: Addison-Wesley, 1977.

[Jard89]
Jardine, L.F., "Digital Image Processing as an Aid to Camouflage Design and Assessment", Ph.D. dissertation, School of Electrical Engineering and Science, Royal Military College of Science (Cranfield), Shrivenham, UK, May 1989.

[Kell73]
Kelly, D.H., and Savoie, R.E., A study of sine-wave contrast sensitivity by two psychophysical methods, *Perception and Psycophysics*, Vol. 14, No. 2, pp. 313–318, 1973.

[King84]

King, M., Stanley, G., and Burrows, G., Visual search processes in camouflage detection, *Human Factors*, Vol. 26, No. 2, pp. 223–234, 1984.

[Lowi76]

Lowitz, G.E., Stability and dimensionality of karhunen-loêve multispectral image expansion, in *Proceedings 3rd International Conference on Pattern Recognition*, pp. 673–677, 1976.

[Mand77]

Mandelbrot, B.B., *Fractals: Form, Chance, and Dimension*, San Francisco, CA: W.H. Freeman, 1977.

[Mand82]

Mandelbrot, B.B., *The Fractal Geometry of Nature*, San Francisco: W.H. Freeman, 1982.

[Pele84]

Peleg, S., Naor, J., Hartley, R., and Avnir, D., Multiple resolution texture analysis and classification, *IEEE Trans. Patt. Anal. Mach. Intell.*, Vol. 6, No. 4, pp. 518–523, 1984.

[Pent84]

Pentland, A.P., Fractal-based description of natural scenes, *IEEE Trans. Patt. Anal. Mach. Intell.*, Vol. 6, No. 6, pp. 661–674, 1984.

[Prat78]

Pratt, W.K., *Digital Image Processing*, New York: Wiley Interscience, 1978.

[Sche59]

Scheffé, *The Analysis of Variance*, New York: Wiley, 1959.

[Schn77]

Schneider, W., and Shiffrin, R.M., Controlled and automatic human information processing: 1. detection, search and attention, *Psychological Rev.*, Vol. 84, No. 1, pp. 1–66, 1977.

[Wata65]

Watanabe, S., Karhunen-loêve expansion and factor analysis, theoretical remarks and applications, in *4th International Conference on Pattern Recognition*, pp. 635–660, 1965.

Appendix A — Analysis of Variance

Analysis of variance (ANOVA) tests for the equality of more than two normal populations. Random samples from the populations are compared, and their significance is tested. ANOVA makes inferences about effects (α_i, β_j) and their interactions in a linear model. Thus the overall observed variable (γ_{ijk}) can be expressed in terms of the effects, their interactions and also an error term, ε_{ijk}, where k is used to indicate replication, i.e.

$$\gamma_{ijk} = \alpha_i + \beta_j + \alpha\beta_{ij} + \varepsilon_{ijk}$$

The usual practice when using ANOVA is to hypothesize that the effects being tested $(\alpha_i, \beta_j$ and $\alpha\beta_{ij})$ are constant (for all values of i and j).[†] Tests are carried out to reveal significant effects, e.g., that the α_i values are different (indicating an α effect), by

---

[†] $\alpha_1 = \alpha_2 = \alpha_3$, etc.

Table A–1. Detection chance means (%) for direction and visual angle.

Direction	Visual Angle						Direction Totals
	0.73°	1.0°	1.3°	2.0°	2.7°	5.0°	
Forward	132	143	139	163	184	215	976
Backward	158	142	160	189	210	210	1069
Visual angle totals	290	285	299	352	394	425	Grand total = 2045

partitioning the total sum of squares (corrected about the mean) into sums of squares due to effects, interactions and error. The corrected sums of squares are distributed as scaled, χ_k^2 (χ_1^2 is the square of the normal distribution). The ratios of the corrected sums of squares of the various components and the residual sum of squares are distributed as F. If the ratio is large (compared with the tabulated F value) then the null hypothesis can be rejected at a given level of significance. Thus, if the ratio is greater than the 5% value of F, less than 1 in 20 samples gives this result if the means are the same. Thus, we reject the null hypothesis at the 95% level of certainty. For a fuller coverage of ANOVA the reader is referred to Scheffe [Sche59].

ANALYSIS OF VISUAL ANGLE AND DIRECTION

The original hypothesis was that both the visual angle (range) and the direction of movement[†] did not affect the subjects' ability to detect the positions of the artificial inserts. ANOVA was performed on all the trials data using the six distances (or visual angles) as one variable and the two directions (forwards and backwards) as the other variable. The means are seen in Table A–1.

From Table A–2 it is possible to reject the null hypothesis that there is no effect from the visual angle at the 0.1% level. The visual angle effect is significant at the 99.9% level; thus, the range (not unexpectedly) is a factor in detection. This shows that the sample was great enough to give statistically meaningful results.

Results for direction were less conclusive and were not found to be significant at even the 5% level, making it impossible to reject the null hypothesis that the direction of movement played no part in detection. Thus, there does not appear to have been a very significant learning effect throughout the trial, which strengthens the validity of the results. It is still possible (and indeed likely) that there was a small learning effect throughout the trials, but it was considerably less significant than the other effects (noise).

ANALYSIS OF VISUAL ANGLE AND BACKGROUND

Again, the original hypothesis was that both the visual angle and the background scene had no effect on the subjects' ability to detect the position of artificial texture inserts.

[†]By direction of movement we mean moving closer to the screen or retreating from it to test for a learning curve.

Table A–2. ANOVA for direction and visual angle.

Source	s.s.	d.f.	M.S.	M.S.R.	F
Analysis of Variance Table					
Between visual angles VA	875	$c - 1 = 5$	175.0	5.1***	$F_{5,108}[0.1\%] \approx 4.76$
Between directions D	72	$r - 1 = 1$	72.0	2.1N.S.	$F_{1,108}[5\%] \approx 4.$
$VA \times D$ interaction	52	$(c-1)(r-1) = 5$	10.4	0.3N.S.	$F_{5,108}[5\%] \approx 2.37$
Residual	3733	$rc(n-1) = 108$	34.6		
Totals (for checking)	4732	$rcn - 1 = 119$			

Table A–3. Detection chance means (%) for background andvisual angle.

Background	Visual Angle						Means Over
	0.7°	1.0°	1.3°	2.0°	2.7°	5.0°	Visual Angle
Hillside	32.2	23.9	32.0	56.4	60.8	64.2	44.9
Heath land	26.8	38.8	36.6	56.1	70.0	80.0	51.4
Fir trees	48.8	22.8	56.1	69.0	69.8	81.5	58.0
Woodland	60.0	61.4	54.9	60.6	82.0	92.0	68.5
Stubble	69.0	76.0	81.0	87.6	89.3	89.2	82.0
Corn field	81.5	88.8	92.8	96.0	91.7	92.6	90.6
Means over background	53.1	52.0	58.9	71.0	77.3	83.3	Overall mean = 65.9

Table A–4. ANOVA for background and visual angle.

Source	s.s.	d.f.	M.S.	M.S.R.	F
Analysis of Variance Table					
Between visual angles VA	2594	$c - 1 = 5$	519.0	13.95***	$F_{5,36}[0.1\%] \approx 5.3$
Between backgrounds B	4765	$r - 1 = 5$	953.0	25.62***	$F_{5,36}[0.1\%] \approx 5.3$
$VA \times B$ interaction	1110	$(c-1)(r-1) = 25$	44.4	1.19	$F_{25,36}[5\%] \approx 1.83$
Residual	1340	$rc(n-1) = 36$	37.2		
Totals (for checking)	9809	$rcn - 1 = 71$			

Part of the initial hypothesis (about visual angle) has already been disproved in the previous section, but this provides a useful reference to the significance of the result for background.

As the direction was found to have a less than significant effect on detection, the decision was to group the data from the two directions together to increase the sample size in order to have enough information to analyze the detection rate by background. Even so, the Hayfield background was omitted due to insufficient sample size. Table A–3 presents this data.

One feature worthy of comment is the decrease in mean detectability when the visual angle increases from 0.73° to 1.0°. This occurs in only two of the six backgrounds, but the effect is strong enough to reverse those of the other four backgrounds. The most likely cause of this is differences in the effectiveness of the camouflage in different areas of the image. The fir tree background was more prone to this than other backgrounds because of strong shape elements (in this case, tree trunks).

Table A–4 shows that the hypothesis that visual angle (or distance) has no effect on detection can be rejected again at the 0.1% level. More importantly, the hypothesis that the background does not affect detection can also be rejected at the same level. This statistically confirms the graphical evidence presented earlier.

Positive Wavelet Representation of Fractal Signals and Images

Graham H. Watson and J. Glynn Jones

Abstract

With appropriate choice of an analysing wavelet in the form of a positive pulse, information concerning the structure of a signal is concentrated economically in the local maxima and minima of the function of two variables, position and scale, given by the wavelet transformation. This information is extracted by a process of correlation detection, in which the analysing wavelet is regarded as a multiple-scale matched filter. Identification of local extrema corresponds to the detection of signal wavelets. The ensemble of such signal wavelets provides a discrete feature-based representation of the given function. In contrast to the standard method of reconstruction by means of the linear inverse wavelet transform, an alternative method of reconstruction from the feature-based representation is demonstrated. Applications of the positive wavelet representation to an elucidation of the fractal structure of measured and simulated turbulence are illustrated. The method extends in a straightforward manner to two dimensions. An application which demonstrates the multiple-scale feature-based representation of a two-dimensional image is presented.

Positive Wavelet Analysis

The (real) wavelet transformation of a given function $g(x)$ takes the form

$$g \to T(y, L) = L^{-1/2} \int_{-\infty}^{\infty} g(x) \, \bar{F}\left\{ \frac{x - y}{L} \right\} dx \qquad (1)$$

where the 'analysing wavelet' is derived from a single prescribed function, $\bar{F}(x)$, through translation by y and dilation by L. Thus, the function $g(x)$ is processed through varying degrees of resolution, or magnification, to reveal components that are localised in both physical (position) and wave number (scale) space.

Under constraints on $\bar{F}(x)$, which include finite energy and zero mean, $g(x)$ is reconstructed from $T(y, L)$ by means of the linear inverse wavelet transform [Kron87; Gros85]

$$g(x) = \frac{1}{C} \int_0^{\infty} \int_{-\infty}^{\infty} T(y, L) \, \frac{\bar{F}\left\{ \dfrac{x - y}{L} \right\}}{L^{1/2}} \, \frac{dL \, dy}{L^2} \qquad (2)$$

where C is a numerical constant that depends on $\bar{F}(x)$.

In the method of positive wavelet analysis (see [Jone92]), $\bar{F}(x)$ is taken to be a positive pulse. Since this violates the condition of zero mean, Eq. (2) is no longer available. Nevertheless, $g(x)$ is reconstructed approximately as a weighted sum

$$g(x) \approx \sum_i m_i \, \bar{F}\left\{ \frac{x - y_i}{L_i} \right\} \tag{3}$$

of 'signal wavelets' $\bar{F}\{(x - y_i)/L_i\}$ located at positions (y_i, L_i) in position–scale space at which there occur local extrema (maxima or minima) in the correlation surface, $T(y, L)$ (Eq. 1). Moreover, the use of such a positive wavelet leads to a concentration of information into the local extrema in $T(y, L)$ and hence to an economical discrete feature-based representation of $g(x)$.

The coefficients m_i in Eq. (3) are found by minimising the residual sum of squares between the two sides of this approximate equality. In the particular case in which the components $\bar{F}\{(x - y_i)/L_i\}$ are nonoverlapping, the coefficients m_i are found by a sequence of independent minimisations at each of the locations y_i, L_i. This process can be interpreted in terms of 'correlation detection' (see [Jone90; Earw90, Earw88] in which the analysing wavelet is regarded as a matched filter, and the identification of the local extrema at positions (y_i, L_i) corresponds to the detection of associated signal wavelets. The result of such local minimisation is

$$m_i = L_i^{-1/2} \, T(y_i, L_i) \tag{4}$$

Substituting into Eq. (3) yields

$$g(x) \approx \sum_i T(y_i, L_i) \frac{\bar{F}\left\{ \dfrac{x - y_i}{L_i} \right\}}{L_i^{1/2}} \tag{5}$$

Note the close formal resemblance to Eq. (2).

In general, the components $\bar{F}\{(x - y_i)/L_i\}$ located at the local extrema in $T(y, L)$ exhibit considerable overlap. Such interaction implies redundancy in the information contained in the numerical values, $T(y_i, L_i)$. The removal of this redundancy is achieved by performing a global minimisation of the residual sum of squares between the two sides of the approximate equality (Eq. 3), in general resulting in weighting coefficients, m_i, which differ from those given by Eq. (4).

The approximate reconstruction given by Eq. (3), with weighting coefficients m_i derived by global minimisation, for many practical purposes provides an adequate approximation, as illustrated in subsequent sections of this paper. However, successively improved approximations can be derived iteratively by subtracting the signal wavelets already detected from $g(x)$ and computing $T(y, L)$ for the resulting difference function. This allows the benefits of exploiting the concentration of information in local extrema to be retained. The new signal wavelets thus uncovered do not produce local extrema in the original function, $T(y, L)$, because other more intense components have 'smothered' them by introducing large gradients which remove stationary points. The iterative method subtracts these more intense signal components, revealing the smothered peaks. To summarise, positive wavelet analysis is characterised by:

a. choosing an analysing wavelet in the form of a positive pulse. Information concerning the structure of a given data function, $g(x)$, is concentrated economically into local extrema in $T(y, L)$ (Eq. 1);

b. extraction of information from such local extrema is achieved by a process of correlation detection [Jone90; Earw90, 88] in which the analysing wavelet is interpreted as a matched filter designed for the detection of signal wavelets. Discrete features (positive pulses) are extracted by recording the positions, scales and amplitudes of the local extrema in $T(y, L)$;

c. information extracted from local extrema in general contains redundancy which can be removed by performing a global minimisation of the residual sum of squares between the given function and the wavelet representation.

d. successively improved approximations are achieved by an iterative method in which the current wavelet representation is subtracted from $g(x)$ and subsequently augmented by signal wavelets located at local extrema uncovered by the subtraction process.

Spectral Transformation

For some applications, such as the representation of turbulence structure, an improved representation is achieved by applying the procedure outlined in the previous section not to the given data function directly, but to a transformed function obtained by prewhitening. If applied directly, the matching criterion based on least-squares (step c) results in the residual error in the approximation (Eq. 3) having a frequency-independent or 'white' power spectrum. However, since measured turbulence records typically have a power spectrum proportional to $(frequency)^{-5/3}$, the resulting approximation has proportionally large errors at the higher frequencies. An improved representation results if the signal-to-noise ratio is independent of frequency. This is achieved by preprocessing the data function by means of a frequency weighting, or spectral, transformation such that the power spectrum of the transformed data function is approximately white. The sequence of steps outlined in the previous section is then applied to this transformed function. The resulting wavelet representation is subsequently subjected to an associated inverse spectral transformation to provide an approximation to the original function.

As a simple example, suppose the given data function has a power spectrum proportional to $(frequency)^{-2}$, which is quite close to that of turbulence velocity quoted previously. The spectral transformation then becomes simply a process of differentiation, and the procedure outlined in the previous section is applied, not to the given function directly, but to its derivative. Each signal wavelet in Eq. (3) then corresponds to a positive pulse in the gradient of the function. On application of the inverse spectral transformation, this becomes a ramp-shaped component in the function itself.

Illustrative Examples

Figures 1a and 1b, respectively, illustrate a wavelet feature in the form of a positive pulse assumed to exist as a component of a given data function, $g(x)$, and of the correlation surface, $T(y, L)$, (see Eq. 1) that results when the analysing wavelet, $\bar{F}(x)$, also takes the form of a positive pulse. In this case, $T(y, L)$ is a positive function of position and scale, characterised by a single maximum from which is inferred the position y, scale L and amplitude m of the pulse in $g(x)$. This inference process is an instance of correlation detection [Jone90; Earw90, 88]. The analysing wavelet, $\bar{F}(x)$, acts as a generalised matched filter with varying position and scale, which detects optimally a pulse in the given data, $g(x)$, with the same shape as $\bar{F}(x)$.

Figure 1b illustrates the limited zone of influence in position–scale space of a single pulse-shaped feature in $g(x)$. When two or more signal components exist, these zones overlap; and a local maximum or minimum in the position–scale correlation function, $T(y, L)$, can then be influenced by more than one signal component. Conversely, an individual signal component can influence more than one extremum. Information extracted from position–scale extrema thus, in general, contains redundancy.

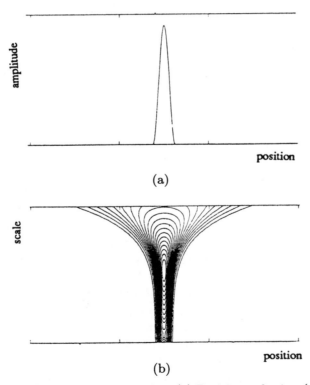

Figure 1. Detection of isolated positive pulse. (a) Positive pulse in $g(x)$; (b) correlation surface $T(y, L)$.

An extreme case, relevant to an understanding of fractal structure, is shown in Figure 2, where the data function, $g(x)$, now consists of two adjacent positive pulses. The correlation surface, $T(y, L)$, then comprises a positive function with three local maxima (see Figure 2b). Two of the peaks correspond to the individual pulses. Since the respective zones of influence do not interact at the peak locations, there is complete information in these two peaks to reconstruct the locations, scales and magnitudes of the given signal components (see Figure 2a).

In addition to these two local maxima, there is a third peak (Figure 2b) that we refer to as a 'phantom peak'. This corresponds to a smoothed, or low resolution, view of the given signal. Provided the information contained in the two peaks of smaller scale is available, the information contained in the phantom peak is entirely redundant. However, the characterisation of a fractal function involves combining information obtained by viewing the function at different resolutions; for this purpose it is necessary to collect information from all the peaks in the correlation surface, $T(y, L)$.

As explained earlier, for the analysis of measured data, such as turbulence velocity, a spectral transformation is first applied to whiten the data. Equation (1) is then applied to the whitened function rather than to $g(x)$ directly. This process leads to the detection of signal wavelets in the whitened data function, each in the form of a positive pulse (Figure 1a). The effect on the shape of the

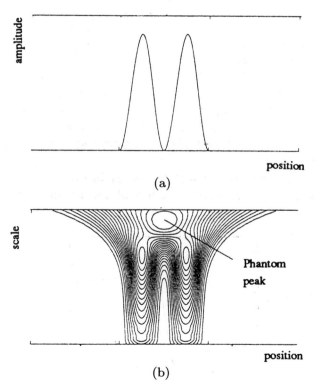

Figure 2. Detection of adjacent pulses. (a) Adjacent pulses in $g(x)$; (b) correlation surface $T(y, L)$.

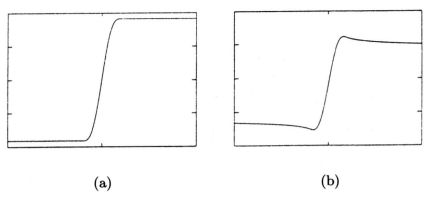

(a)   (b)

Figure 3. Signal wavelets detected using prewhitening. (a) $B = 2$; (b) $B = 5/3$;
(c) $B = 1$.

detected signal wavelet of subsequently applying an associated inverse spectral
transformation is shown in Figure 3. Figures 3a, b and c show the shapes of the
signal wavelets detected in this manner when the given data function is assumed
to have a power spectrum proportional to (frequency)$^{-B}$ where B takes the
respective values 2, 5/3, 1. In each case the signal wavelet comprises a smooth
incremental ramp, embedded in 'tails' whose rate of decay depends upon the
values of the spectral exponent, B. The profile in Figure 3b is that used in
subsequent illustrations in which positive wavelet analysis is applied to records
of turbulence velocity.

Figure 4 illustrates the analysis of a measured sample of atmospheric turbulence [Fost89]. Figure 4b shows the correlation surface, $T(y, L)$, corresponding
to the data record (see Figure 4a) following a spectral transformation based on
an assumed data spectrum proportional to (frequency)$^{-5/3}$ supported by spectral measurements [Fost89]. Figure 4c shows the detected locations of the local
extrema in $T(y, L)$, the 'plus' symbols corresponding to up ramps in the data,
and the 'zero' symbols to the down ramps.

In Figure 5, the process of reconstruction is illustrated for a short sample
of turbulence data. To clarify the location of the reconstructed features, the

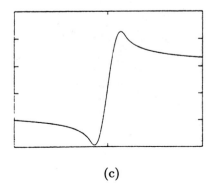

(c)

Figure 3. (*Continued*.)

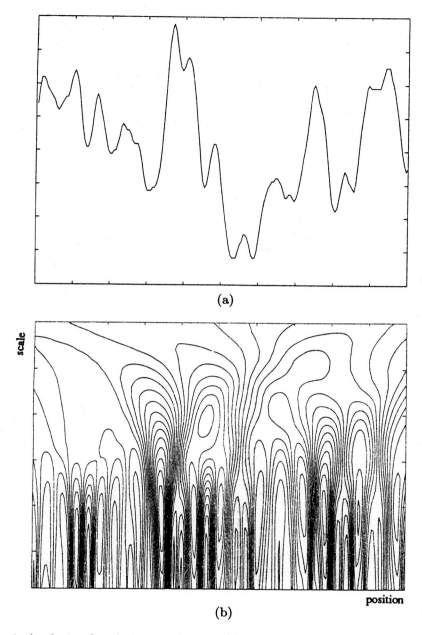

Figure 4. Analysis of turbulence velocity. (a) Measured data record; (b) correlation surface, $T(y, L)$; (c) location of local extrema in $T(y, L)$.

prewhitening, for this example, is based on an assumed spectrum proportional to (frequency)$^{-2}$. Following the inverse spectral transformation, the resulting signal features are ramp profiles embedded in regions of constant signal amplitude (see Figure 3a). Figure 5a shows the wavelet analysis applied over a limited band of scales. The result is that one peak and two troughs are detected in the

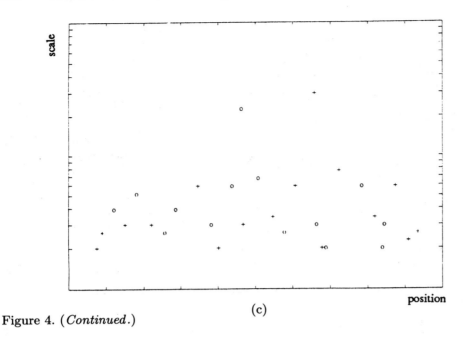

Figure 4. (*Continued.*)

(c)

correlation surface, $T(y, L)$. For this illustration contours are omitted, and just the locations of the local extrema in position–scale space are shown. The three extrema correspond to a down-up-down sequence of ramps in the data. Also shown here is a reconstruction based on the information in these three extrema.

In Figure 5b the wavelet analysis is extended to include larger scales. As shown, a third trough is now located. This corresponds to a large-scale downward ramp, which covers the previously found sequence of three ramps of alternating sign. Whilst this fourth extremum contains redundant information, it also introduces new information as evidenced by the modified reconstruction.

Figure 6 illustrates reconstruction using local extrema detected over limited bands of scale. In Figure 6a, only extrema in $T(y, L)$ detected at large scales above the scale boundary shown are incorporated. In this case the spectral transformation is based on an assumed spectrum proportional to $(\text{frequency})^{-5/3}$, and the signal wavelets used in the reconstruction take the form illustrated in Figure 3b. In contrast, Figure 6b shows the corresponding reconstruction using only local extrema detected at small scales, below the scale boundary shown (the same scale boundary as in Figure 6a). The lower limit of the locations of the local extrema detected corresponds to the boundary imposed at very small scales by the discrete sampled nature of the data.

In Figure 6c we see the reconstruction based on the full range of scales. Note that this is *not* the sum of the reconstructions shown in Figures 6a and 6b. These reconstructions over limited ranges of scale contain mutual redundancy, which was removed from the reconstruction shown in Figure 6c by the process of global optimisation described earlier.

Figure 7 illustrates the method of iteratively subtracting feature-based partial reconstructions of the signal in order to approximate the latter to any required

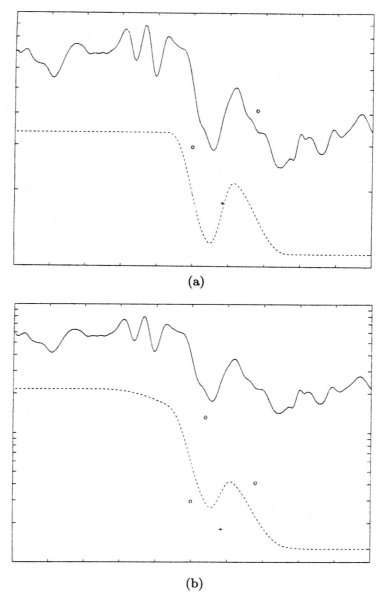

(a)

(b)

Figure 5. Detail of reconstruction method (a) using one peak and two troughs; (b) incorporating largest scale trough.

accuracy. As explained earlier, less intense features sometimes do not result in peaks in the correlation function, $T(y, L)$, because these stationary values are 'smothered' by more intense overlapping features. The more intense features need to be subtracted from the signal before the less intense features produce peaks; these are then detected in the usual way.

The square pulse in Figure 7a is an extreme example of the need for feature subtraction. When an analysing wavelet of the shape shown in Figure 1a is

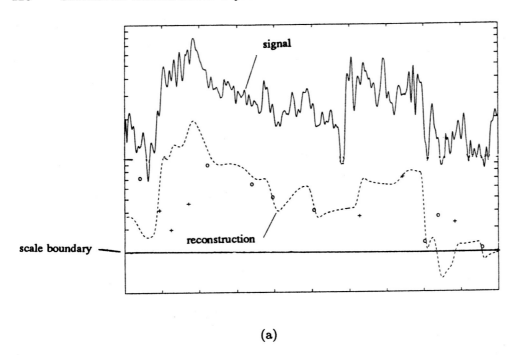

(a)

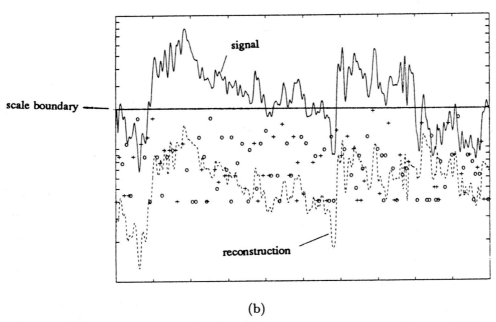

(b)

Figure 6. Reconstruction using information over prescribed bands of scale. (a) Large scale signal wavelets only; (b) small scale signal wavelets only; (c) full range of wavelets.

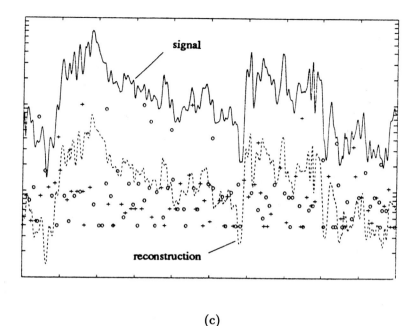

(c)

Figure 6. (*Continued.*)

applied, the correlation function, $T(y, L)$, has only one extremum, as shown in the contour plot of Figure 7b. The dashed line in Figure 7a shows the best feature-based approximation to the square pulse based on the single feature detected from the peak in $T(y, L)$. The result of subtracting the single feature detected in $T(y, L)$ is shown in Figure 7c, along with the five peaks in the new correlation function; a contour plot of the latter is shown in Figure 7d. There are now six features available for characterising the square pulse, one from the peak in the original correlation function, and five from peaks in the correlation surface of the pulse with the single feature subtracted. The best approximation of the square pulse using these six features is shown by the dashed line in Figure 7e, together with the six peaks in position–scale space.

The process of subtracting the best feature-based approximation can be repeated several times to produce feature-based characterisations of arbitrarily high accuracy. Figure 7f shows a 19-feature characterisation with a residual sum of squares error of only 0.32%.

Cascade Model for Turbulence

In order to obtain a better insight into the structure of measured fractal data, a feature-based cascade model for turbulence was developed. Examples of synthetic turbulence data were generated, and comparisons between this and real measured turbulence made, using positive wavelet analysis.

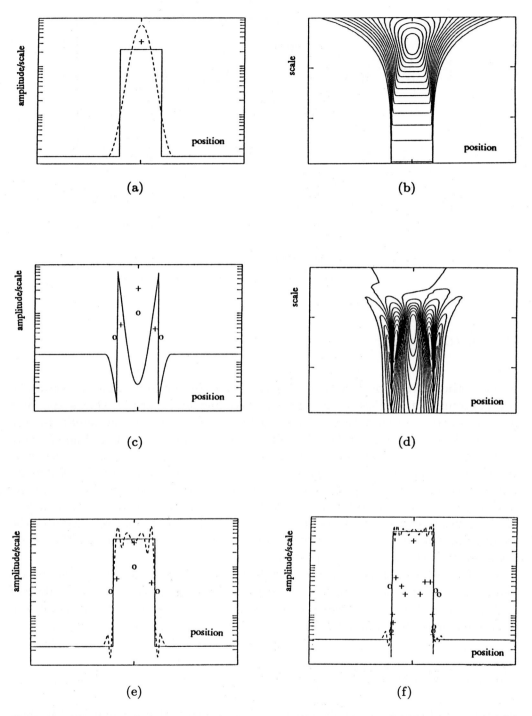

Figure 7. Feature subtraction method on square pulse data. (a) Square pulse $g(\mathrm{x})$ with initial approximation; (b) correlation surface $T(y, L)$; (c) single subtraction; (d) correlation surface of single subtraction; (e) approximation after single subtraction; (f) approximation after several subtractions.

The cascade model starts with a single elementary pulse feature spanning the whole signal; that is, the position is half way along the signal, and the scale is the length of the signal. The next stage is to replace this feature with a pattern of smaller features of different amplitudes, positions and scales. The amplitudes, positions and scales are all derived from those of the single feature being replaced.

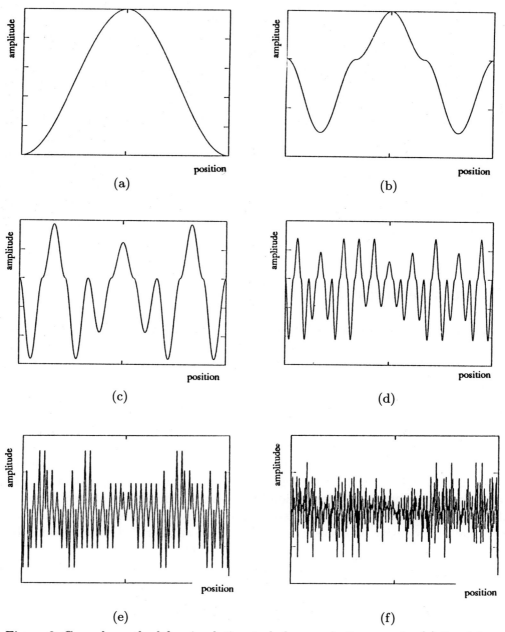

Figure 8. Cascade method for simulating turbulence velocity records. (a) Level 1; (b) level 2; (c) level 3; (d) level 4; (e) level 5; (f) level 8.

The replacement procedure is then applied recursively to each of the elementary features just created. The recursion continues until the scale of each feature is significantly below the sample interval for the signal. In our case, the threshold scale chosen is a quarter of the sample interval. Finally, for each feature below the scale threshold an impulse function with the same position and amplitude as the feature is generated.

Randomness is introduced into the model by selecting each replacement pattern at random from a library of patterns. To illustrate the method a very simple library with only two patterns is used. But this nevertheless produces a realistic simulation of whitened turbulence. Figure 8 shows levels 1, 2, 3, 4, 5 and 8 of recursion in the cascade process; at each level, the features at the previous level are replaced by one of the two patterns in the library. In this example, the cascade process terminates at the eighth level of recursion.

The final stage is to unwhiten the simulated data by applying an inverse spectral transformation. Measured turbulence data has a spectrum very close to $(\text{frequency})^{-5/3}$, but the finest structure is lost due to smoothing caused by signal processing. Therefore, a smoothing filter is applied to the transformed data to simulate the spectral properties at the smallest scales. Figure 9 illustrates the processes of unwhitening and smoothing, and compares the result with measured turbulence data.

Phantom Features

A special case of redundant information between features occurs when a large scale feature is comprised almost entirely of embedded smaller scale features, with little or no additional information at the largest scale. An example of such a feature, referred to here as a phantom, is shown in Figure 2.

The occurrence of phantom features provides information about the fractal structure of chaotic signals, such as turbulence records. Of particular interest is whether large scale structure is entirely comprised of smaller scale structure, or whether there are smooth large scale structures which cannot be decomposed in this way and hence contain nonredundant information. To answer this question, a new measure of intensity, referred to as information intensity, is defined. This represents the amount of information in a feature which is not shared by any of the smaller scale features embedded within. A true phantom feature has zero information intensity, whereas a feature with no smaller feature embedded has the same information intensity as ordinary intensity.

Figure 10 compares the distributions of ordinary and information intensity at different scales. Figure 10a is for turbulence records. Figure 10b is for simulated turbulence using the cascade model described above. Figure 10c is for Gaussian noise with spectral properties similar to turbulence. In all three cases the

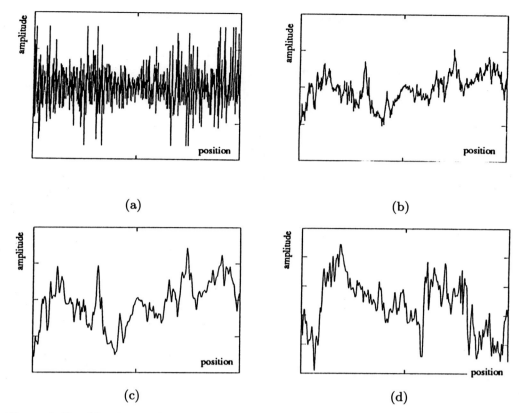

Figure 9. Dewhitening and smoothing of simulated turbulence. (a) Result from cascade model; (b) dewhitened version of (a); (c) smoothed version of (b); (d) actual turbulence measurements.

relationship between ordinary and information intensities is quite similar, with information intensities falling to zero at larger scales. These results imply that all three types of large scale structure, in this case ramp features, are comprised almost entirely of smaller scale ramps, with very little independent information at larger scales. Figure 6 also illustrates the redundancy at larger scales; the large scale ramps shown in Figure 6a are accounted for mostly by sequences of the smaller scale ramps shown in Figure 6b. There is very little difference between the reconstruction in Figure 6b, based on small scale features only, and the reconstruction of Figure 6c, which incorporates features at all scales.

Image Representation

Positive wavelet analysis is also used to generate a feature-based representation of two-dimensional images. Figure 11 shows an application to a Landsat image. Following a prewhitening spectral transformation, a two-dimensional equivalent to Eq. (1) is applied to the data shown in Figure 11a, with the analysing wavelet,

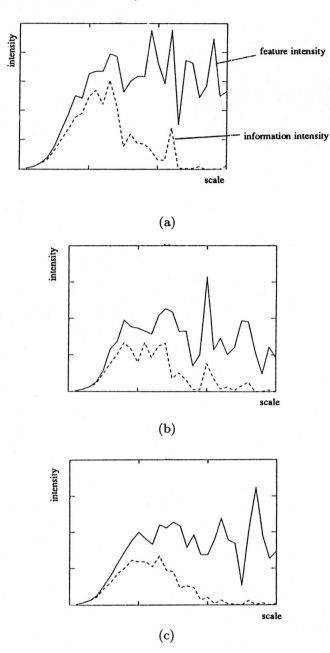

Figure 10. Variation of information intensity with scale. (a) Measured turbulence; (b) simulated turbulence; (c) Gaussian noise.

$\bar{F}$, in the form of a positive bar detector which is subjected to the operations of translation, dilation and rotation. Figure 11b shows the locations, scales and orientations of the corresponding bar-shaped signal wavelets detected through the occurrence of local extrema in the correlation surface resulting from the wavelet transformation. As in one dimension, information which is contained in these local extrema contains redundancy which can be removed by performing a global minimisation of the residual sum of squares between the (whitened) image and the wavelet representation. The effect of applying an inverse spectral transformation to this feature-based representation is shown in the reconstructed image, Figure 11c.

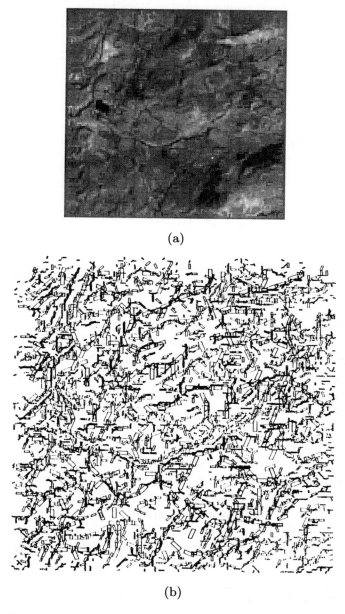

(a)

(b)

Figure 11. Analysis of 2D image data. (a) Landsat image; (b) bar-shaped feature characterisation; (c) reconstruction from bar features.

(c)

Figure 11. (*Continued*.).

Conclusions

This paper presents a new method [Jone92] of characterising fractal signals in terms of discrete features by detecting positive wavelets using matched filtering over multiple scales. The analysing wavelets used are positive pulses, unlike those used in the standard wavelet transform which have zero mean. The positions and scales of the detected discrete features correspond to extrema in the position–scale correlation surface. Such features allow an economical discrete feature-based representation of a signal, because the positions and scales of the features are chosen to give the best local approximation to the signal.

A global approximation to the signal is achieved by minimising the residual sum of squares between the signal and the feature-based reconstruction. The signal is represented to an arbitrarily high level of accuracy using this technique, with the aid of feature subtraction to uncover additional peaks in the correlation surface.

Spectral transformations are applied to analyse signals whose background power spectrum is not white. Such transformations allow feature-based approximations which minimise the signal-to-noise ratio for more general noise models. A whitening transformation is first applied to the signal, and then a discrete feature characterisation of the transformed signal is obtained. Finally, the inverse transformation is applied to each feature. This has the effect of introducing new feature shapes into the representation of the signal, for example ramp-shaped features.

The discrete feature characterisation method was demonstrated on air turbulence records in order to determine the breakdown of structure within. It was found that large scale features (ramps) are almost entirely comprised of embedded smaller scale features, with little or no new information content. The same property was observed in simulated random processes, in particular Gaussian noise and a signal generated by a cascade process.

An application to image representation is illustrated, in which the analysing wavelet now takes the form of a positive bar detector covering a range of locations, scales and orientations. Feature detection is again based on the identification of local extrema in the wavelet transformed space, and global optimisation removes redundancy.

Acknowledgments. The authors thank Sharon Watson of SD-Scicon UK Ltd, who implemented the software used in the production of Figure 11.

REFERENCES

[Earw88]
  Earwicker, P.G., Correlation detection in self-similar noise, Royal Aerospace Establishment, Tech. Report 88032, 1988.

[Earw90]
  Earwicker, P.G., and Jones, J.G., Correlation detection using multiple-scale filters and self-similar noise models, in *Mathematics in Signal Processing II*, McWhirter, J.G., Ed., Oxford, UK: Clarendon Press, 1990.

[Fost89]
  Foster, G.W., and Jones, J.G., Analysis of atmospheric turbulence measurements by spectral and discrete gust methods, *Aero. Jour. Royal Aeronautical Society*, Vol. 93, pp.162–176, 1989.

[Gros85]
  Grossman, A., and Morlet, J., Decomposition of functions into wavelets of constant shape, and related transforms, in *Mathematics and Physics, Lectures on Recent Results*, Vol. 1, Streit, L., Ed., Singapore: World Scientific, 1985.

[Jone90]
  Jones, J.G., Earwicker, P.G., and Foster, G.W., Multiple-scale correlation detection, wavelet transforms and multifractal turbulence, IMA Conf. on Wavelets, Fractals and Fourier Transforms, Cambridge, UK, December 1990.

[Jone92]
  Jones, J.G., Positive wavelet representation, Defence Research Agency, Farnborough, England, Tech. Memo. TM MTC28, 1992.

[Kron87]
  Kronland-Martinet, R., Morlet, J., and Grossman, A., Analysis of sound patterns through wavelet transforms, Int. Jour. Patt. Recognition and Artificial Intell., Vol. 1, No. 2, pp. 273–302, 1987.

Application of Fractal Geometry to Geological Site Characterization

Michael D. Impey and Peter Grindrod

Abstract

In this paper we apply fractal geometry to a problem of practical significance in geosciences, that of generating a rock transmissivity field with realistic detail over a range of length scales from a relatively small number of measured values. We discuss a conceptual rock-property model based on statistically self-affine fractals. Then we demonstrate a methodology based on this model for generating realizations of the transmissivity field with spatial variability over a range of scales. We estimate a fractal dimension directly from the measured data, and assess, in a quantitative manner, the 'goodness-of-fit' of the fractal model to the measured data. The goodness-of-fit test indicates that it is realistic to interpret the measured data in terms of a fractal model. Thus, we can be confident that the model can be used to generate physically realistic transmissivity fields. The Intera code AFFINITY is applied to measured field data to generate fractal transmissivity fields that have the correct dimension and interpolate the field data. AFFINITY is also used to compute flow and tracer transport through the fractal transmissivity fields. These computations exhibit channelling and dispersive phenomena. These phenomena are of significant practical interest in the assessment of the geological properties of a rock formation.

Introduction

Fractal geometry, pioneered by Benoit B. Mandelbrot, now provides both a description and a mathematical model for many complex forms and patterns observed in nature. The use of fractals has gained popularity rapidly over recent years, providing a bridge between pure mathematical research and the natural and physical sciences.

Of course, the applied scientist or analyst may well wish to impose practical cut-off limits at extremely large or small scales. This is always necessary from a computational point of view, but it can also be required from technical or physical constraints on the systems under consideration. This has always been an accepted part of modelling and simulation employing fractal geometries. The important aspect is that the object under consideration shows a self-similarity, a self-affinity, or even merely a statistical self-affinity, over spatial scales differing by one or more orders of magnitude. Space-filling curves and volume-filling surfaces are well known. There is an ongoing interest in employing such tools to provide a realistic description of naturally occurring quantities, or geometries.

Fractals are particularly suited to the modelling of nonsmooth media, since

the degree of roughness is easily controllable;

the fractals are generated by simple iterative procedures which are highly efficient when implemented on computers.

In this paper we apply a statistically self-affine fractal conceptual model to an *inverse* problem from the geosciences. These problems arise as part of the process of characterization of the geology of an underground site, especially in areas where ground water flow and particle transport through the region is of primary concern. One parameter of fundamental interest is the rock permeability, or transmissivity, which is measured directly by drilling boreholes into the region under investigation. It has long been recognized that flow and transport phenomena, such as channelling and dispersion, are strongly dependent on the spatial variability of the transmissivity over a range of scales (possibly down to very small scales). But for reasons of cost and maintaining site integrity, the number of transmissivity measurements is usually rather small. We are thus faced with the problem of interpolating the measured data with realistic detail over a range of scales. In the following sections we outline a methodology for tackling such inverse problems, and demonstrate the application of this methodology to typical measured data values from a geological site.

Statistically Self-affine Fractals

Consider a single function $v(x)$ satisfying

$$\gamma_v(h) = \left\langle |v(\vec{x} + \vec{h}) - v(\vec{x})|^2 \right\rangle \propto h^{2p} \tag{1}$$

where $h = |\vec{h}|$ and p is a constant in (0,1). Here the brackets $\langle \ \rangle$ denote a spatial average over all points $\vec{x}$. The function v shows a statistical scaling behaviour since, if the spatial scale is changed by a factor r, then the corresponding increments in v, $\Delta v = |v(\vec{x} + \vec{h}) - v(\vec{h})|$, are, on average, changed by a factor, r^p. Formally

$$\left\langle \Delta v(r\vec{h})^2 \right\rangle = r^{2p} \left\langle \Delta v(\vec{h})^2 \right\rangle$$

This scaling property is known as *self-affinity* and is distinct from self-similarity, where the scalings for x and Δv are the same (the function appears to repeat exactly under straightforward magnification). Since the self-affine property only holds 'on average' (i.e., not necessarily exactly), this is referred to as *statistical self-affinity*. It is important not to confuse γ_v with similar quantities defined for random functions where the average is taken over all possible realizations of a random field for fixed $\vec{x}$ and $\vec{h}$.

Fields, v, possessing a scaling law as in Eq. (1), valid as $h \to 0$, are not generally smooth. Instead they can define curves or surfaces which are *fractal*, that is, objects with noninteger dimension. For example, the pathline executed by a particle subject to Brownian motion has topological dimension one (it can be parameterized by time, for example) yet is space-filling, self-similar and has a fractal dimension of 1.5.

In our construction above, if $\vec{x} \in \Re^n$, the graph of a continuously defined field, $v(\vec{x})$, has a topological dimension equal to n (that is, it is basically parameterized by $\vec{x}$). However, its fractal dimension, D_f, is given by

$$D_f = n + 1 - p$$

Thus, if $p = 1$ the graph of v is relatively 'smooth', whereas for $p \in (0, 1)$ the graph of v is a fractal object of dimension $n + 1 - p$ embedded in $(\vec{x}, v)$ space $(\equiv \Re^{n+1})$.

It is illustrative to work with discrete Fourier transforms (restricting our interest in v to a cube in $\Re^n$), i.e.

$$v(\vec{x}) = \sum_{\vec{k}} a_{\vec{k}} e^{2\pi i \vec{k} \cdot \vec{x}}$$

where $\vec{k} = (k_1, \ldots, k_n)$. The nonsmoothness of v is characterized by its properties on smaller and smaller scales. These are, of course, determined by the manner in which the Fourier transform behaves for large $|\vec{k}|$. The result is that the coefficients, $a_{\vec{k}}$, should satisfy

$$\left\langle |a_{\vec{k}}|^2 \right\rangle \sim |\vec{k}|^{-(n+2p)}$$

so that the surface is statistically self-affine. This condition ensures that when the truncated series

$$v(\vec{x}) = \sum_{|\vec{k}| < N} a_{\vec{k}}^{2\pi i \vec{k} \cdot \vec{x}}$$

is employed, the self-affinity is realized on spatial scales above that of the cut-off, $\sim 1/N$.

It is interesting to note the connection between the notions of fractal dimension and smoothness presented above with the more conventional techniques of applied functional analysis. For the continuous transform, the condition

$$|a(\vec{k})|^2 \sim |\vec{k}|^{-(n+2p)} \qquad \text{as} \qquad |\vec{k}| \to \infty$$

implies $v(\vec{x})$ is in the Sobolev space, $H_q = W_{2,q}(\Re^n)$, the collection of functions whose generalized derivatives up to order q are square integrable over $\Re^n$, if and only if $q < p$. Note that to ensure that v is differentiable (in a weak sense), we require it to be in H_q for some $q > 1 + n/2$ (by the Sobolev Lemma). This clearly is generally not the case for the fields we defined.

A Geosciences Fractal Model

Consider the following inverse estimation problem:

> Given M observations of a scalar field, $v(\vec{x})$, at locations $\vec{x}_1, \ldots, \vec{x}_M$, estimate the values taken by v at any other location, $\vec{x}_0$.

The fundamental difficulty about any inverse problem when posed in this most naked form is its nonuniqueness. To tackle such problems, assumptions are usually made regarding the statistical properties of the field, the smoothness of the field or even the field's algebraic representation.

In this section we set out a fractal conceptual model for interpolating irregularly placed observations. Instead of searching for $v^*(\vec{x})$ from within a certain class of smooth functions, we restrict our attention to a space of functions which possesses an appropriate type of statistical self-affinity. This is motivated by two major factors:

> the spatial variability (as represented by the fractal scaling law) can be inferred directly from the observed data and utilized directly to generate the interpolating field. There are no random functions introduced at this level; we use only the point measurements;

> if sampled, the interpolating field reproduces the scaling behaviour of the original data.

THE CONCEPTUAL MODEL

The spatial variability of the observed field, v, is represented by the behaviour of the quantity

$$\gamma_v(h) = \left\langle [v(\vec{x} + \vec{h}) - v(\vec{x})]^2 \right\rangle$$

where $h = |\vec{h}|$ and the brackets denote the expected value from a large number of samples at points $\vec{x}$ and $\vec{x} + \vec{h}$. We assume that the scaling properties are represented by a law of the form

$$\gamma_v(h) = qh^{2p} \tag{2}$$

for $p \in (0, 1)$, constant q, and for all h less than the inter-measurement distances, in particular as $h \to 0$. We also assume that $\gamma_v(h) \to$ constant for large h.

A realization, $v(\vec{x})$, must be generated which interpolates the observed data, possesses the desired self-affine scaling and also matches the mean and variance of the available site observations:

$$\langle v \rangle \equiv \tilde{v} = \text{the mean of the observed data;}$$
$$\left\langle (v - \tilde{v})^2 \right\rangle = \text{the variance of the observed data.}$$

The last condition fixes the sill ($\lim \gamma_v$ as $h \to \infty$). Thus, both small and large scale structure is inferred from the data.

One of the key steps is the determination of the parameter, p. The technique we use is based on chi-squared estimation, which gives an indication of the goodness-of-fit of the measured data to the conceptual model as well as providing an estimate for the value of p. This is, of course, a valuable aid in building confidence in the fractal conceptual model.

CHI-SQUARED ESTIMATION

To determine whether a given data set, $v(\vec{x}_i)$ $(i = 1, \ldots, M)$ satisfies the fractal power law (Eq. 2) and to derive the parameters p and q, we first bin the data using the following steps:

define intervals, or 'bins', of $h = |\vec{h}|$, $[h_0, h_1], [h_1, h_2], \ldots, [h_{N-1}, h_N]$;

associate each pair of data points $(\vec{x}_i, \vec{x}_j)$ with one bin by determining in which bin $|\vec{x}_i - \vec{x}_j|$ lies;

compute the bin average, $\bar{\gamma}_k$, of $[v(\vec{x}_i) - v(\vec{x}_j)]^2$ over the points in the kth bin $(k = 1, \ldots, N)$.

We next fit the N data points $(\tilde{\gamma}_k, \tilde{h}_k) = (\ln[\bar{\gamma}_k], \ln[\bar{h}_k])$, where $\bar{h}_k$ is the midpoint value of h in the kth bin, to the model curve obtained by taking the logarithm of Eq. (2)

$$\tilde{\gamma}(h; p, r) = r + 2p \ln[h] \tag{3}$$

where $r = \ln[q]$. There is an error associated with the bin-averaging which is represented by the standard deviation, σ_k, of $\ln[\bar{\gamma}_k]$ in each bin. In this case, the standard method for finding the maximum likelihood (i.e. best-fit) estimate of the model parameters is to minimize the quantity

$$\chi^2 = \sum_{k=1}^{N} \left(\frac{\tilde{\gamma}_k - \tilde{\gamma}(h_k; p, r)}{\sigma_k} \right)^2 \tag{4}$$

called chi-squared [Mood88]. In theory, the chi-squared minimization fit requires that the measurement errors be independent and normally distributed in each bin. Recourse to the Law of Large Numbers and the Central Limit theorem indicates the second condition is approximately satisfied providing there are a large number of measurements in each bin.

The linear nature of the model curve (Eq. 3) means that the maximum likelihood best-fit parameters are easily derived. Furthermore, the uncertainty in the best-fit parameters, p and r, due to the measurement errors incurred during binning can also be quantified. The standard deviation of the best-fit parameters, σ_p and σ_r, is easily computed [Mood88]. We also examine the goodness-of-fit of the data to the model. Although this is rather a qualitative concept, it is important to establish that it is reasonable to fit the data with the chosen fractal model

(Eq. 2). The basis for deciding on the goodness-of-fit is that the probability distribution for different values of χ^2 at its minimum is given by the chi-squared distribution of $N - 2$ degrees of freedom, i.e.

$$f(\chi^2) = \frac{\chi^{2(\nu/2-1)}e^{-\chi^2/2}}{2^{\nu/2}\Gamma(\nu/2)} \tag{5}$$

where $\nu = N - 2$ and Γ is the standard Gamma function. The confidence level, Q, defined by

$$Q = \int_{\chi^2}^{\infty} \frac{x^{2(\nu/2-1)}e^{-x^2/2}}{2^{\nu/2}\Gamma(\nu/2)} \, dx \tag{6}$$

gives the probability that chi-squared exceeds the measured value if the data points are chosen at random. If Q is small for some particular data set, then the apparent discrepancies are unlikely to be due to chance fluctuations and the proposed model should be called into question. Alternatively, if Q is too large ($\approx 100\%$) then the fit is, in a sense, too good to be true. This tends to happen if errors are over-estimated.

In practice, a fit is regarded as realistic if Q is greater than about 10% but not too close to 100% (e.g., $\leq 80\%$). We must make choices about the various binning parameters when evaluating the scaling parameter, p. It is tempting to rank estimates for p using different types of bins in terms of the confidence level, Q. This temptation should be resisted, because the confidence level, Q, only indicates whether it is reasonable to fit the model curve (Eq. 3) to the binned data — an attempt to say if one fit is 'more reasonable' than another is logically flawed! However, if a particular binning gives a confidence level that is very much lower than the general level of other binnings, it is reasonable to reject this binning as inappropriate.

Application to Measured Data

We have applied the techniques described above to measurements from a number of separate geological regions. The results obtained are, of course, site-specific; but for the purposes of demonstrating the application of the fractal conceptual model we focus on one data set. A full discussion of the issues that have arisen during application of the model to a range of data from a number of geological regions is beyond the scope of this paper, but the data set and the results we discuss exhibit several 'typical' features. The measured data set is listed in Table A1 in Appendix A. It consists of only 35 measured transmissivity values, distributed in an irregular pattern in a region approximately 20km by 27km. The transmissivity values are measured in a thin horizontal geological formation extending throughout a region under investigation. The thinness of the formation allows us to make an approximation that the rock properties are averaged in the vertical direction, and so the transmissivity values are regarded as functions

$\Re^2 \to \Re$. The value of p found was 0.24 with a confidence of 62% corresponding to a fractal transmissivity field dimension of 2.76 (see Figure 1 and Table 1).

This high value of confidence indicates that it is physically realistic to interpret the measured data in terms of the fractal conceptual model discussed in this paper. This model was implemented by Intera within the AFFINITY code [Grin91] to generate fractal transmissivity fields with the correct dimension. These transmissivity fields interpolate the site data. The AFFINITY code is also used to compute flow and tracer transport through the generated transmissivity fields. Plates 10 and 11 show typical results. The four transmissivity fields shown in Plate 10 all have fractal dimension 2.76 and interpolate the measurement points, thus are statistically indistinguishable. The differences highlight the nonuniqueness inherent in a statistical approach. All the realizations were produced on a 128×128 grid. Regions of highest transmissivity, i.e., $T = \mathrm{O}(1)$, are marked in white, and regions of lowest transmissivity, where $T = \mathrm{O}(10^{-14})$, in black. Intermediate transmissivities are marked in yellow, green, orange, red, blue and purple, in order of decreasing transmissivity on a logarithmic scale.

The four transmissivity fields show common features, including regions of low transmissivity towards the eastern boundary of the region and regions of high

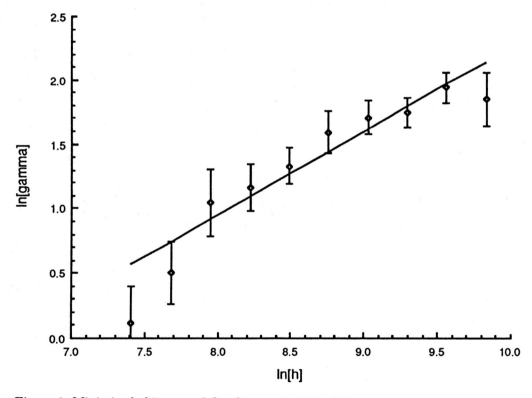

Figure 1. Minimized chi-squared fit of transmissivity data.

Table 1. Values of chi-squared minimization fit parameters.

p	σ_p	r	σ_r	confidence Q
0.2374	0.0227	−1.449	0.8195	62.81%

transmissivity towards the western edge. The fields all exhibit a general east–west trend, with relatively less variation in the north–south direction. This is almost certainly a function of the conditioning of the fractal fields on the measured data, which shows similar behaviour. It is also of interest to note that the fractal transmissivity fields all exhibit similar-sized local low transmissivity regions with similar east–west coordinates, but that the north–south coordinates show some variation. This suggests that the availability of more data from the east of the region might enable more precise identification of the position of regions of very low transmissivity if they are of particular interest. Thus, visualizations of transmissivity fields such as these are potentially useful in planning the spatial distribution of data collection points.

The computed flows through the transmissivity fields are shown in Plate 11. In the diagrams white indicates velocities of O (1), and black indicates velocities of $O(10^{-14})$. The intermediate velocities are marked in orange and red on a logarithmic scale, with darker colours indicating lower velocities. It is clear that the Darcy velocity flow fields again show common features. The narrow regions of high-speed flow, often referred to as channels, are of great interest and significance in practical assessment of the geological formation. The influence of the channelling is apparent in the tracer transport calculations shown in Figure 2, which shows the variation with time of the position of 10,000 particles initially

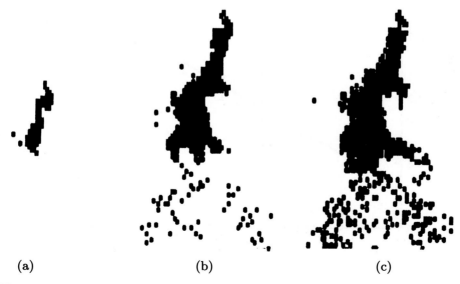

(a)   (b)   (c)

Figure 2. Tracer transport calculations showing the positions of 10,000 particles initially released from a single point at times (a) 5,000; (b) 10,000; (c) 15,000 years.

released from a single point in the transmissivity field shown at the top left in Plate 11. A large number of the particles rapidly move down the high-speed channels, with a smaller number moving in a more diffusive manner through the rock formation.

Conclusions

We discussed a conceptual rock-property model based on statistically self-affine fractals, and we demonstrated the suitability of a methodology based on this conceptual model for generating realizations of the transmissivity field with spatial variability over a range of scales. We paid particular attention to two steps in the methodology which involve the measured data: the derivation of a scaling parameter, p, which characterizes the spatial variability of the measured transmissivity data, and the conditioning of generated fractal fields on the measured data points.

Using minimized chi-squared fits, we estimated the value of an appropriate fractal dimension directly from the measured data. We also assessed the goodness-of-fit of the conceptual rock-property model (in which p is defined) to the measured data. The goodness-of-fit test indicates that it is realistic to interpret the measured data in terms of our conceptual rock-property model. Thus, we are confident that the conceptual model employed is appropriate. The conceptual model is incorporated in the Intera code AFFINITY applied to the measured data to generate fractal transmissivity fields that have the same dimension as the measured data and interpolate the data. The AFFINITY code is also used to solve for flow and tracer transport through the fractal transmissivity fields. These computations exhibit channelling and dispersive effects which are of significant practical interest.

Appendix A: Transmissivity Data

The transmissivity data indicates the (x, y) coordinates of the measurement points in metres from the southwest corner of the region under investigation, as well as the $\log_{10}$ transmissivity value at each of the measurement points.

Table A1. Transmissivity data.

x coordinate (m)	y coordinate (m)	$\log_{10}[T](m^2/s)$
10277	13201	-7.27
11040	13149	-7.69
9980	12428	-6.29
11300	9988	-7.20
6812	16766	-9.83
13110	16612	-3.96
15590	7348	-1.58

Table A1. (*Continued.*)

x coordinate (m)	y coordinate (m)	$\log_{10} [\,T\,]\,(m^2/s)$
9726	166	−3.04
730	9873	−10.14
8350	10899	−4.07
6677	7941	−9.00
11359	11859	−8.40
8385	13580	−9.47
10331	13726	−7.47
7982	9419	−8.82
11436	14671	−6.68
8497	12058	−4.86
10017	16820	−3.23
14616	13892	−2.53
13076	10241	−9.91
9774	9034	−7.13
9990	15054	−9.72
11056	15747	−3.41
9961	14186	−8.19
17315	16631	−2.51
19686	15042	−1.69
19274	25837	−2.27
12434	26216	−4.38
9979	21223	−8.71
10004	13490	−7.94
10509	9559	−8.50
8747	447	−3.77
17238	4904	−2.13
14998	11007	−6.48
2574	22383	−8.58

REFERENCES

[Mood88]
  Mood, A.M., Graybill, F.A., and Boes, D.C., *Introduction to the Theory of Statistics*, London: McGraw-Hill, 1988.

[Grin91]
  Grindrod, P., Robinson, P.C., and Williams, M.J., The art of noise: self-affinity, flow and transport, Intera Sciences internal report, 1991.

Analysis, Generation and Compression of Pavement Distress Images Using Fractals

Maaruf Ali, Michael A. Gennert
and Trevor G. Clarkson

Abstract

The vast amount of data generated by automated surface distress evaluation equipment far exceeds the storage capabilities of current digital data storage systems. A study using fractals is being carried out to alleviate the data storage problem, since fractal image compression offers the largest compression ratio of the available image compression algorithms. This paper discusses the use of fractals to analyse, compress and generate pavement distress features, i.e., cracks in the road surface. Much of the following is abridged from a paper by LeBlanc [LeBl91]. A method for calculating the fractal dimension of cracks is presented and values for pavement cracks reported. Several methods for fractal image compression are explained, especially the midpoint displacement algorithm to generate pavement distress images and iterated function system codes. The use of fractal techniques to generate standard images for testing an automated surface distress evaluation system is proposed.

Introduction

The deterioration of transportation systems in the United States is a problem of major concern to local, state and federal agencies and to the public. Highways in the United States are deteriorating at an alarming rate due to the normal aging process, as well as being subject to greater and more severe traffic loads. This problem is compounded by decreases in available funding for restoration of this vital element of the infrastructure. Improvements are not predicted as maintenance and construction costs rise due to inflation in material and labour costs and as revenues decline. The need for a pavement management system to provide accurate assessment of the condition of various types of highway pavement is of critical importance in addressing highway maintenance needs.

Pavement management systems require systematic monitoring of pavement surface to determine preventive and corrective maintenance. The process involves accumulation of large amounts of visual data, typically obtained from site visitation. The pavement surface condition is then correlated to a pavement distress index that is based on a scoring system previously established by the various state Departments of Transportation (DOTs). The scoring system determines if the pavement section requires maintenance, overlay or reconstruction.

A large amount of data is required to establish a pavement distress index. The computation process is currently computerised. However, the raw data are still input manually, a laborious and expensive task. This, coupled with the difficulty and impracticality associated with field measurements of pavement surface cracks in areas with high traffic density, emphasises the need for an automated visual crack measuring device.

The objective of this project is to develop a system for processing video images of pavements and to identify, quantify and classify pavement distress. The basic strategy for automated acquisition and analysis of video images for evaluating pavement distress is straightforward: a vehicle (see Figure 1) travels along the road taking pictures of the pavement, which are analysed to evaluate the type, severity and distribution of surface cracks and patches.

Road images are taken by a moving vehicle and the data are analysed in real time; only summary information about distress severity and extents is recorded (see Table 1). This solves the data rate and storage problem, but since the raw data is discarded many useful functions cannot be carried out by the pavement maintenance engineer. These functions include, for example, evaluating the cause of distress and comparison of records to determine pavement wear. The second

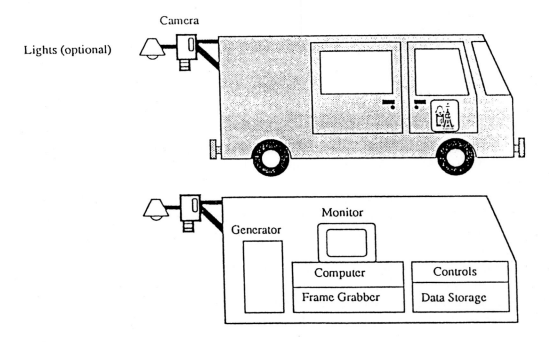

Figure 1. Schematic drawing of a pavement data collection system [LeBl91].

approach retains the raw data by using commercial video cameras and recording equipment for data analysis at a later time. But the major problem of using currently available recording equipment is that its limited bandwidth is incapable of meeting the system specifications, i.e., low resolution images.

A solution elaborated in this paper is to use a special purpose high resolution image acquisition system with data compression to allow recording raw image data at moderate road speeds (45 mph) using commercial equipment. The compressed images are stored and reconstructed at a later time for evaluation by the pavement engineer or can be input directly for image processing by automated machine vision systems.

Fractal coding is chosen because it satisfies the condition of image equivalency and offers a very high compression ratio. Human to computer evaluation is not considered. Equivalency in terms of this project is defined to be:

> the reconstructed image is equivalent to the original uncompressed image as judged by humans;

> machine vision image processing determines that both the uncompressed and compressed images show the same distress, distress extent and severity.

This paper reports ongoing research being conducted by Worcester Polytechnic Institute, Massachusetts, USA, and King's College London, University of London, England, in using fractals to compress images. Initially, simple distress features are being modelled, namely simple longitudinal, transverse and diagonal cracks. Complete image reconstruction accuracy is not the objective of the work. Sufficient data must be retained to allow accurate assessment of severity and extent of pavement distress by both humans and computers.

Data Reduction

THE NEED FOR DATA REDUCTION

The volume of data to be processed is enormous. If P is the number of points per square inch to be analysed, and assuming a 14-foot lane width, $10,644,000 \times P$ points per mile of highway are needed. If 10,000 miles of highway per year are

Table 1. Simplified inspection system technical specifications.

Maximum Inspection speed:	45mph (72km/h)
Inspection width:	14′ (4.3m)
Road coverage:	continuous (100% inspected within a lane)
Minimum crack width:	1/16″ (1.6mm)
Maximum joint width:	1″ (25mm)
Pavement Surface:	bituminous or portland cement concrete
Pavement condition:	new to severely worn
Aggregate:	any material, not worn shiny-smooth
Lighting conditions:	any natural combination of sun and skylight

to be covered (not unreasonable for many states) at a resolution of 1/16 inch (to guarantee detection of cracks 1/16 inch wide) with $P = 256$, 27.1 trillion points per year need to be processed. To acquire this data at 45 miles per hour would need 222 hours of road time; thus, data acquisition can be safely restricted to periods of favourable weather. Data needs to be acquired at a rate of 33.9 million points per second. This can be processed off-line at a much lower rate, as computers can run 365 days a year, 24 hours per day. Thus, 8,760 hours are available to process data that required 222 hours to acquire, for an effective rate of 0.86 million points per second.

Data Reduction Methods

Ignoring Other Than Pavement Distress Features

One type of information that does not contribute to pavement distress evaluation is image texture due to aggregate. Aggregate has a signature that is easy to characterise: it has a roughly circular texture at a regular frequency. Methods for detecting and eliminating most, if not all, of the signal directly attributable to aggregate are explored. This enables information storage requirements to be reduced to four bits per pixel or less, thus halving storage requirements at the cost of some decoding prior to processing.

Further compression of the aggregate-free images is possible using the simple but powerful method of image encoding known as Run Length Encoding. In Run Length Encoding, consecutive runs of pixels with identical values are efficiently represented by storing the intensity value only once, with a repetition count telling how many times the given value is to be repeated. On a typical image this results in a compression ratio of 10 to 100 over the original image, and with filtering provides even greater compression.

Image Compression

Image compression is reducing the number of bits required to represent an image in such a way that either an exact replica of the image (lossless compression) or an approximate replica (lossy compression) of the image can be retrieved.

Fractals

Computer Description of Natural Objects

The natural graphics system encodes pictures by assigning an address and colour attribute for each point of the object, resulting in a long list of addresses and attributes. The problem is alleviated by using a newer class of geometrical shapes that are both flexible and controllable. These geometrical shapes can be made to conform to clouds, feathers, leaves and other natural objects and are found in the domain of fractal geometry.

ADVANTAGES OF USING FRACTAL TRANSFORMS

A Fractal is described as "... a highly complex structure ... generated from a simple concise kernel of data which is easy to produce. (Such large database amplification is a primary advantage of fractal techniques in general.)" [Oppe86]

FRACTALS — A BRIEF INTRODUCTION

Coastlines, mountains and clouds are not easily described by traditional Euclidean geometry. We use Mandelbrot's fractal geometry to describe and mathematically model the natural objects. This is another reason image compression using fractal transforms is studied. Mandelbrot first coined the word fractal in 1975 [Mand75].

PROPERTIES OF FRACTALS

The property of self-similarity, or scaling, is one of the central concepts of fractal geometry. Also, a fractal has a fractional dimension, from which the word fractal is derived; Euclidean shapes have integer dimensions only.

Self-similarity

The property of objects whereby magnified subsets appear similar or identical to the whole and to each other is known as self-similarity. It sets fractals apart from Euclidean shapes, which generally become smoother. Thus, fractal shapes are self-similar, independent of scale or scaling and possess no characteristic size. This describes a pavement distress image: a magnified segment of a crack appears the same as the unmagnified segment. Thus cracks are effectively represented by fractals.

Fractal Dimension

The classic example of a self-similar curve is that of a coastline, the length of which increases as the dimension of the ruler used to measure it decreases. Thus, unlike a straight line a fractal's measured length depends on the ruler's length. This dependence is described by the fractal dimension, D. Other fractal dimension measures exist, such as the similarity dimension. A detailed discussion of fractal dimension is beyond the scope of this paper. For pavement analysis purposes, a method for calculating the fractal dimension of cracks is required and presented, and conversely, the generation of cracks given a fractal dimension.

The distance or the number of rulers, N, obtained by measuring a straight line, L, using a ruler of length K is

$$N = \frac{L}{K}$$

When the curve is not straight but convoluted N, the number of rulers needed to fit the curve, grows by an exponential factor, D, as

$$N = \left(\frac{L}{K}\right)^{D}$$

For a straight line, $D = 1$. D must be less than 2, otherwise the line has space and contradicts the Euclidean definition of a line.

Measuring the Fractal Dimension of a Crack

We measure the fractal dimension of a crack using a modified Calliper method, which has produced the most consistent results and is most suitable for measuring the fractal dimension of linear structures.

First, segment the distress features from the pavement image. An example of a Portland Cement Concrete (PCC) pavement image is shown in Figure 2. Figure 3 shows the segmented image of the distress. Here the pavement's grey level is altered to white, whilst those pixels associated with the distress itself are black. Segmentation is a major problem in itself; ongoing research is being conducted at Worcester Polytechnic Institute to segment an image more efficiently.

Next, skeletonize the segmented image, that is, reduce the width of the pixels to a single pixel. This is carried out to determine the morphology of the distress. Figure 4a shows a segmented transverse crack taken from Figure 3, and Figure 4b shows the same crack after skeletonization.

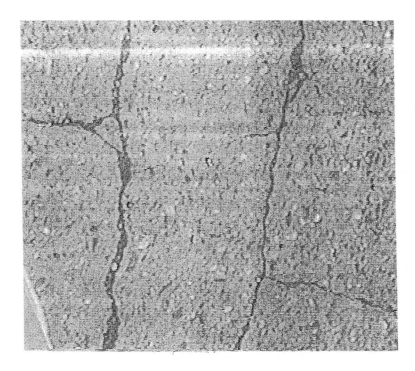

Figure 2. Image of a distressed PCC pavement [LeBl91].

Figure 3. Segmented image of the distress in Figure 2 [LeBl91].

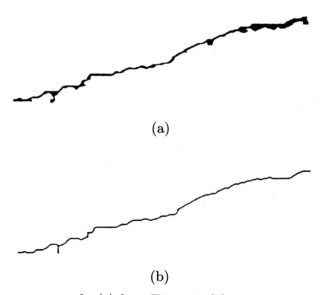

(a)

(b)

Figure 4. Transverse cracks (a) from Figure 3; (b) same crack skeletonized.

Then, the measured length, M, in pixels of the skeletonized crack is determined using a variety of ruler lengths, K, also in pixels. Following Smith [Smit89], a log-log plot of M (log curve length) as a function of K (log ruler length) is plotted, as shown in Figure 5.

Finally, the slope, S, is computed to find the fractal dimension, D, from the expression

$$D = 1 - S$$

The value obtained for this example is $D = 1.08$.

For small K values, the discreteness of the digital image means the left portion of the curve is generally flat, since pixels are larger than points and self-similarity breaks down at the pixel level. For large values of K the behaviour of the curve is explained by quantization error because the length is not an integral number of ruler lengths.

Point selection for determining the slope was arbitrary; ruler lengths of 10 to 100 pixels give the most repeatability. A more rigorous slope measurement method must be developed to fully automate fractal dimension measurements.

From the study of both PCC and asphalt cement (AC) pavements, the fractal dimension was found to lie in the range

$$D = 1.1 \pm 0.05$$

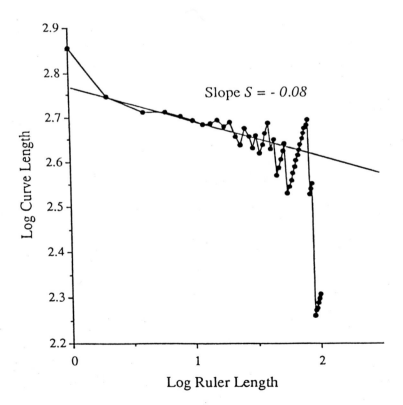

Figure 5. Log-log plot of curve length versus ruler length from Figure 4b [LeBl91].

Joints in PCC pavements have fractal dimensions below this range. Curves with fractal dimensions above this range are too convoluted (see Figure 6). Due to the difficulty of segmenting distress features in digitised pavement images (about 20), the population of the data is not large enough to derive statistical information concerning the fractal dimension, such as the standard deviation, nor to claim that the fractal dimension range is universal. No theories for this observation have yet been formulated.

The Simulation of Pavement Surface Distress Using Fractals

The first technique to be described generates fractals by iterative applications of 'generator' functions to Euclidean objects. In the case of simulation of pavement distress, a straight line, the Euclidean object, is dissected into smaller line segments by the generator. The resulting line segments are further dissected by the same generator, until the dissections are smaller than the screen or output device resolution. No general theory exists in designing or selecting the required optimal fractal generator to simulate pavement distress. The approach undertaken was to search for the generator and build up a library of generators that produce the different types of distress by subjective comparison of the results with the real distress.

A technique described later in this paper attempts to find the appropriate iterated function system (IFS) code to generate the distress by the moment matching method.

Fractal Generating Functions

DETERMINISTIC FRACTAL GENERATING FUNCTIONS

A Koch snowflake is a classic example of a fractal produced by deterministic fractal generating functions. The fractal is brought into existence by applying the generator shown in Figure 7b at each iteration. The generator trisects a line segment, shown in Figure 7a, replacing the central segment with two segments of equal length after the application of the generator G times. The curve produced for $G = 3$ is shown in Figure 7c. The resulting curve has 3^G segments. The

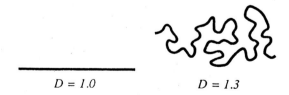

$D = 1.0$ $D = 1.3$

Figure 6. Curves with fractal dimensions outside the range $D = 1.1 \pm 0.05$ [LeBl91].

curve is only a fractal as G approaches infinity. For practical purposes G must be larger than the logarithm, base 2, of the image size in pixels. If the image size is 2^8 pixels wide, then G need only be equal to or greater than 9.

What most people do not understand is that the human eye is incapable of ever seeing a fractal. It cannot resolve the infinite detail present in a fractal, thus only an approximation of the fractal is sensed.

The Koch snowflake does not resemble a pavement distress in any way. Two reasons for this observation are:

> The fractal dimension of the Koch snowflake is greater than the measured range of pavement distress dimensions and is given as (see [Voss88])

$$D = \frac{\log N}{\log \frac{1}{R}}$$

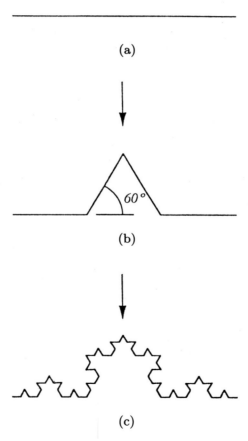

(a)

(b)

(c)

Figure 7. An example of a deterministic fractal generating function. (a) Line segment used for generating a fractal; (b) Koch snowflake generator; (c) curve after three iterations of the generator [LeBl91].

where N is the number of segments into which the line is dissected, and R is the ratio of the new line segment length to the original line length. For the Koch snowflake $N = 4$, $R = 1/3$ when $D = 1.262$ (3 d.p.), which is outside the distress dimension range.

The Koch snowflake is too regular.

From these observations we deduce that control of the fractal dimension is required in order to produce more irregular fractals and fractals whose fractal dimension lies in the range where distress fractals exist.

STOCHASTIC FRACTAL GENERATING FUNCTIONS — STOCHASTIC MIDPOINT DISPLACEMENT ALGORITHM

Irregular fractals are produced by randomly varying the lengths and orientations of the basic generator function at each iteration. In the deterministic case, the generator bisects the line segment by displacing the midpoint to produce two new line segments. The displacement is always the same, as shown in Figure 8a. This generator function displaces the midpoint in an orthogonal direction by a quarter of the original line length. Figure 8b shows the case for the stochastic midpoint displacement generator, where both the magnitude, r, and the direction, θ, of the displacement are selected randomly. The midpoint is only displaced uniformly within the closed circle of radius, p. The displacement angle, θ, is therefore uniformly distributed within the circle with the probability density of the angle, θ, given by

$$P_\theta(\theta) = \frac{1}{2\pi}$$

To obtain a uniform distribution, the probability density of any displacement magnitude, r, is

$$P_r(r) = \frac{2r}{p^2}$$

The equation used to calculate the Koch snowflake is still used to calculate the fractal dimension. In this case, where $N = 2$ and $R = E\{l_1\}$, the average or expected value of l_1. l_1 is the length of the line $P_1 M'$, the line connecting an endpoint to the displaced midpoint in Figure 8b. The other line segment, $P_2 M'$, obeys the same statistics; the expected lengths are equal, and this is given by

$$E\{l_1\} = E\{l_2\} = \int_0^P \int_0^{2\pi} P_r(r) P_\theta(\theta) l_1(r, \theta) \, dr \, d\theta$$

From the geometry of Figure 8b l_1 is

$$l_1(r, \theta) = \sqrt{0.25 + r^2 + r \cos \theta}$$

A plot of the fractal dimension, D, against the parameter p is given in Figure 9. The values of p, found to lie in the range $0.25 \leq p \leq 0.425$, produce cracks whose fractal dimensions lie in the range of pavement distress. For p values greater

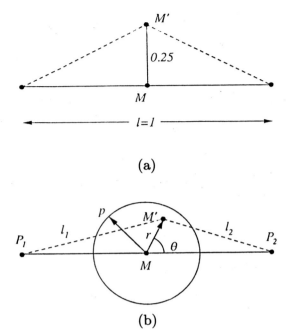

Figure 8. Midpoint displacement generators. (a) Deterministic; (b) stochastic. [LeBl91].

than 0.5, the curves are too convoluted to resemble pavement distress; above 0.85, the fractal dimension exceeds two, and the curves are area-filling in nature. Conversely, for p values less than 0.25 the curves are too straight. Some curves obtained by using this algorithm are given in Figure 10.

Crack Width Algorithm

The fractal curve produced above had no width. To render the curve it was necessary to assign a pixel width of one or two. With this the curve has constant width, which is contrary to real pavement distress. To obtain a more realistic distress, a crack width algorithm is implemented. The input parameters for this are the width at one end of the crack and the minimum and maximum widths. Points are constructed at both segment ends a constant perpendicular distance from the segment by defining a constant width box around the segment. The width of the box is randomly generated and is constrained by the upper and lower width boundaries. Too, it cannot vary by more than a pixel from the previous line segment of the fractal curve. To make the curve appear continuous and with no abrupt width changes, the box endpoints are connected end to end by shaped polygons. The final stage consists of replacing the line segments by the boxes and polygons to render the final crack. Figure 11 shows the crack of Figure 10b after application of the crack width algorithm. No theoretical foundation exists for this algorithm; its use is purely for the purpose of generating realistic looking cracks.

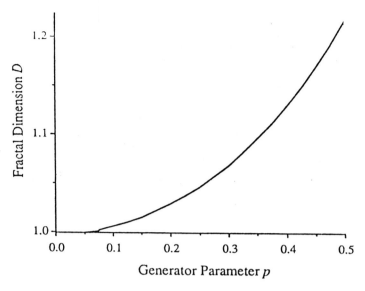

Figure 9. Fractal dimension as a function of the generator parameter [LeBl91].

Generating Pavement Images and Image Compression

Real distress features not only have a nonconstant width but also a nonconstant grey level with colour variation as well. The grey level of the pavement depends upon, for example, the material, lighting conditions and the geometry of the distress. To simulate new pavement images to reflect lighting or material, other pavement images can be combined and processed with the application of computer models to compute the correct grey levels. To construct an image this way (see Figure 12) we first use the segmented image of Figure 3 as a mask

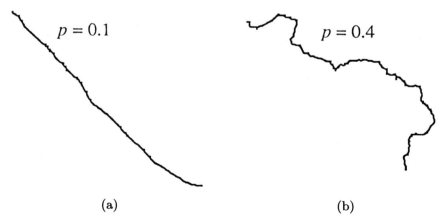

Figure 10. Fractals produced by a stochastic midpoint displacement generator [LeBl91].

Figure 11. A fractal curve with algorithmically produced width [LeBl91].

to remove the distress from the image of Figure 2. Then we superimpose the computed distress of Figure 11 onto Figure 2, adjusting the grey levels. Only 13 parameters are required to achieve this:

the crack endpoint coordinates (xstart, ystart, xstop, ystop — four values);

the fractal dimension;

the minimum crack width;

the maximum crack width;

initial crack width;

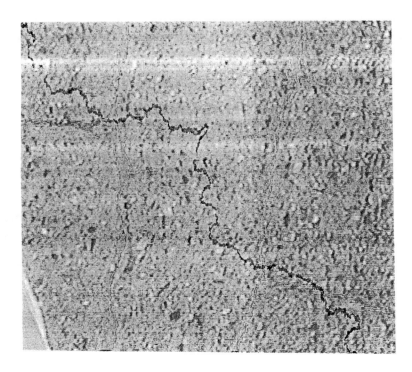

Figure 12. Simulated image of a distressed PCC pavement [LeBl91].

the assumed crack depth;

the average pavement surface reflectivity;

two illumination angles;

the ratio of directed to ambient illumination.

Note that the last six parameters are only needed for synthesizing crack images and might not be needed for crack analysis (and might be very difficult to recover). Thus one normally only needs the first seven parameters for analysis. This holds only for simple cracks. For more complicated cracking patterns consisting of N crack segments, less than $7N$ parameters are needed, since crack endpoints are necessarily shared among multiple cracks. The data used is 1/500th of the data in the original image; thus an effective compression ratio of 500:1 is achieved.

Iterated Function Systems (IFS)

IFS: THEIR USE IN IMAGE COMPRESSION

Using fractals to simulate natural effects is not new. The innovation is to start with an actual image and find the fractals that imitate it to the required degree of accuracy (see [Barn88; Zorp88]). Since these fractals are represented in a compact way, the whole image is represented by a highly compressed data set. Thus, data compression is achieved. Iterated Function System (IFS) codes are used to represent the fractal transforms. IFS codes use affine transformations which express relations between parts of an image. They define and convey intricate details of a picture.

Fractal compression is a lossy compression technique. The high compression ratio is increased further by applying the best lossless compression algorithm currently available to the IFS code itself.

AFFINE TRANSFORMATIONS

Affine transformations are combinations of rotations, scalings and translations of the coordinate axes in n-dimensional space. Figure 13 shows an example of a contractive affine transformation, W, operated on a smiling face, F, lying in the xy plane and moving it to a new face, $W(F)$. W always moves points closer together — it is contractive. The general form of an affine transformation is

$$W \begin{pmatrix} x \\ y \end{pmatrix} = \begin{pmatrix} a & b \\ c & d \end{pmatrix} \begin{pmatrix} x \\ y \end{pmatrix} + \begin{pmatrix} e \\ f \end{pmatrix} = \begin{pmatrix} ax + by + e \\ cx + dy + f \end{pmatrix}$$

If the translations, rotations and scalings that make up W are known in advance, then the coefficients are calculated by

$$a = r \cos \theta \qquad b = -s \sin \phi$$
$$c = r \sin \theta \qquad d = s \cos \phi$$

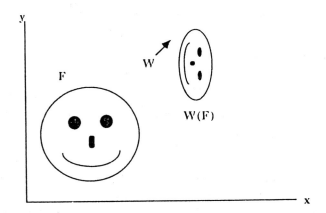

Figure 13. An example of a contractive affine transformation, W.

where r = scaling factor on x s = scaling factor on y

θ = angle of rotation on x ϕ = angle of rotation on y

e = translation on x f = translation on y

What is an IFS?

An IFS is a collection of contractive affine transformations that express relations between parts of an image. The relations define and convey intricate details of a picture. An IFS code for the generation of a fractal fern leaf consisting of four affine transformations in matrix form is

W	a	b	c	d	e	f	p
1	0	0	0	0.16	0	0	0.01
2	0.2	−0.26	0.23	0.22	0	1.6	0.07
3	−0.15	0.28	0.26	0.24	0	0.44	0.07
4	0.85	0.04	−0.04	0.85	0	1.6	0.85

An IFS consists of m affine transformations, W_1, W_2, ..., W_m, each with an associated probability. The probabilities affect the rate of filling-in of the various regions and attributes of the image.

The Complex Form of IFSs

The points (x, y) in the real 2D space can be seen as points z in the complex plane. Then the affine transformation, ω_i, expressed in the complex form $\omega_i(z)$ is

$$z = x + iy$$

$$\omega_i(z) = c_i z + (d_i z^*) + b_i \qquad i = 1, \ldots, N$$

where $z^* = x - iy$

Comparing this with the polar form of the affine transformation, the complex variables of the affine transform are

$$c_i^r = \frac{1}{2}\left(r\cos\theta + s\cos\phi\right) \qquad\qquad r^2 = (c_i^r + d_i^r)^2 + (c_i^c - d_i^c)^2$$

$$c_i^c = \frac{1}{2}\left(r\sin\theta + s\sin\phi\right) \qquad\qquad \tan\theta = \frac{c_i^c - d_i^c}{c_i^r + d_i^r}$$

$$d_i^r = \frac{1}{2}\left(r\cos\theta - s\cos\phi\right) \qquad\qquad s^2 = (c_i^r - d_i^r)^2 + (c_i^c + d_i^c)^2$$

$$d_i^c = \frac{1}{2}\left(-r\sin\theta + s\sin\phi\right) \qquad\qquad \tan\phi = \frac{c_i^c + d_i^c}{c_i^r - d_i^r}$$

$$b_i^r = e$$

$$b_i^c = f$$

The probabilities stay the same in either case.

RELATIONSHIP BETWEEN THE COMPLEX MOMENT AND THE COMPLEX FORM OF IFS

The moment of an IFS is defined as [Barn86]

$$M_n = \int_k z^n d\mu(z) \qquad n = 0, 1, 2, \ldots$$

where z represents the points generated by the affine transformation ω_i.

Consider our fractal image to be made up of m points z_k. Then the moment, M_n, is

$$M_n = \sum_{k=1}^{m} (z_k)^{n/m}$$

For an IFS with $r = s$ and $\theta = \phi$ (for example, of the form $\omega_i(z) = a_i z + b_i$, $i = 1, \ldots, N$) then

$$M_n = \sum_{i=1}^{N} p_i \int_k (a_i z + b_i)^n d\mu(z)$$

Expanding using the binomial theorem yields

$$M_n = \sum_{i=1}^{N} p_i \sum_{j=0}^{n} (^nC_j) \int_k (a_i z)^j b_i^{n-j} d\mu(z) = \sum_{i=1}^{N} p_i \sum_{j=0}^{n} (^nC_j) a_i^j b_i^{n-j} \int_k z^j d\mu(z)$$

where

$$^nC_j = \frac{n(n-1), \ldots, (n-j+1)}{j!}$$

and

$$j! = j(j-1)(j-2)\ldots 1$$

Since $\int_k z^j d\mu(z) = M_j$, M_n is simplified to

$$M_n = \sum_{i=1}^{N} p_i \sum_{j=0}^{n} (^nC_j) a_i^j b_i^{n-j} M_j = \sum_{i=1}^{N} p_i \sum_{j=0}^{n-1} (^nC_j) a_i^j b_i^{n-j} M_j + \sum_{i=1}^{N} p_i a_i^n M_n$$

Taking M_n to the LHS and rearranging yields

$$M_n = \left(1 - \sum_{i=1}^{N} p_i a_i^n\right)^{-1} \sum_{i=1}^{N} p_i \sum_{j=0}^{n-1} (^nC_j) a_i^j b_i^{n-j} M_j$$

An equation is obtained giving M_n with the previous moments, $M_j, j = 0, \ldots, n-1$, and the form of the affine transformation, a_i, b_i and $p_i, i = 1, \ldots, N$. Since $M_0 = 1$, the rest of the moments are calculated without the need to generate the points z_k. Valuable computation time where 10,000 or more points need to be generated to obtain accurate moments is thus saved.

Thus, an IFS that describes an image is found by attempting to make the moments of the IFS as close to the moments of the image as possible. This only holds for the case $r = s$ and $\theta = \phi$. For the more general case, the general moment definition is

$$M_{jk} = \int_k z^j z^{*k} d\mu(z) \qquad j, k = 0, 1, 2, \ldots$$

Here, a matrix equation for the moments M_{jk}, with $j + k = n$, must be solved in the form (see [Wils88])

$$-[C] = ([A] - [I]) [M]$$

where $[M] = $ vector $[M_{0n}, M_{1(n-1)}, M_{2(n-2)}, \ldots, M_{n0}]^T$;

$[A] = $ matrix of dimension $(n+1) \times (n+1)$ whose elements are IFS parameter dependent;

$[I] = $ Identity matrix $I_{ii} = 1$, $I_{ij} = 0$ if $i \neq j$;

$[C] = $ vector whose elements depend upon the IFS parameters and moments M_{jk} (where $j + k < n$).

Thus, using the IFS code and $M_{00} = 1$, the moment M_{jk} can be solved.

The Moment Library Search Method

The moments must be normalised so that fractal images which are the same except for a global scaling can be compared. By having a large database of IFS codes and its associated normalised moments, this library is used to search for an IFS code whose moment is closest to the normalised moment of an image to be encoded. This IFS code is then retained and passed as the fractal transform of that image segment to directly compress that segment; otherwise, the IFS code obtained is used as a starting point to a nonlinear solution method to find a closer IFS code for that segment.

Newton's Method to Find an IFS Code Close to an Image

Newton's method is used to solve an equation of the form $f(\vec{x}) = 0$. The problem is essentially

$$f(\vec{x}) = f_1(\vec{x}) - f_1(\vec{x}_{\text{image segment}})$$

where $f_1(\vec{x}) = $ normalised moments function of an IFS code;

$\qquad f_1(\vec{x}_{\text{image segment}}) = $ normalised moments of image calculated explicitly from the points of the image.

When $f(\vec{x}) = 0$ the vector form of the IFS code, $\vec{x}$, has been found.

Simulated Annealing Method to Find an IFS Code Close to an Image

The simulated annealing method (see [Kirk83]) to find an IFS code close to an image is a better method of minimising functions of many variables because it does not immediately go to the local minimum of a function, a problem inherent with the Newton method. The problem concerns the thermodynamics of metal cooling and annealing given by

$$\text{Prob}(E) \approx \exp \frac{-E}{kT}$$

where $E = $ the energy of the system;

$\qquad T = $ temperature (Kelvin);

$\qquad k = $ Boltzmann's constant.

The method requires parameters that are analogues of T, whose value is decreased as the method gets closer to the minimum, and energy, E, where E is the value of the system to be minimised.

At initial higher Ts, changes to higher energy states are much more likely to be accepted. It is this feature of the method that allows the algorithm to find the global minimum of a function rather than one of many local minima. The method is used to find an IFS whose moments are close to a given set of moments. The following conditions are required:

description of the system — use the vector $\vec{x}$ of size N_{ofx}, where N_{ofx} is the number of points in the image segment

$$\vec{x} = \left(c_1^r, c_1^c, d_1^r, d_1^c, b_1^r, b_1^c, \ldots, d_{N_{affine}}^r, d_{N_{affine}}^c, b_{N_{affine}}^r, b_{N_{affine}}^c \right)^T$$

a random system change generator — this is accomplished by the random vector, $\vec{dx}$, a variable of a length randomly chosen between 0 and the given length, δ_l. δ_l and T were decreased simultaneously, creating a new vector, $\vec{x}_{new}$

$$\vec{x}_{new} = \vec{x}_{old} + \vec{\delta x}$$

The vector was checked for valid IFS code production. If the code obtained was invalid, then a new $\vec{dx}$ was generated;

the energy of the system, E, whose minimisation is required, is

$$E = |f(\vec{x})|^2 = \sqrt{\sum_{i=1}^{N_{ofx}} f_i(\vec{x})^2}$$

where $f(\vec{x}) = f_1(\vec{x}) - f_1(\overrightarrow{\text{image}})$. Unnormalised moments are used for $f_1(\vec{x})$ and $f_1(\text{image})$;

the parameter T and a method of decreasing T; T governs the changes in the function E. The value of E should be considered carefully, since it affects the energy changes, ΔE, which are acceptable.

How to Decode an IFS Code

The Random Iteration Algorithm

A summary of the random iteration algorithm (see [Barn88]) given in pseudocode form is:

1. initialise variables, $x = 0$, $y = 0$;
2. for $n = 1$ to Number_of_points_in_image, do steps (3) and (4);
3. choose k to be one of the numbers $1, 2, \ldots, m$, with probability P_k;
4. apply the transformation, W_k, to the point (x, y) to obtain (x', y');
5. set (x, y) equal to the new point, $x = x'$, $y = y'$;
6. if $n >$ Number_of_points_required_to_obtain_attractor, then plot (x', y');
7. loop.

More points are added to an image by increasing the variable Number_of_points_in_image. This can be required to obtain an image with a greater resolution. Zooming is also achieved by using an increased scale factor. The variable Number_of_points_required_to_obtain_attractor is around 100 but can be minimised by empirical methods. The ability of the random iteration algorithm to produce the same image independent of the random sequence of events chosen is proven in two ways:

by carrying out computer graphic mathematical experiments;

by the rigorous theoretical foundation of the mathematician John Elton of Georgia Institute of Technology, Atlanta, Georgia, USA (see [Elto87]).

Conclusions

The attempts to simulate pavement distress using fractal techniques illustrate the problems of image equivalency. There is no objective test for image equivalency such as there is for image accuracy. The project illustrates that the fractal dimension can be used to assess image accuracy by using the fractal dimension to generate the fractal curve and by comparing the calculated fractal dimension of the same curve.

This paper shows the suitability of using fractal techniques for image compression and generation related to pavement distress, such as the variation of the midpoint displacement algorithm and IFS coding techniques. Pavement test images can also be generated and used for testing and developing automated pavement evaluation systems. The advantage of test images is that their geometric and photometric characteristics are known in advance. Further work is required to improve and integrate this new technology into an operational automated pavement surface distress evaluation system.

A modified method of calculating the fractal dimension (Calliper method) of linear structures has been explained. Table 2 shows the values of the generator, p, and its associated fractal dimensions, theoretical and measured. The maximum discrepancy between the measured and the calculated fractal dimension was 5.4%, whereas the least was only 0.2%! This shows the reliability of the method. The major discrepancy in the work can be attributed to the difficulty in determining the slope of the log-log plots, such as seen in Figure 5. This requires further research and development.

The major advantage of using fractal techniques is that they offer a very large image compression ratio. The work being conducted using the fractal dimension has given compression ratios of 500:1. This figure is obtained by comparing the information required to generate the distress with the raw data of the pavement that included the distress and the aggregate — most of the data is required to synthesize the aggregate. Since only distress data is of concern to the pavement maintenance engineer, a library of pavement surface images can be stored on a CD. When a pavement image is reconstructed from the compressed data, the distress is superimposed on the relevant aggregate image selected from the CD; hence, a large compression ratio of 500:1 or even higher is easily attained. A fractal method for synthesizing the aggregate from the IFS code is being studied.

Table 2. Comparison between theoretical and measured fractal dimension.

Image	Generator 'p'	Generator 'D'	Measured 'D'	Percentage error between measured & calculated D
Figure 10a	0.1	1.006	1.06	+5.4%
Figure 10b	0.4	1.129	1.11	−1.7%
Figure 7c		1.262	1.26	−0.2%

Using Iterated Function System codes — a type of fractal equation — to compress image segments has been explained. The difficult inverse problem of finding a suitable IFS code whose fractal image is to represent the real image and hence achieve compression is being studied through the use of

a library of IFS codes and complex moments;

the method of simulated annealing for solving nonlinear equations of many parameters.

The application of simulated annealing is still under development.

IFS codes are robust, thus they are ideal for transmission through noisy distortion-inducing communication channels, since small deviation of the IFS codes still produces recognisable images with minimal distortion. Figure 14 shows an example of a pavement distress generated entirely from a file of IFS codes whose size is only 926 bytes.

Segmentation probably plays the most significant part in fractal image compression. The success of achieving a large compression ratio effectively rests on an efficient segmentation algorithm. Work being conducted at Worcester Polytechnic Institute on a fractal model-based segmentation technique is producing promising results. A basis of the algorithm is to determine the fractal dimension of the segment and compare it with the range of fractal dimensions of, for example, pavement distress features, to see if the segment is that of the object of interest. Block-based coding is also under investigation to avoid the problems associated with segmentation.

Acknowledgments. I thank Drs. N. Wittels, M. Ward and T. El-Korchi for their help and cooperation during my stay at Worcester Polytechnic Institute in Massachusetts, USA. A special thank you to my professor, Dr. Mike Gennert. This

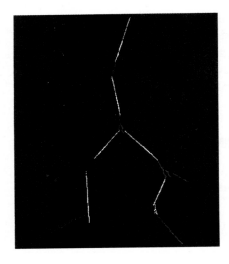

Figure 14. An example of an IFS-generated pavement distress.

paper is an abridged version of [LeBl91]. I am also grateful to Dr. D.M. Monro (Bath University, England) for supplying the material by Wilson [Wils88].

REFERENCES

[Barn86]

Barnsley, M.F., Ervin, V., Hardin, D., and Lancaster, J., Solution of an inverse problem for fractals and other sets, *Proc. Nat. Acad. Sci.*, USA, Vol. 83, pp. 1975–77, April 1986.

[Barn88]

Barnsley, M.F., and Sloan, A.D., A better way to compress images, *BYTE*, January 1988, pp. 215–223.

[Elto87]

Elton, J.H., An ergodic theorem for iterated maps, *Ergod. Th. & Dynam. Sys.*, Vol. 7, pp. 481–488, 1987.

[LeBl91]

LeBlanc, J., Gennert, M.A., Wittels, N., and Gosselin, D., Analysis and generation of pavement distress images using fractals, *Transportation Res. Rec.*, No. 1311, pp. 158–165, 1991.

[Kirk83]

Kirkpatrick, S., Gelatt, C.D., Jr., and Vecchi, M.P., Optimisation by simulated annealing, *Science*, Vol. 220, No. 4598, pp. 671–679, 13 May 1983.

[Mand75]

Mandelbrot, B.B., *les objects fractals: forme, hasard et dimension*, Paris: Flammarion, 1975.

[Oppe86]

Oppenheimer, P.E., Real time design and animation of fractal plants and trees, *Comput. Graph.*, Vol. 20, pp. 55–64, 1986 (Siggraph 86).

[Smit89]

Smith, T.G., Jr., Marks, W.B., Lange, G.D., Sheriff, W.H., and Neale, E.A., A fractal analysis of cell images, *Jour. Neuroscience Methods*, Vol. 27, pp. 173–180, 1989.

[Voss88]

Voss, R.F., Fractals in nature: From characterization to simulation, in *The Science of Fractal Images*, Peitgen, H.-O., and Saupe, D., Eds., New York: Springer-Verlag, 1988, p. 29.

[Wils88]

Wilson, D., 'Fractal Image Compression', computer science M.Sc. project report, September 1988, Imperial College of Science, Technology & Medicine, University of London, England.

[Zorp88]

Zorpette, G., Fractals: not just another pretty picture, *IEEE Spectrum*, October 1988, pp. 29–31.

Multifractals and the Local Connected Fractal Dimension:
Classification of Early Chinese Landscape Paintings

Richard F. Voss and James C.Y. Wyatt

Abstract

Local and global applications of multifractals to the analysis of digitized image intensities, $I(x, y)$, are discussed. The magnitude of the local slope, $|\nabla I(x, y)|$, is shown to be a more useful measure than $I(x, y)$. A global fractal dimension, D, can be estimated from the spectral density, $S(\vec{k})$, the angle-averaged pair-correlation, $C(r)$, and mass-radius $M(R)$. The concept of local fractal dimension can be used to construct a color-coded dimensional image. Applications to the classification of early Chinese landscape paintings, however, suggest that the local connected fractal dimension provides the best agreement with the human eye for highlighting and discriminating between images.

Fractals: From Self-similarity to Self-affinity and Multifractals

The term fractal was invented and developed by IBM mathematician Benoit Mandelbrot in 1975 [Mand75] to characterize a previously disjoint and little-known collection of mathematical techniques and models applicable to irregular shapes and time series [Mand82, 77, 75]. Since that time, fractal geometry has become a scientific discipline in its own right and has achieved tremendous impact on other fields of science, technology and art.

The initial exposition of fractals focussed on the concept of self-similarity or dilation symmetry, in which a small part of a shape mimicked the characteristics of the whole [Mand77, 75]. When a shape is described as consisting of N sub-shapes, each scaled down by a factor $r < 1$ from the original, it is characterized by a fractal dimension, D, where

$$D = \frac{\log N}{\log \frac{1}{r}} \tag{1}$$

Although extremely useful, the concept of fractal dimension is, strictly speaking, only applicable to sets, collections of points or regions that are specified according to some membership rule. In other words, use of a fractal dimension assumes a black and white, or binary, view of the world. A specific point is either a member of the set of interest or not.

Most views of the world (and most scientific problems) are not so clear-cut and require continuous shades of gray in their description. Fractal geometry spawned two strategies for dealing with this problem. Self-affinity is used to describe functions of time or space [Mand85, 68; Voss88, 85]. Models for self-affine functions $X(t)$, such as fractional Brownian motion (fBm) [Mand68], typically involve the addition of perturbations, $f(t/\tau)$, each having a typical size, τ

$$X(t) = \sum_\tau a(\tau) f\left(\frac{t}{\tau}\right) \tag{2}$$

Self-similar shapes are constructed from subshapes scaled equally in all directions. With self-affinity the subshapes can be scaled differently in different directions. For a Brownian motion or random walk, the displacement, ΔX, scales with time change Δt as $\Delta X \propto \Delta t^{1/2}$. When the time scale is changed by 4, the distance scale is changed by 2. Consequently, the original concept of fractal dimension, which was based on self-similarity, must be used with great care for self-affine functions [Voss88, 85; Mand85]. Different procedures for estimating D, that give the same answer for self-similar shapes, in general give different answers for self-affine shapes. A single procedure, moreover, can give a different D for different spatial scales.

Multifractals, on the other hand, are used to describe mathematical measures [Mand89, 88, 74]. Models for multifractals, such as the Besicovitch measures, typically involve the multiplication of perturbations, $f(\tau)$, each having a typical size τ

$$X(t) = \prod_\tau a(\tau) f\left(\frac{t}{\tau}\right) \tag{3}$$

As seen from Eqs. (2) and (3), there can be a great deal of similarity between self-affine and multifractal descriptions of a problem. A measure can be converted to an arbitrary number of sets. For example, one set includes all points for which $X > X_0$. Since each X_0 produces a different set with a possibly different D, multifractals are typically characterized by their distributions, or histogram, of D values.

Measures and Mass Dimension

The fractal analysis techniques described here are first illustrated in 1D and then extended to 2D images. The basic problem is the fractal description of a measure or local mass density, $m(x)$.

As shown in Figure 1, even a discrete distribution of point masses becomes approximately continuous under coarse-grained averaging. Most experimental data, and digitized images in particular, represent a coarse-grained average of

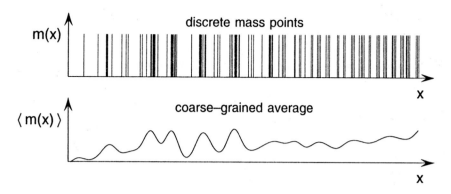

Figure 1. A sample discrete-point mass distribution and its coarse-grained average.

some underlying point process (such as the actual locations of photons reaching a CCD or film).

There are a number of standard techniques for characterizing random functions, $m(x)$, and their correlations [Robi74; Reif65]. The autocorrelation or pair-correlation function, $C(r)$, is a quantitative measure of how the fluctuations in $m(x)$ are related at x and $x + r$

$$C(r) = \langle\, m(x)\ m(x+r)\,\rangle$$

where the brackets $\langle\dots\rangle$ denote sample or ensemble averages. $C(r)$ is that probability of finding another mass point a distance, r, from an existing mass. Similar information is provided by the mass-radius relation. $M(R)$ is the conditional total average 'mass' within a distance, R, of an existing point

$$M(R) = \int_0^R C(r)\, dr \propto R^D \tag{4}$$

for a set of mass points characterized by a fractal dimension, $0 < D < 1$. Thus

$$C(r) \propto \frac{1}{r^\eta} \propto \frac{1}{r^{1-D}} \tag{5}$$

for a fractal set in 1D.[†]

An alternate characterization is provided by the Fourier coefficients, $m(k) \propto \int e^{-2\pi i k x}\, dx$, and the spectral density, $S(k) \propto |m(k)|^2$, in frequency or k space. $S(k)$ and $C(r)$ are not independent. In most cases they are related by the Wiener-Khintchine relations [Robi74; Reif65]

$$S(k) \propto \int C(r) \cos 2\pi k r\, dr \tag{6}$$

and

$$C(r) \propto \int S(k) \cos 2\pi k r\, dk \tag{7}$$

[†]For a detailed discussion of some of the mathematical subtleties, see Vassilicos and Hunt [Vass91].

Fast Fourier Transform (FFT) algorithms allow efficient direct computation of $S(k)$ from sample sequences and the estimation of $C(r)$ and D from $S(k)$ using Eqs. (5) and (7).

For 2D image analysis, the measure, $m(x, y)$, becomes a function of x and y, as does

$$G(\vec{r}) = C(r_x, r_y) = \langle\, m(x,y)\ m(x+r_x, y+r_y)\,\rangle$$

The familiar $C(r)$ of Eq. (5) now represents the average of $C(\vec{r})$ over all angles such that $r^2 = r_x^2 + r_y^2$. Here

$$M(R) = \int_0^R C(r)\, r\, dr \,\propto\, R^D \qquad (8)$$

so

$$C(r) \propto \frac{1}{r^\eta} \,\propto\, \frac{1}{r^{2D}} \qquad (9)$$

for a fractal set in 2D where $0 < D < 2$.

As with the 1D case, 2D FFT algorithms allow efficient computation of the 2D $S(\vec{k})$ from $m(x, y)$, $C(\vec{r})$ using the 2D equivalent of Eq. (7), and the estimation of D from $C(r)$ or $M(R)$ by averaging over angles. This procedure is illustrated in Figure 2. $S(\vec{k})$ was estimated for each 512 by 512 binary image using a 2D FFT. The 2D cosine FFT of $S(\vec{k})$ gives $C(\vec{r})$, and averages over all angles produce $C(r)$. Least-squares power-law fits to $C(r) \propto 1/r^\eta$, and $S(k) \propto 1/k^\beta$ are shown as solid lines. The angle average is the last step in the procedure. Angle averaging the 2D $S(\vec{k})$ to produce the 1D $S(k)$ and using Eq. (7) for $C(r)$ introduces errors.

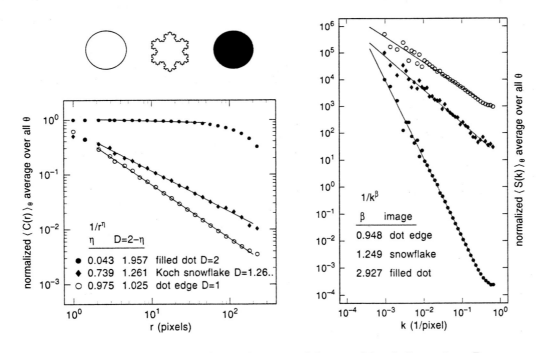

Figure 2. $C(r)$ image analysis of test shapes with known fractal dimension, D.

Local Image Gradient and the Statistics of Natural Images

As shown in Figure 2, this 2D global characterization by a single fractal dimension, D, works well for test images of well-defined fractal sets. There are, however, numerous problems in trying to apply this procedure directly to digitized images. What measure, $m(x, y)$, should be measured? If $I(x, y)$ represents the coarse-grained image intensity (photon flux striking the sensor at x, y), any nonzero background, sensitivity changes across the image, or sharp edges seriously corrupt $S(\vec{k})$ and $C(\vec{r})$.

Although Field [Fiel87] describes typical 'natural scenes' as having $S(k) \propto 1/k^2$, his choice of test scenes avoided the common light–dark edge, such as the land–sky boundary of many natural scenes. As shown in Figure 3, natural scenes that include such a prominent boundary (e.g., the Norwegian coast scenes) have $S(k)$ that is indistinguishable from a simple test edge (sharp transition from white to black) with $S(k) \propto 1/k^3$. $1/k^\beta$ power-law fits to $S(k)$ are shown as solid lines. Only the gumtree image in Figure 3, which was cropped to eliminate large-scale boundaries, has $S(k) \propto 1/k^2$ as reported by Field [Fiel87].

The major difficulties with $I(x, y)$ as the image measure, $m(x, y)$, for analysis are eliminated by using the local image gradient, $|\nabla I(x, y)|$. This image gradient

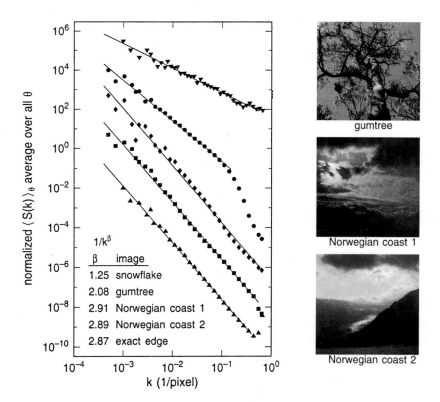

Figure 3. $S(k)$ for $I(x, y)$ image analysis of test shapes and natural scenes that contain a prominent edge, such as land–sky boundary.

emphasizes the edges in an image.[†] Figure 4, which shows $|\nabla I(x,y)|$ spectral analysis for the same images as Figure 3, demonstrates that the effects of large-scale gradients, uniform background and prominent edges are all greatly reduced. The use of $|\nabla I(x,y)|$ rather than $I(x,y)$ allows distinguishing even natural scenes with prominent edges from the $S_{|\nabla|}(k) \propto 1/k$ of a test edge. All of the natural scenes now show $S_{|\nabla|}(k) \propto 1/k^\beta$ with $\beta \approx 1.5$–1.6. $1/k^\beta$ power-law fits to $S_{|\nabla|}(k)$ are shown as solid lines in Figure 4.

Indeed, perceptual experiments on random fractal images [Rogo90] show that human estimates of fractal characteristics are based primarily on edge characteristics. Solid-filled and outline shapes have the same effect.

Local Fractal Mass Dimension

The procedures discussed in the previous section provide a global characterization of an image by a single fractal dimension, D. In many cases, particularly when the objects of interest represent only a subset of the original image, this is inappropriate. A more accurate and useful data reduction follows the multifractal lead and studies the distribution of local fractal dimensions.

Equation (8) represents the global average of $M(R)$ over all positions, x, y, that have mass. One can also study $M(R)$ about a particular point, $\vec{r}_0$

$$M_{\vec{r}_0}(R)g \propto \int_0^R m(\vec{r}_0 + \vec{r})\, d^2\vec{r} \propto R^{D(\vec{r}_0)} \tag{10}$$

This $D(\vec{r}_0)$, or D_{local}, is roughly equivalent to the standard multifractal use of the Holder exponent, α. D_{local} is not strictly a dimension, and it can take values outside the normal range, $D < 0$ or $D > 2$, in 2D. Image measures $m(x,y)$ are now characterized by histograms of D_{local} similar to the usual $f(\alpha)$ of multifractal measures.

Classification of Early Chinese Landscape Paintings

Use of D_{local} for image analysis is illustrated with an art history classification problem. The representation of space in Chinese landscape painting underwent a basic change during the Sung dynasty (960–1279 A.D.), a period which saw the highest development of this art form in China. The paintings in Figure 5 represent the stylistic phases that illustrate this change. The early phase is represented by two paintings in the upper left corner. The middle left painting is by Fan Kuan, who worked in the beginning of the eleventh century, and the

---

[†] $|\nabla I(x,y)|$ is estimated by a local fit of $I(x,y)$ in the neighborhood of x, y to the form $a\Delta x + b\Delta y + I(x,y)$. This gives $|\nabla I(x,y)| = (a^2 + b^2)^{1/2}$.

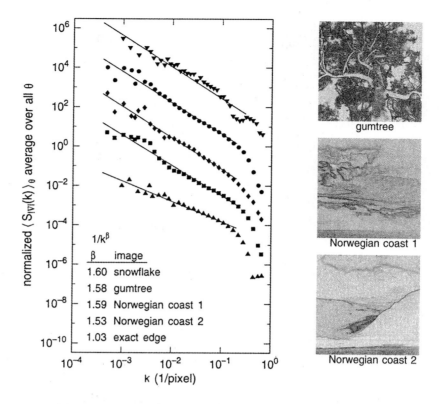

Figure 4. $S_{|\nabla|}(k)$ for $|\nabla I(x,y)|$ analysis of the same images as Figure 3.

top left painting is by Kuo Hsi from 1072 A.D. In these landscapes, emphasis was placed on the so-called three-distances (sanyuan): height, level and depth. These distances were not considered related in a geometric construction like the three dimensions implied in a Western perspective drawing. They do not converge on a point. In particular, the level-distance describes a plane that can stretch to infinity. Height-distance is suggested by a lofty mountain that towers over the landscape in the middle distance and foreground. The effect of depth-distance is achieved by a series of overlapping buildings in a valley or a series of overlapping mountains in ever-decreasing scale. Painters of this period usually worked from nature or by direct observation of natural landscape in the open.

In the twelfth to thirteenth centuries, painters in the imperial academy seem to have abandoned the attempt to represent the three-distances. The academy was then located in the Southern Sung capital in Hangchou, and there were no lofty mountains in the immediate vicinity. By concentrating on the foreground and leaving half the pictorial space blank, a feeling of openness or infinite recession is suggested. This style is represented by the three paintings on the right.

The painting in the lower left corner is by Hsü Tao-ning, another eleventh century painter. This work is judged by art historians to date from about 1050 A.D. and thus predates the Kuo Hsi (top left) by some twenty years. Nevertheless,

Figure 5. Sample digitized images, $I(x, y)$, of six early Chinese landscape paintings illustrate stylistic changes during the Sung dynasty (960–1279 A.D.).

this painting seems to presage a later development as it preserves the representation of level- and depth-distances without the height-distances. Stylistically it occupies a position between Fan Kuan and the academic painters of the later part of the Sung dynasty.

Thus, although Chinese painters did not use the same perspective techniques as developed in Europe beginning with the Renaissance, they did use repetition of similar shapes on smaller scales to covey a sense of depth. This technique is particularly noticeable in the two upper left paintings in Figure 5. The later paintings on the right seem more linear, with less repetition on smaller scales. Can these visual impressions be quantified with the methods developed here?

Figure 6 shows the local image slope, $|\nabla I(x,y)|$, for the six images from Figure 5. This is used as the fundamental image measure, $m(x,y)$, in Plate 15, which shows the corresponding D_{local} image. Each pixel is colored according to the least-squares estimate of $M_{\text{local}}(R) \propto R^{D_{\text{local}}}$ including all $|\nabla I(x,y)|$ within $R < 32$ pixels. Such a coloring yields few differences between the images. This is confirmed with the D_{local} histogram in Figure 8a. Each image has $\langle D_{\text{local}} \rangle$ in the range 1.6–1.7, and the histograms are not readily distinguished. Tails of the histograms are highlighted in Figure 8 for easy visual comparison.

Local Connected Fractal Dimension

To improve the classification it is necessary to take a lesson from percolation theory [Stau85; Voss82]. Here the important fractal shapes require a consideration of local connectivity. As illustrated in Figure 7, connectivity highlights important fractal shapes. The left image shows a 128 by 128 square array in which sites are randomly occupied (black) with probability $p = 0.6$. At larger scales, for example when viewed from a distance, the image becomes a uniform gray, with $D_{\text{local}} = 2$. The right image, however, shows the corresponding four largest connected clusters which are known to be fractal, with $D \approx 1.89$ [Stau85; Voss82]. This concept can be applied to image analysis by including in $M(R)$ only those mass points that are connected to $\vec{r}_0$. In practice this involves selecting some minimum threshold, m_0. Neighboring pixels with $|\nabla I(x,y)| = m(x,y) > m_0$ are considered connected. D_{conn} now represents the least-squares exponent of the connected $M_{\text{conn}}(R) \propto R^{D_{\text{conn}}}$.

The difference between D_{local} and D_{conn} is clarified if one considers an image of closely spaced but disconnected parallel lines of spacing, δ. For $R > \delta$, $D_{\text{local}} \approx 2$ while $D_{\text{conn}} \approx 1$. For the case of paintings, D_{conn} follows the local brush strokes. Plate 16 shows the D_{conn} image[†] for the six landscapes, where each pixel is now colored according to the least-squares estimate of connected $M_{\text{local}}(R) \propto R^{D_{\text{conn}}}$. $M_{\text{local}}(R)$ includes only the connected $|\nabla I(x,y)|$ within

---

[†]The choice of threshold, m_0, can be based on the image statistics for a particular class. Given the quantized $|\nabla I(x,y)|$ histogram, H_m, for the images in Figure 6, m_0 was defined as the weighted average, $m_0 = \sum m H_m / \sum H_m$.

Figure 6. Local slope $|\nabla I(x, y)|$ for the Chinese landscape paintings of Figure 5.

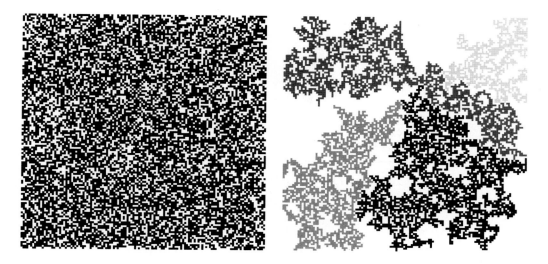

Figure 7. 2D percolation illustrates how connectivity emphasizes shapes.

$R < 32$ pixels. Obviously, D_{conn} provides a superior classification to the D_{local} in Plate 15. This is confirmed with the D_{conn} histograms in Figure 8b, where the two earliest landscapes (upper left) have $\langle D_{\text{conn}} \rangle$ in the range 1.3–1.4, while the three later academic paintings (right) have $\langle D_{\text{conn}} \rangle$ in the range 1.07–1.13. The lower left painting, which is intermediate stylistically, has an intermediate $\langle D_{\text{conn}} \rangle$ of 1.14. Recall that tails of the histograms are highlighted in Figure 8 for easy visual comparison.

Discussion

The human perceptual system evolved over millions of years in a natural fractal environment. Only recently, by evolutionary time scales, have we found ourselves in a primarily Euclidean environment of straight lines and few spatial scales. Our visual system shows a particular response to random fractals [Rogo90]. Nevertheless, it has proven extremely difficult to quantitatively mimic with fractal analysis the classification and feature detection that the eye performs with ease.

As demonstrated here with early Chinese landscape paintings, significant image processing is required to reliably distinguish between the classes of images. Care must be taken in the decision of which measure to measure. For many natural scenes the image edges $|\nabla I(x,y)|$ are far less prone to artifacts than the original intensities, $I(x,y)$.

For local enhancement and feature detection, the concept of local fractal dimension (D_{local}) can be defined analogous to the multifractal, $f(\alpha)$. Even with $|\nabla I(x,y)|$, however, D_{local} detects few of the differences perceived by eye. The critical step here is the use of local connected fractal dimension, D_{conn}, analogous to percolation theory. D_{conn} only considers the local connected portions of the measure. Histograms of D_{local} are the best fractal tool for quantifying the

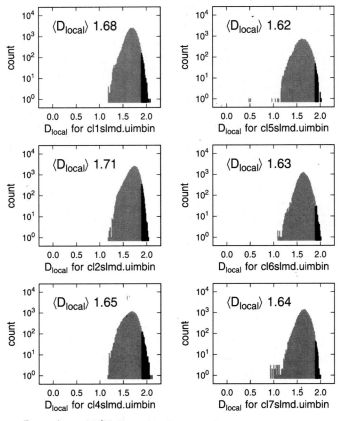

D_{local} from M(R) fits with R<32 pixels D>1.9 darkest

(a)

Figure 8. Comparison of D_{local} and D_{conn} for classification of the Chinese landscape paintings of Figure 5. (a) D_{local} from local fits of $M_{local}(R)$ to R^D including all $|\nabla I(x,y)|$ within R. (b) Corresponding D_{conn} which includes only the connected $|\nabla I(x,y)|$ within $R < 32$ pixels.

early Chinese landscape paintings. Numerous other applications (for example, medical images) are currently being investigated.

REFERENCES

[Fiel87]

Field, D.J., Relations between the statistics of natural images and the response properties of cortical cells, *Jour. Opt. Soc. Amer.*, Vol. A4, pp. 2379–2394, 1987.

[Mand68]

Mandelbrot, B.B., and van Ness, J.W., Fractional Brownian motion, fractional noises and applications, *SIAM Review*, Vol. 10, pp. 422–437, 1968.

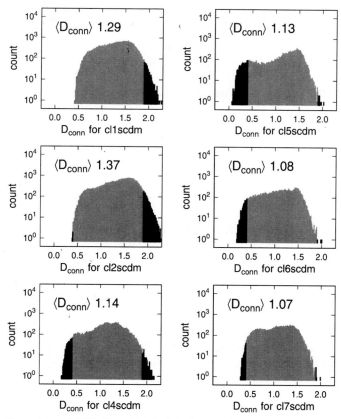

D_{conn} from M(R) fits with R<32 pixels   D<0.4 D>1.9 darkest

(b)

Figure 8. (*Continued.*)

[Mand74]
Mandelbrot, B.B., Intermittent turbulence in self similar cascades; Divergence of high moments and dimension of the carrier, *Jour. Fluid Mechs.*, Vol. 62, pp. 331–358, 1974.

[Mand75]
Mandelbrot, B.B., *les objects fractals: forme, hasard et dimension*, Paris: Flammarion, 1975.

[Mand77]
Mandelbrot, B.B., *Fractals: Form, Chance, and Dimension*, San Francisco, CA: W.H. Freeman, 1977.

[Mand82]
Mandelbrot, B.B., *The Fractal Geometry of Nature*, San Francisco: W.H. Freeman, 1982.

[Mand85]
Mandelbrot, B.B., Self-affine fractals and fractal dimension, *Physica Scripta*, Vol. 32, pp. 257–260, 1985.

[Mand88]
Mandelbrot, B.B., An introduction to multifractal distribution functions, in *Fluctuations and Pattern Formation (Cargese 1988)*, Stanley, H.E., and Ostrowsky, N., Eds., Boston: Kluwer, Dordrecht, pp. 345–360, 1988.

[Mand89]
Mandelbrot, B.B., Multifractal measures for the geophysicist, *Pure and Applied Geophysics*, Vol. 131, pp. 5–42, 1989.

[Reif65]
Reif, F., Irreversible processes and fluctuations, Chap. 15 in *Fundamentals of Statistical and Thermal Physics*, New York: Mc-Graw Hill, 1965.

[Robi74]
Robinson, F.N.H., *Noise and Fluctuations*, Oxford: Clarendon Press, 1974.

[Rogo90]
Rogowitz, B.E., and Voss, R.F., Shape perception and low dimension fractal boundary contours, in *Proc. Conf. on Human Vision: Methods, Models and Applications*, Rogowitz, B.E., and Allenbach, J., Eds., SPIE/SPSE Symposium on Electronic Imaging, Vol. 1249, Santa Clara, CA, 1990.

[Stau85]
Stauffer, D., *Introduction to Percolation Theory*, London: Taylor and Francis, 1985.

[Vass91]
Vassilicos, J.C., and Hunt, J.C.R., Fractal dimensions and spectra of interfaces with application to turbulence, *Proc. Roy. Soc. London Ser. A*, Vol. 435, pp. 505–534, 1991.

[Voss82]
Voss, R.F., Laibowitz, R.B., and Alessandrini, E.I., Fractal (scaling) clusters in thin gold films near the percolation transition, *Phys. Rev. Lett.*, Vol. 49, pp. 1441–1444, 1982.

[Voss85]
Voss, R.F., Random fractals: characterization and measurement, in *Scaling Phenomena in Disordered Systems*, Pynn, R., and Sjeltorp, A., Eds., New York: Plenum Press, 1985.

[Voss88]
Voss, R.F., Fractals in nature: from characterization to simulation, in *The Science of Fractal Images*, Peitgen, H.-O., and Saupe, D., Eds., New York: Springer-Verlag, 1988.

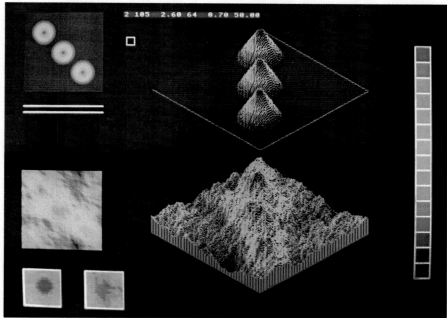

Plate 1. A more evolved object generated with the construction from Figure 12, form F.

Plate 2. Example of a 'tailored Mandelbrot surface'.

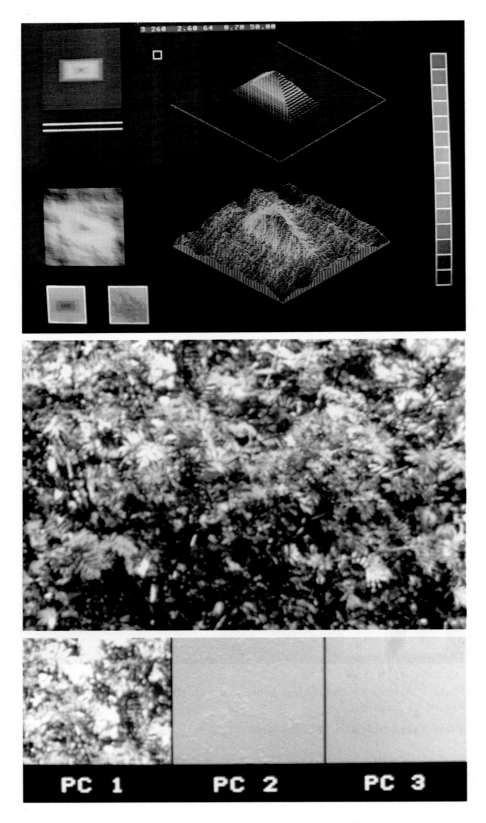

Plate 3. Another example of a 'tailored Mandelbrot surface'.

Plate 4. Rowan tree test picture.

Plate 5. Reconstructions from each principal component of the rowan tree picture.

Plate 6. Stubble background with inserts.

Plate 7. Fir trees background with inserts.

Plate 8. Heathland background with inserts.

Plate 9. Hillside background with inserts.

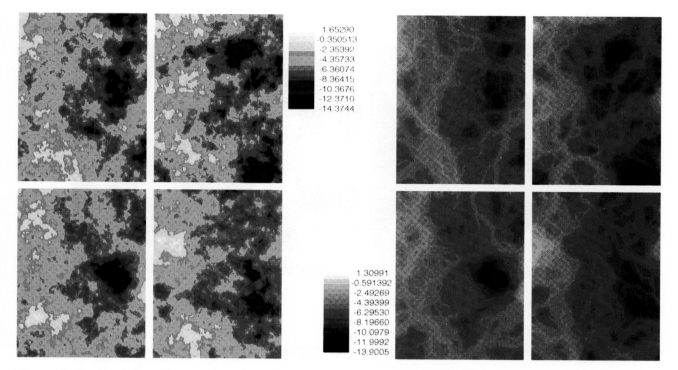

Plate 10. Realized fractal transmissivity
fields with dimension 2.76 conditioned on
the measured data.

Plate 11. Magnitude of the Darcy velocity
of flow through the fractal transmissivity
fields shown in Plate 10.

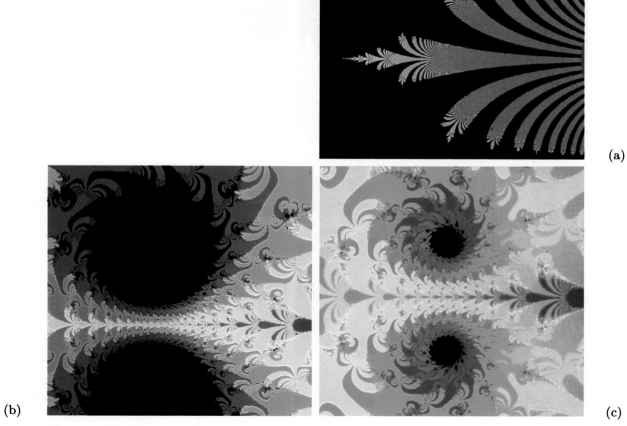

Plate 12. Explosion in the exponential family. (a) $\lambda = 1/e$; (b) $\lambda > 1/e$; (c) $\lambda > 1/e$
recomputed with more iterations.

Plate 13. The Julia set of (a) $0.66i \cos z$; (b) $0.68i \cos z$.

Plate 14. Julia set for (a) $\sin z$; (b) $(1 + .1i) \sin z$; (c) $(1 + .2i) \sin z$; (d) $(1 + .4i) \sin z$.

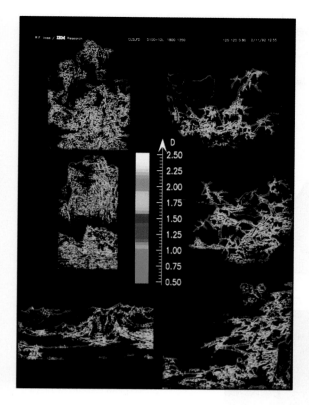

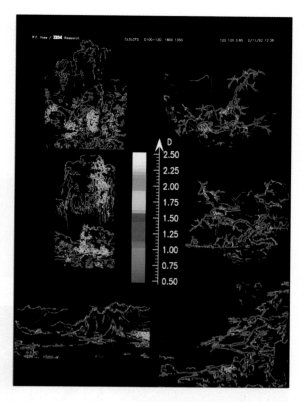

Plate 15. D_{local} colored images for the Chinese landscape paintings of Figure 5. Different colors represent different D_{local} from local fits of $M_{\text{local}}(R)$ to R^D.

Plate 16. D_{conn} colored images for the Chinese landscape paintings of Figure 5. Different colors represent different D_{conn}.

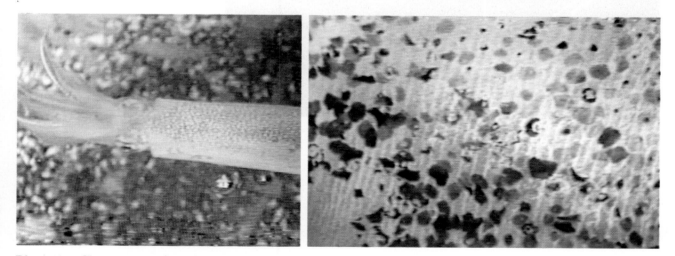

Plate 17 . Close-up still (right) from a videotape of pigment spot activity on the surface of the squid. Coordinated changes in the size of these pigment spots gives spatio-temporal patterns over the skin.

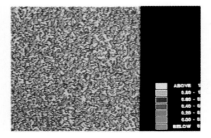

Plate 18. Spatio-temporal irregularity and coherence in a two-dimensional, diffusively coupled logistic coupled map lattice. Initial conditions were random, a= 4 and e= 0.1. This weak coupling imposes local coherence.

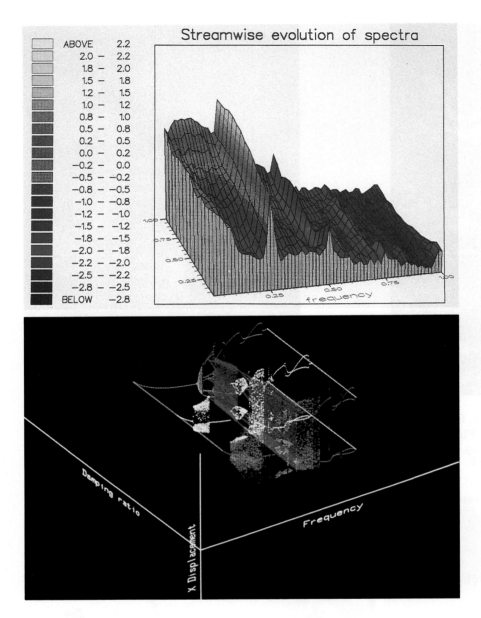

Plate 19. Isometric graph of power spectra over a range of streamwise locatons.

Plate 20. Three-dimensional bifurcation diagram, with damping ratio varying from 0.075 to 0.125, Ω/ω_1 varying from 2 to 3, $k_2/k_1 = 30$, $g = 0.5\,\text{mm}$ and $\delta = 0.5\,\text{mm}$.

2 Applications of Chaos

Chaotic Bursts in Complex Dynamical Systems

Robert L. Devaney

Abstract

In this paper we investigate the behavior of a certain very special but nevertheless extremely important and beautiful class of dynamical systems known as entire transcendental functions. We pay special attention to the set of chaotic orbits of this system, the Julia set. We show how this set may change its shape dramatically as a parameter varies, and we illustrate this by showing the computer graphics experiments which led to this discovery.

Dynamical Systems

Recent advances in the branch of mathematics known as nonlinear dynamical systems promise to revolutionize the way scientists view many different kinds of evolutionary processes. These processes occur in all branches of science, ranging from the fluctuations of temperature, pressure, wind speed and so on in meteorology to the ups and downs of the stock market in economics. Any physical, chemical or biological process which evolves in time is an example of a dynamical system. Some systems are simple, e.g., the motion of a pendulum which gradually damps down to a stable resting position. Others are much more complicated, e.g., the motion of the galaxies in the universe, or a fluid tumbling over an obstacle.

The basic goal of scientists who work with dynamical systems is to develop methods which accurately predict the future behavior of the system. Sometimes this can be accomplished by direct observation or experimentation: years of waking up each morning have convinced us that the sun will rise again tomorrow. But other evolutionary processes, such as the weather or the stock market, are much more difficult to predict. Therefore the scientist seeks other methods to make predictions.

One of the most common methods for making predictions is first to set up a mathematical model of the system at hand, and then to solve the resulting equations. The scientist uses accepted laws, such as Newton's Laws or Hooke's Law, to set up this mathematical model, which is often a differential equation or a difference equation. The solutions of these equations then yield the desired predictions.

Sometimes the solution of these equations is easy. Most often this occurs when the equations are linear, i.e., involve all of the constituent variables in the simplest possible manner: no squares or cubes, logarithms or sines, etc. When the equations are nonlinear, the situation changes drastically. There are very few mathematical techniques available to explicitly solve such equations. Thus, the scientist must use other methods to 'solve' the equations. Very often this necessitates the use of a computer and various approximation techniques to gain at least partial insight into the solutions. But this approach, as we shall see, is not altogether satisfactory. One of the main advances in recent years in the study of nonlinear dynamics is the recognition that such computer solutions may be totally meaningless, for many systems behave so erratically or unpredictably that the slightest error or approximation used in their formulation or solution leads to completely erroneous predictions. This is the phenomenon known as 'chaos.'

Chaos

Chaos is the mathematical term for the behavior of a system which is inherently unpredictable. Unpredictable phenomena are readily apparent in all areas of life. Fluctuations in the stock market and the weather make long term predictions in these areas nearly impossible. One might argue that the large numbers of factors which influence economic or meteorological systems is the reason for this unpredictability. But chaos can also occur in systems which have few degrees of freedom. For example, a damped, forced pendulum is well known to possess motions that are quite chaotic.

The critical ingredient in this example is what mathematicians call sensitive dependence on initial conditions. If you make even the slightest change in the initial configuration of the system, then the resulting behavior of the system may be dramatically different. The system is extremely sensitive to initial measurements. This should be contrasted with the unforced pendulum example, where, no matter how fast we initially start the pendulum swinging, it eventually winds down to a simple resting position. This dynamical system is not at all chaotic.

When viewed on a computer graphics screen, the solutions of a chaotic system tend to oscillate or wander about randomly, with no apparent order to the motion. If we consider another solution which begins near our original solution, then this solution also seems to behave randomly. However, after an initial period of similarity, the two solutions eventually look completely different from each other.

One of the principal recent discoveries in dynamics is that this type of chaos can be present in completely deterministic systems. That is, even if we can write down the equations which govern the motion explicitly, without recourse to probabilistic terms, the solutions themselves can behave in a manner which is seemingly totally random. Moreover, even the simplest mathematical models can possess this complicated behavior. Let us illustrate this using the logistic equation from mathematical biology. The logistic equation is a model for the growth of an idealized population consisting of only one species. This system was put forth as a simple model for population growth by the ecologist Robert May [May76] in the middle 1970s.

To be precise, let us suppose that there is a single species whose population grows and dwindles over time in a controlled environment. Suppose we measure the population of the species at the end of each generation. Rather than produce the actual count of individuals present in the colony, suppose we measure instead the percentage of some limiting number or maximum population. That is, let us write P_n for the percentage of population after generation n, where $0 \leq P_n \leq 1$. One simple rule which an ecologist can use to model the growth of this population is the logistic equation

$$P_{n+1} = kP_n(1 - P_n)$$

where k is some constant that depends on ecological conditions, for example the amount of food present. Using this formula, the population in the succeeding generation can be deduced from a knowledge of only the population in the preceding generation and the constant, k.

Note how trivial this formula is. It is a simple quadratic formula in the variable P_n. Given P_n and k, we can compute P_{n+1} exactly. In Table 1 we have listed the populations predicted by this model for various values of k. Note several things. When k is small the fate of the population seems quite predictable. Indeed, for $k = 0.5$ the population dies out, whereas for $k = 1.2$, 2 and 3 it tends to stabilize or reach a definite limiting value. Above 3, different values of k yield startlingly different results. For $k = 3.1$ the limiting values tend to oscillate between two distinct values. For $k = 3.4$ the limiting values oscillate between four values. And finally, for $k = 4$ there is no apparent pattern to be discerned. One initial value, $P_0 = 0.5$, leads to the disappearance of the species after only two generations, whereas $P_0 = 0.4$ leads to a population count that seems to be completely random.

This is the unpredictable nature of this process. Certain k values, such as $k = 1.2$, lead to results which are quite predictable — a fixed or periodically repeating limiting value. But other k values lead to results which are, for all intents and purposes, random.

The reader might object that the quite limited table of values for P_n when $k = 4$ can in no way be interpreted as a proof that the values do behave randomly. Nevertheless, this is a fact which can be proven quite easily with techniques from dynamical systems theory.

This example illustrates one of the major consequences of the discovery of chaos in deterministic systems: the output of the computer can no longer be trusted. Indeed, at virtually each stage of the computation of P_n the computer makes approximations or round-off errors. As illustrated in the table, these small changes can lead to vastly different eventual values for P_n.

The existence of chaos in deterministic systems has a number of important consequences in both mathematics and the physical sciences. First of all, it

Table 1. Values of P_n for various k values.

$P_{n+1} = kP_n(1 - P_n)$							
$k = 0.5$	$k = 1.2$	$k = 2$	$k = 3$	$k = 3.1$	$k = 3.4$	$k = 4$	$k = 4$
0.5	0.5	0.5	0.5	0.5	0.5	0.4	0.5
0.125	0.3	0.5	0.675	0.775	0.85	0.96	1
0.055	0.252	0.5	0.592	0.540	0.434	0.154	0
0.026	0.226	0.5	0.652	0.770	0.835	0.520	0
0.013	0.210	0.5	0.613	0.549	0.469	0.998	0
0.006	0.199	0.5	0.641	0.768	0.847	0.006	0
0.003	0.191	0.5	0.622	0.553	0.441	0.025	0
0.002	0.186	0.5	0.635	0.766	0.838	0.099	0
0.001	0.181	0.5	0.626	0.555	0.461	0.358	0
0.000	0.178	0.5	0.632	0.766	0.845	0.919	0
0.000	0.176	0.5	0.628	0.556	0.446	0.298	0
0.000	0.174	0.5	0.631	0.765	0.840	0.837	0
0.000	0.172	0.5	0.629	0.557	0.457	0.547	0
0.000	0.171	0.5	0.630	0.765	0.844	0.991	0
0.000	0.170	0.5	0.629	0.557	0.448	0.035	0
0.000	0.170	0.5	0.630	0.765	0.841	0.135	0
0.000	0.169	0.5	0.629	0.557	0.455	0.466	0
0.000	0.168	0.5	0.630	0.765	0.843	0.996	0
0.000	0.168	0.5	0.629	0.557	0.450	0.018	0
0.000	0.168	0.5	0.630	0.765	0.851	0.070	0
0.000	0.168	0.5	0.630	0.557	0.455	0.261	0
0.000	0.168	0.5	0.630	0.765	0.843	0.773	0

means that no matter how accurately we measure the physical quantities which determine the system we may never be able to accurately predict the resulting motion. Secondly, it indicates that the search for individual, specific solutions to the system may be useless. After all, any small change produces a vastly different solution, perhaps necessitating completely new methods or analysis in order to generate the solution. This may be impractical or even impossible.

What does a mathematician do in the face of chaos? Obviously, by the very nature of a chaotic system the search for a specific solution of the equations is not especially fruitful. Hence the mathematician takes a more global viewpoint. Instead of seeking specific solutions, the mathematician seeks to describe the totality of all possible solutions. Although the particular behavior of a solution may be unpredictable, the totality of all of these solutions may be identifiable. In a certain sense this may even be more important than finding specific solutions.

As an example, the meteorologist may not be able to predict whether it will be rainy or sunny on a given day of July in Rome, but he knows that it will not be snowing on that day. Thus there are limits to the unpredictability of a system, and finding these limits is an important task. Toward that end there have been a number of remarkable advances in recent years.

Strange Attractors

A profound development in recent years is the discovery of strange attractors. In nature, all processes seem to tend toward some sort of stable state or equilibrium. This state is, to a mathematician, an attractor — in terms of a dynamical system, an attractor is an object toward which all nearby solutions tend as time moves on.

For years scientists believed that the attractors toward which physical systems tend should be quite simple. They should either be rest points or equilibrium points such as the rest position of a pendulum, or else they should be limit cycles or repeating configurations such as often occur in population biology or economic systems. Experiments or simulations which did not tend to equilibrium or steady state were often viewed with suspicion. Either the experiment itself was flawed (too much noise) or else the process terminated too soon.

Now, however, we know that this is by no means the case. There are other much more complicated attractors — called strange attractors — which often arise. In the early 1960s Stephen Smale [Smal64] proposed several geometric models of new attractors which were much more complicated than rest points or limit cycles. The dynamics of these attractors was chaotic, not steady state or periodic. Later R.F. Williams [Will74] showed that these attractors are stable in the sense that small changes in the basic system did not destroy them.

So strange attractors exist as mathematical objects, but do they exist in nature? While this has not yet been definitively answered, every indication is that the answer is yes. In the early 1960s the meteorologist E.N. Lorenz [Lore63] from MIT suggested a simplified model of meteorological turbulence. His model is a differential equation in three dimensions. When viewed on a computer graphics terminal, each solution curve of the system tends toward the same object — the Lorenz attractor. Once near the attractor, the solution oscillates about one of two lobes of the attractor. The important fact is that the number of oscillations about each lobe seems to be random and depends very much on which solution curve is followed. This, of course, is chaos. Consequently, the Lorenz system never settles down to equilibrium or periodic behavior, but rather continually cycles chaotically. Since Lorenz's discovery, similar strange attractors have been found in a variety of scientific disciplines. For example, strange attractors may provide the key to understanding turbulence in fluid and aerodynamic problems.

The Chaotic Set

The above considerations lead us to try to understand at the outset the set of all chaotic orbits of a dynamical system rather than the behavior of individual orbits. In general, it is a difficult problem to try to find the set of unpredictable orbits. But there are some classes of systems for which there are techniques available. One such class is the class of complex analytic dynamical systems. These systems have a rich and beautiful history in mathematics. They were first studied in the 1920s by the French mathematicians Fatou [Fato26] and Julia

[Juli18] and their co-workers. But the full beauty of these dynamical systems was not realized until the late 1970s and early 1980s, when computer graphics showed the startling beauty and complexity of the chaotic set for these systems, the so-called Julia set. For the remainder of this paper we concentrate on the structure and properties of this class of analytic functions. We show how to find and to compute the Julia sets for these functions. We also describe in detail how these chaotic sets sometimes change in configuration in a quite unexpected manner: sometimes these sets undergo a burst or explosion as parameters are varied.

We consider only iterated mappings of the complex plane, $\mathbf{C}$, for example $E_\lambda(z) = \lambda \exp(z)$, or $S_\lambda(z) = \lambda \sin(z)$. Here λ should be interpreted as a complex parameter, $\lambda = \lambda_{re} + i\lambda_{im}$, where λ_{re} and λ_{im} are the real and imaginary parts, respectively, of λ, and $i = \sqrt{-1}$. Similarly, the state variable, z, is complex: $z = x + iy$, with real numbers as the two components of z.

Consider the problem of iterating a complex function, F. That is, for a given initial complex number, z_0, we compute successively

$$z_1 = F(z_0)$$

$$z_2 = F(z_1) = F(F(z_0)) = F^2(z_0)$$

$$z_3 = F(z_2) = F^3(z_0)$$

$$\vdots$$

$$z_n = F^n(z_0)$$

Note that F^n means the n-fold iteration of F, not F raised to the nth power. The set of points $\{z_0, z_1, z_2, \ldots\}$ is called the orbit of the initial point, z_0. As above, the basic goal of dynamical systems theory is to understand the ultimate fate of all orbits of a given system. This is precisely the problem we encountered in the logistic equation. That is, the question is what happens to $F^n(z_0)$ as n tends to ∞?

There are many possible fates for a given system. For example, an orbit may behave relatively tamely by simply tending to a fixed point, as illustrated by the simple mapping $F(z) = z^2$. If z_0 is a complex number with absolute value less than one, then a simple computation shows that successive squarings yield an orbit which tends to 0 in the limit. That is, all complex numbers inside the circle of radius one tend to 0 under iteration of $F(z) = z^2$. This is stable behavior: all sufficiently nearby initial choices of z_0 lead to the same fate for the orbit.

As another example, consider the exponential function, $E_\lambda(z) = \lambda \exp z$, with $\lambda > 0$. If we use only real values of z, then Figure 1 shows that the graph of E_λ assumes two different forms depending upon whether $\lambda > 1/e$ or $\lambda < 1/e$, where $e \approx 2.7128\ldots$ and satisfies $\ln e = 1$. In Figure 1a, E_λ has two fixed points, q_λ and p_λ, i.e., $E_\lambda(q_\lambda) = q_\lambda$, and $E_\lambda(p_\lambda) = p_\lambda$. One can check that all points in the interval $-\infty < x < p_\lambda$ lead to orbits which tend to q_λ as n tends to ∞. On the other hand, in the interval $p_\lambda < x < \infty$ all points have orbits which tend to ∞ under iteration. For values of $\lambda > 1/e$, all points have orbits which tend to ∞. This is easily checked with a calculator by simply iterating $\lambda \exp(x)$ for various choices of initial x. The rigorous proof is also easy. Thus we see that the dynamical system, E_λ, has two vastly different behaviors on the real line, depending upon whether $\lambda > 1/e$ or $\lambda < 1/e$. We will see that this is an example of a burst into chaos when viewed as a dynamical system in the complex plane.

Before considering this we digress to discuss the behavior of a completely chaotic dynamical system. There are a number of different definitions of chaos in the literature. We adopt the following definition: a completely chaotic system must exhibit unpredictability, indecomposability and recurrence. For precise definitions we refer to Devaney [Deva89], but we list the following somewhat imprecise definitions which are satisfactory for our special case. An iterated mapping is unpredictable if it exhibits sensitive dependence on initial conditions; i.e., given any initial state z_0, there must be a nearby state, w_0, whose orbit diverges from that of z_0. That is, the distance between z_n and w_n must eventually be large. We therefore think that any numerical computation of the orbit of z_0 must be suspect; a small initial error, perhaps because of round-off error, may yield a completely different orbit, thus rendering numerical study inaccurate.

The dynamical system is indecomposable if there is an orbit which eventually enters any preassigned region, no matter how small, in the plane. Thus this orbit comes arbitrarily close to any point whatsoever in $\mathbf{C}$, and we cannot separate the given system into two essentially separate subsystems which behave independently.

Finally, a dynamical system exhibits recurrence if, given an initial condition, z_0, there is another initial condition, w_0, which is arbitrarily close to z_0 and which is periodic. That is, there is an iteration, n, for which

$$F^n(w_0) = w_0$$

Consequently, $w_{n+1} = w_1$, $w_{n+2} = w_2$, etc., and the orbit of w_0 is a cycle or

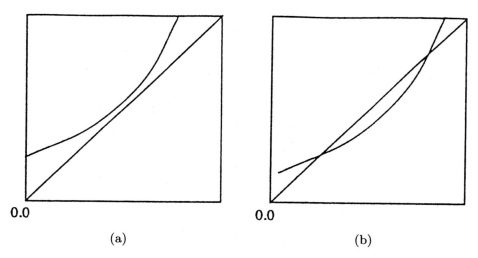

0.0   0.0

(a)   (b)

Figure 1. Graph of E_λ. (a) $\lambda > 1/e$; (b) $\lambda < 1/e$.

periodic orbit. Periodic orbits are usually regarded as among the most important motions in a dynamical system, so our assumption is that they abound.

To summarize, a dynamical system in $\mathbf{C}$ is completely chaotic if it exhibits all three of the above properties. This definition is intended to mirror the properties of physical systems which exhibit turbulence.

Spurred on by the computer graphics of Mandelbrot [Mand82], D. Sullivan [Sull85] gives effectively computable criteria for a dynamical system to be completely chaotic. For example, in the case of systems such as $\lambda \exp(z)$ or $\lambda \sin(z)$ all we need to do is follow the critical orbits of the system. For the exponential this is the orbit of 0 (the omitted value), and for sine these are the orbits of the critical points $\pm \pi/2$ (where the maxima and minima occur on the real line). Technically, the critical orbits are defined to be the orbits of the critical and asymptotic values. Critical values are simply the images of the critical points. Note that sine has infinitely many critical points but only two critical values and no asymptotic values, so checking the above criteria is straightforward. One consequence of Sullivan's recent No Wandering Domains theorem [Sull85] is that, if all critical orbits of these maps tend to infinity, then the dynamical system is completely chaotic on the whole plane. In the example $E_\lambda(z) = \lambda \exp(z)$ where $\lambda > 1/e$, it is easy to check that 0 indeed tends to infinity, so E_λ is completely chaotic in the whole plane when $\lambda > 1/e$.

Now let us contrast this with the case $0 < \lambda < 1/e$. Consider the vertical line, $x = 1$, in the complex plane. Via Euler's formula

$$e^{x+iy} = e^x e^{iy} = e^x(\cos y + i \sin y)$$

this vertical line is mapped to the circle, Γ, of radius $\lambda \cdot e^1 < 1$. Moreover, each point in the plane to the left of this vertical line is mapped inside the circle Γ. Thus, the whole left half plane (real part of $z \leq 1$) is contracted inside itself and, in fact, inside Γ. Now apply E_λ again; Γ is contracted further inside itself. Continuing in this fashion, we see that E_λ cannot be chaotic in this half-plane; for example, there cannot be any cycles or periodic points outside of Γ. Indeed, one can check that the only cycle to the left of $x = 1$ is the fixed point, q_λ, discussed above.

Thus, we see that as λ increases through $\lambda = 1/e$ there is a dramatic change in the set of points on which the dynamical system is chaotic. When $\lambda < 1/e$ there are no such points to the left of $x = 1$, whereas when $\lambda > 1/e$ E_λ is completely chaotic on the entire plane. This is the burst into chaos.

The Julia Set

The set of points in the complex plane for which a dynamical system such as $\lambda \exp(z)$ or $\lambda \sin(z)$ is completely chaotic is called the Julia set. It is known that this set is often a fractal [Mand82] and so can assume spectacular geometric shapes. There are a number of different techniques for plotting the Julia sets numerically. A procedure that works for polynomials is described by Blanchard

[Blan84] and Douady and Hubbard [Doua82]. For the transcendental maps that we are considering there is a special and rather simple algorithm due to John Hubbard[†] which allows for easy plotting of the Julia set. It is known that the Julia set of a map such as $\lambda \exp(z)$ or $\lambda \sin(z)$ is the closure of the set of points whose orbit tends to ∞ (see Devaney [Deva87]). That is, any point whose orbit tends to ∞ and any limit point of such points lies in the Julia set. Note an apparent contradiction: periodic cycles must occur arbitrarily close to any point in the Julia set by our notion of recurrence, but so too must points whose orbits tend to ∞. Indeed, bounded and unbounded orbits accumulate at all points of the Julia set, giving further indication of the unpredictability of these systems on the Julia set.

Using Hubbard's algorithm, we can thus plot the outline of the Julia set by iterating a grid of points in the plane a preselected number of times N. If the orbit of the point remains bounded for all N iterations, we assume that the point does not lie in the Julia set and color it black. If, however, the orbit escapes to infinity (i.e., becomes too large for the computer), we assume that the point lies in (or, more appropriately, near) the Julia set. To capture the dynamics on the Julia set, we color such a point according to a scheme which assigns the color depending upon the number of iterations which occurred before escape. Points which are colored shades of red escape very quickly. Points are then colored shades of orange, yellow, green, blue and violet in increasing order, so that violet points escape only after a number of iterations close to N.

We plotted the results for $\lambda \exp(z)$ in Plate 12. Note the small chaotic region for a particular $\lambda < 1/e$. Indeed, in this picture almost the entire plane is black. Black points never lie in the Julia set; indeed, all of these points are attracted to the fixed point which we denote by q_λ. No matter how large N is chosen a similar picture results. The two different pictures for $\lambda > 1/e$ are computed with different values of N and different values of λ. We set N equal to 50 in Plate 12b; choosing N larger results in the disappearance of the black region as more points have a chance to escape. N was chosen to be 200 in Plate 12c.

The results above, together with many similar bursts, were suggested initially by mathematical experimentation. The idea of experimentation is becoming increasingly important in mathematics as the computer becomes the mathematician's laboratory. Experimentation has led to a number of significant new ideas, particularly in dynamical systems. As further examples of this, the above algorithm can be used with minor adjustments to find bursts in other families of complex entire functions. For example, there is a burst which occurs in the family $i\lambda \cos(z)$ when $\lambda \approx .67$. There is another burst which occurs at $\lambda = 0$ in the family $(1 + \lambda i) = \sin z$ (see Plate 13).

Each of these bursts can be rigorously proven to occur (see Devaney [Deva84]). For the cosine family, the mechanism that produces the burst is entirely analogous to that which occurs in the exponential family: the elementary saddle-node bifurcation occurs at the critical parameter value and allows the critical orbits to

---

[†]Private communication with Hubbard.

slip away to ∞. For the sine family, however, the mechanism is entirely different. The family $\mu \sin z$ experiences an elementary bifurcation as μ increases through the value 1. This bifurcation is reminiscent of the period, doubling bifurcation as described by Devaney [Deva89] or Feigenbaum [Feig78], although it is technically somewhat different. It is well known that such a bifurcation does not lead to a burst into chaos; rather, the states both before and after the bifurcation are quite stable. Nevertheless, if a different route in parameter space is chosen through the value $\mu = 1$, then a burst is possible (see Plates 14a–c). Indeed, we can prove that there are parameter values arbitrarily close to 1 for which the corresponding Julia set is the whole plane (see Devaney [Deva86]). In fact, the above results suggest that any elementary bifurcation in complex dynamics (for entire transcendental functions) is accompanied by a direction in parameter space which leads to a similar burst.

REFERENCES

[Blan84]
Blanchard, P., Complex analytic dynamics on the Riemann sphere, *Bull. AMS.*, Vol. 11, pp. 85–141, 1984.

[Deva89]
Devaney, R.L., *An Introduction to Chaotic Dynamical Systems*, Addison Wesley: Redwood City, CA, 1989.

[Deva87]
Devaney, R.L., Chaotic bursts in nonlinear dynamical systems, *Science*, Vol. 235, pp. 342–345, 1987.

[Deva86]
Devaney, R.L., Exploding Julia Sets, in *Chaotic Dynamics and Fractals*, Barnsley, M., and Demko, S., Eds., Academic Press: Orlando, FL, p. 141, 1986.

[Deva84]
Devaney, R.L., Bursts into chaos, *Phys. Lett.*, Vol. 104, pp. 385–387, 1984.

[Doua82]
Douady, A., and Hubbard, J., Itération des polynômes quadratiques complexes, *C.R. Acad. Sci. Paris.*, Vol. 294, pp. 123–126, 1982.

[Fato26]
Fatou, P., Sur l'itération des fonctions transcendentes Entières, *Acta Math.*, Vol. 47, pp. 337–370, 1926.

[Feig78]
Feigenbaum, M., Quantitative universality for a class of nonlinear transformations, *J. Stat. Phys.*, Vol. 21, p. 669, 1978.

[Juli18]
Julia, G., Itération des applications fonctionelles, *J. Math. Pures Appl.*, Vol. 4, pp. 47–245, 1918.

[Lore63]
Lorenz, E.N., Deterministic nonperiodic flows, *Jour. Atmospheric Sci.*, Vol. 20, pp. 130–141, 1963.

[Mand82]

Mandelbrot, B.B., *The Fractal Geometry of Nature*, San Francisco: W.H. Freeman, 1982.

[May76]

May, R.B., Simple mathematical models with complicated dynamics, *Nature*, Vol. 261, pp. 459–467, 1976.

[Smal64]

Smale, S., Diffeomorphisms with Many Periodic Points, in *Differential and Combinatorial Topology*, Cairns, S.S., Ed., Princeton, NJ: Princeton Univ. Press, pp. 63–80, 1964.

[Sull85]

Sullivan, D., Quasiconformal maps and dynamical systems I, Solutions of the Fatou-Julia problem on wandering domains, *Ann. Math.*, Vol. 122, pp. 401–418, 1985.

[Will74]

Williams, R.F., Expanding attractors, *IHES Publ. Math.*, Vol. 43, pp. 169–203, 1974.

Chaos, Complexity and Design Applications

John Lansdown

Abstract

Chaos theory is beginning to lead us towards a new view of reality and an understanding of how computers might help us handle its complexity. Setting the complexity of some current imagery into the context of narrative underpinning and compositional structure, we go on to suggest that a new paradigm is arising by virtue of our appreciation of complexity. This paradigm sees computation as a process of managing complexity rather than one of simplifying it. The implications of this for design applications are examined.

Introduction

The current great interest shown by scientists, mathematicians, artists, designers and the public generally in chaos theory is, I think, of more than passing significance. Undoubtedly the interest is partly visual. This comes about in appreciation of the beautiful, though highly complex, 'organic' imagery that chaos theory investigations sometimes produce (Figure 1). In this type of imagery, temporal randomness combines with spatial order to present us with patterns of a form different from those normally arising by use of conventional geometry or in natural pictures. But there is also a significance that goes beyond the imagery.

Visual Complexity of the Past

Our recent times generally are marked by the way we have become accustomed to an unprecedented degree of visual complexity in art and design. This seems a strange — not to say perverse — claim in the face of some complex examples of imagery from the past, for instance illuminated manuscripts, with their convoluted and intertwined knot work; or early maps with their florid and, some would think, superfluous decorations [Sout82]; or paintings such as, e.g., Altdorfer's 1529 *Alexander's Victory over Darius* (a reproduction of which can be seen in [Hook89]). This painting, with its myriad of horsed soldiers replete with lances, flags and accoutrements of war in the foreground, towns, mountains and lowering clouds in the background all shown in splendid detail, cannot by any definition be called simple. But the complexity of this and similar works is made

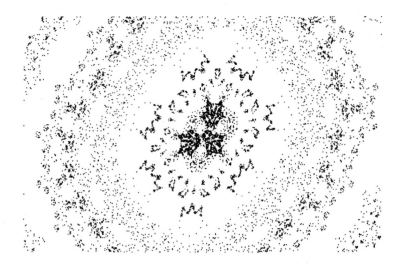

Figure 1. Typical chaos theory output.

understandable to us by two time-honoured devices, narrative underpinning and visual composition. Thus, the sweep of the lances and the disposition of the massed troops leads the eye inexorably to the major protagonists: Alexander, golden and triumphant, situated in the lower centre of the picture, with his lance pointing to charioted Darius hurrying off to the middle left. In this process a 'story' is told. This is made all the more coherent by the familiarity of the general theme and the visual disposition of the picture elements.

The New Imagery

The complexity of modern imagery is usually of a different order to this. Its narrative, if it exists at all, is often collapsed and overlain with obscuring detail. Its visual composition is frequently restless and fragmented and owes little to classical concepts. Undoubtedly, the demands of cinematography and television have had much to do with this change in our perception of what makes a telling image. Nowadays, pictures of raw actuality dominate our television screens and, hence, our visual lives. These images are often hurriedly acquired under difficult, sometimes dangerous, circumstances where opportunity exists only for the most elementary compositional ideas. Sequences are then edited in haste to meet the insatiable demand for instant eyewitness reporting. This, in its turn, has influenced our understanding of all imagery. Thus, contemporary feature films, pop videos, commercials and even still images aiming to emulate the sense of urgency, confusion and realism of actuality are easily understood by us in ways that were hardly possible prior to the 1950s and 1960s. Further, despite the fact that our perceptual mechanisms of attention are essentially serial (see, for instance, [Mora87; Wild82]), current communication methods usually require us to, as it were, 'multiplex' the action of receiving information. Thus, many television programmes, particularly those aimed at young audiences, overlay visual, textual and aural matter so that we are simultaneously presented with images, narration, sounds and running subtitles all giving different messages, often only tenuously related to one another. I have commented elsewhere on the mood-enhancing efficiency but possible educational inefficiency of such an approach [Lans92].

All this is in sharp contrast to the cinematic images and sequences of the earlier film-makers, even when montage was employed. Films by, for example, Eisenstein were painterly and carefully designed according to the principles of classical composition [Leyd85; Eise49]. Such forms have now been replaced by those of film-makers such as Peter Greenaway (see especially [Gree91a, 91b, 85]). This popular British film-maker's images and sequences are no less painterly and carefully crafted than those of earlier times but derive from a different sense of narrative and compositional appropriateness.

This view of imagery is summarised in Figure 2, which sets selected forms within a framework of narrative underpinning on one axis and compositional structure on the other. In examining this figure we might question why random dot patterns are shown to have any dimension at all in the direction of narrative underpinning. This is because of the way we try to make sense of any imagery by associating it with other things. Patterns in the fire, the 'man in the moon', the 'canals of Mars' are all examples of this propensity we have for trying to make sense of essentially random images. Thus, any 'information' whatever in the

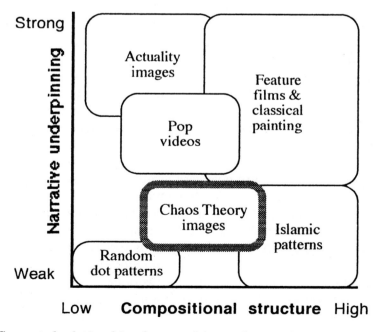

Figure 2. Suggested relationship of composition and narrative.

image is transformed with varying degrees of success into some form of narrative. This is one reason why raw, bit-counting, communication theory à la Shannon and Weaver [Shan49] has little relevance to the matters we are addressing here. Because of our own perceptions of a message and its context, there is often more information in a signal than can be measured by the bits received.

Beyond the Visual

But the popularity of chaos theory has more significance than just the visual. Chaos theory allows us at last to appreciate that many phenomena are fundamentally unpredictable and that many of those we once thought were (or might one day come to be) under our control are simply not amenable to rational direction at all. Phenomena falling into this category are not just natural ones such as, for example, atmospheric turbulence or weather. We now know, as many have long suspected, that a series of apparently rational human decisions can, under certain conditions, give rise to chaotic outcomes. For example, Mosekilde et al. [Mose90], looking at business-like activities, tell us that "Our results provide direct experimental evidence that chaos can be produced by the decision-making behaviour of real people in managerial systems". Thus, in circumstances where we know that certain conditions give rise to chaos it is probably more useful to avoid the circumstances than attempt to control the outcome.

The recent discovery by researchers at the University of Maryland does not invalidate this basic point. Ott, Grebogi and Yorke [Corc91] showed that chaotic motion consists of an amalgam of infinitely many periodic motions. They suggest that by continually applying small forces to some systems of this nature one can control them by 'nudging' them back into orbits of regular, periodic motion. It seems to me, however, that this process, depending on feedback as it must, might simply add another potentially chaotic element into the system.

Computer-based research into those complex systems amenable to chaos theory has also helped us realise that the simplistic and sometimes reductionist models of phenomena that dominated our thinking in the pre-computer past are not the only ones we are capable of handling. This realisation, in its turn, is having a profound effect on our view of computing. It is leading us to see computing not just as a method of simplifying complexity but as a process for more readily managing it. Thus, we are now very aware of the essential complexity of things. If we are to progress in our understanding of them, our models should try to cope with their complexity as it is and not as we would like it to be. This is a view that has particular significance for design modelling. In some areas of computer aided design (CAD), modelling tends towards oversimplification to the extent that, very often, CAD systems do no more than automate empirical methods originally set up to facilitate manual working.

More than a decade ago Maver and colleagues [Mave88; ABAC79], in the context of building energy design, showed how reliance on such methods can produce effects opposite to the intended ones.

Design Modelling for Team-working

Because of this simplified and reductionist approach most existing CAD systems, too, are based on models of the design process derived from considerations of designing as a single-person activity. But few artefacts nowadays are designed by just one person, even when computers are used. Almost everything, from widgets to buildings, from computer chips to aeroplanes, are products of team-working. However, it is only comparatively recently that CAD systems have been designed to facilitate team-working (and then only on an experimental basis). This has required CAD system designers to take into account such things as multiple design viewpoints and incompatibilities of analysis. Ishii et al. [Ishi90] give an interesting view of one of these fairly rare systems. The potential of computer-supported cooperative work — already seen elsewhere as an enabling mechanism — is only just being recognised as a possible solution to the problem of team-based designing (see, for instance, [Kyng91; Brot90; Enge91]).

But it would be wrong to suggest that these new developments arise directly from an appreciation of chaos theory, and I do not think they do. Nor has there been a sudden 'paradigm shift'. They do arise, though, from our change in perception of the nature of reality, a perception that has allowed us to see a new meaning in complexity and to devise new models and descriptions based on this. Jasperson [Jasp86] has persuasively argued that what superficially seem, in historical retrospect, to be major stylistic changes in the appearance of designed objects are, in fact, simply changes in public perception of existing features which have been undergoing a continuous process of change. So, too, with our view of chaos and complexity.

Types of Complexity

Much has been written on all aspects of complexity since Weaver's well-known and influential 1968 paper [Weav68], in which he suggested that there are three levels of complexity in 'natural' systems. Nothing in these more recent works invalidates Weaver's classifications, which are:

> *organised simplicity*, which characterises systems that can be described by a small number of parameters linked to one another deterministically. The parameters of such systems are not all equally important, and the effects of some of them can often be neglected. Newtonian mechanics is a classic example of such a system.

> *disorganised complexity*, which arises in systems characterised by a large number of distinct nondeterministic parameters. Such systems can be described by statistical methods.

> *organised complexity*, which characterises systems having a large number of interrelated but deterministic parameters, all of which contribute significantly to the system and hence cannot be neglected. In my view, these form the bulk of social, economic and man-made systems.

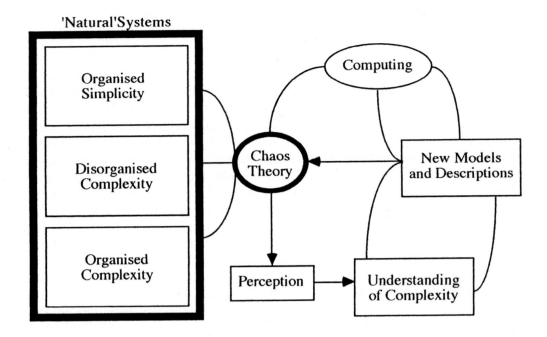

Figure 3. Chaos theory and complexity.

We tend to act as though all systems are in the first category. Even when we know they are not, we simplify our models to make them amenable to our concepts of organised simplicity. As Figure 3 indicates, chaos theory allows us to understand something of the possibilities inherent in the other categories. This can only improve our understanding of reality. For chaos and complexity dominate; it is these that are real. Our perceptions create the mirage.

REFERENCES

[ABAC79]
  ABACUS and VALTOS, Deemed to satisfy, *Architects Jour.*, 24 October 1979.

[Brot90]
  Brothers, L., Sembugamoorthy, V., and Muller, M., ICICLE: Groupware for code inspection, in *CSCW90*, Bikson, T.K., Ed., New York: ACM, 1990.

[Corc91]
  Corcoran, E., Ordering chaos, *Sci. Amer.*, Vol. 265, No. 2, pp. 82–83, 1991.

[Eise49]
  Eisenstein, S.M., *Film Form*, London: Faber and Faber, 1949 (and films, especially such as *Alexander Nevsky*, 1938 and *Ivan the Terrible*, 1944-46).

[Enge90]
  Engelbart, D.C., Knowledge-domain interoperability and an open hyperdocument system, in *CSCW90*, Bikson, T.K., Ed., New York: ACM, 1990.

[Gree85]

Greenaway, P., *A TV Dante*, A Channel 4 short film on Canto V of Dante's *Inferno*, created with Tom Phillips, 1985.

[Gree91a]

Greenaway, P., *Prospero's Books*, London: Chatto and Windus, 1991 (and a film of that name based on Shakespeare's last play, *The Tempest*).

[Gree91b]

Greenaway, P., *Not Mozart*, A BBC short film directed by Peter Greenaway, 1991.

[Hook89]

Hooker, D., Ed., *Art of the Western World*, London: Guild Publishing, p. 169, 1989.

[Ishi90]

Ishii, K., Goel, A., and Adler, R.E., A model of simultaneous engineering design, in *Artificial Intelligence*, Gero, J.S., Ed., Berlin: Springer-Verlag, 1990.

[Jasp86]

Jasperson, T., Perception changes in the realm of design, *Environment and Planning B*, Vol. 13, No. 1, pp. 85–126, 1986.

[Kyng91]

Kyng, M., Designing for cooperation; Cooperating in design, *CACM*, Vol. 34, No. 12, pp. 65–73, 1991.

[Lans92]

Lansdown, J., Mnemotechnics and the challenge of hypermedia, in Cunningham, S., and Hubbold, R.J., Eds., *Interactive Learning Through Visualisation: The Impact of Computer Graphics in Education*, New York: Springer-Verlag, 1992.

[Leyd85]

Leyda, J., and Voynow, Z., *Eisenstein at Work*, London: Methuen, 1985.

[Mave88]

Maver, T., Software tools for the technical evaluation of design alternatives, in *CAAD87 Futures*, Maver, T., and Wagter, H., Eds., Amsterdam: Elsevier, 1988.

[Mora87]

Moray, N., Attention, in Gregory, R.L., Ed., *The Oxford Companion to the Mind*, Oxford, UK: Oxford Univ. Press, pp. 59–61, 1987.

[Mose90]

Mosekilde, E., Larsen, E., and Sterman, J., Coping with complexity: Deterministic chaos in human decision making behaviour, in Casti, J.L., and Karlqvist, A., Eds., *Beyond Belief: Randomness, Prediction and Explanation in Science*, Boston: CRC Press, 1990.

[Shan49]

Shannon, C.E., and Weaver, W., *A Mathematical Theory of Communication*, Urbana, IL, USA: Illinois Univ. Press, 1949.

[Sout82]

Southworth, M., and Southworth, S., *Maps: A Visual Survey and Design Guide*, Boston: Little, Brown and Co., 1982.

[Weav68]

Weaver, W., Science and complexity, *Amer. Scientist*, Vol. 36, pp. 536–544, 1968.

[Wild82]

Wilding, J.M., *Perception: From Sense to Object*, London Hutchinson Univ. Library, 1982.

Computing with the Unpredictable:
Chaotic Dynamics and Fractal Structures in the Brain

Arun V. Holden, Julie Hyde and Henggui Zhang

Abstract

The brain is made up of a large number of interacting component neurones, where a neurone can have a fractal structure and can exhibit chaotic dynamics. Interactions between periodically active neurones can produce chaotic activity, and signals recorded from large populations of neurones have been identified as chaotic. The identification, quantification and modelling of these irregular processes have been facilitated by the methods of interactive computer graphics. Current problems deal with spatio-temporal irregular patterns in neural systems; here quantitative measures are poorly developed, but pseudocolour visualisations provide a promising approach.

Introduction

Sherrington [Sher46] described the patterns of electrical activity in the waking brain as "the head-mass becomes an enchanted loom where millions of flashing shuttles weave a dissolving pattern, always a meaningful pattern though never an abiding one; a shifting harmony of subpatterns". Even though most of our understanding of neural function is based on measurements of activity of one, or a few, single neurones [Gers60], or on measurements at a few points of summed activities of very large numbers of heterogeneous neurones [Free75], Sherrington's poetic description dominates our ideas of how neural assemblies function. "A dissolving pattern, always a meaningful pattern though never an abiding one," suggests the importance of (long-lived) transients in neural functioning: attractors (the ω-limiting sets of dynamical systems) can be met in controlled laboratory experiments, but rarely in normal neural function. "A harmony of subpatterns" suggests self-similar, perhaps even chaotic, dynamics, while "meaningful pattern" emphasises that neural activity is not simply a formal pattern, but is related to the functioning of the nervous system.

As experimental preparations and techniques are developed for recording the activity of large numbers of neurones simultaneously, or for obtaining high resolution images of the spatio-temporal pattern of neural activity [Kaue88; Harr86;

Phel82; Laut73], the problem arises of how to characterise these patterns. In order to simulate spatio-temporal patterned activity in a neural system, we require a representation for:

the dynamics of the neurones;
the connectivity patterns;
the connectivity dynamics.

Even if such a simulation of a neural system were to be exact, in the sense that the electrical activity in all the neurones was reproduced faithfully, it would not necessarily allow us to interpret the behaviour and to discover what computational processes the network is performing. We also require a general theoretical framework for simulating and analysing the computational behaviour over time of a network of processing elements. A general theory of deterministic parallel computation that allows us to formally study models of neural systems is the theory of *synchronous concurrent algorithms*. A synchronous concurrent algorithm (SCA) is a network of processing elements, computing and communicating in parallel and synchronised by a discrete clock; an SCA can process an infinite stream of data. The theory of SCAs makes precise ideas about computation by deterministic networks and allows the formulation of theoretical questions concerning computational aspects of models of neural systems (see [Hold91a, 91b]).

Here we consider the visualisation and modelling of spatio-temporal patterning and irregularity in neural systems, chaotic behaviour in real and modelled nerve cells, fractal measures of neuronal geometry and the simulation of neuronal dendritic growth. We consider as well chaotic behaviour in simple neural networks and the identification and quantification of chaos in the human electroencephalogram. This demonstration of chaotic processes at many different levels of neural activity suggests that chaotic dynamics is an integral part of the normal functioning of neural systems.

Spatio-temporal Patterns in Neural Networks

Most of neurophysiology is in fact neurone physiology, the physiology of single neurones. Although it is easy to record the activity of a single neurone, techniques for recording the activity of many neurones are poorly developed. Thus, most of our understanding of brain function is based on studies of single neurones. Sherrington's "harmony of subpatterns" can be imagined but not visualised.

However, there are some situations where the pattern of outflow from the nervous system can be directly visualised. The skin of some marine cephalopod molluscs (squid, cuttlefish, octopus) provides a preparation where it is possible to directly visualise space-time patterns that are simple mappings of those produced by the nervous system. The skin of these molluscs contains pigment spots that can constrict: in the absence of an innervation, these spots constrict rhythmically. In the presence of a motor innervation, the behaviour of the pigment spot is under neural control. An increase in the discharge rate of the motor fibre to a cluster of pigment spots leads to a contraction and hence a change in pigment spot size. One nerve fibre innervates several neighbouring pigment spots. There is a somato-topic mapping from the surface of the ganglion to the skin surface, so that neighbouring points on the skin correspond to neighbouring points on the surface of the ganglion. Thus, a video-tape recording of the patterns on the skin surface provides a direct record of patterns of activity generated by a neural system [Hold89, 88].

The types of skin pattern seen in the freely behaving animal in the wild — static and dynamic camouflage patterns, attack patterns and sexual displays — are meaningful patterns that are irregular yet structured. The attack patterns consist of a sequence of waves passing over the body and tentacles, and the camouflage patterns are irregular and reminiscent of fractals. Analysis of these patterns provides a means of analysing patterned activity that is a direct mapping of patterned activity in neural systems. The modules that form these patterns, the pigment spots, are illustrated in Plate 17.

A current problem is to develop measures to quantify such granular, spatio-temporal patterns [Mark86]. One approach is to evaluate measures of spatio-temporal patterning on pseudodata generated by simple formal models that produce spatio-temporal waves, patterning and irregularity. A simple type of model is a cellular automaton on a regular lattice [Toff91, 87; Wolf84]. However, a problem with such cellular automata is that the microscopic structure of the lattice is projected into the macroscopic structure of patterns evolving on the lattice. This can be avoided by using a randomised cellular automaton [Mark91; Gerh90]. Another approach is to have a large number of states, which in the limit gives a continuous state model based on interval maps.

A *coupled map lattice* (CML) is a dynamical system with discrete time, discrete space and continuous states [Kane86]. Consider a CML with elements at N sites and one continuous variable, x_i, at site i ($i = 1, 2, \ldots N$). At each lattice site, i, the activity, x_i, evolves as a nonlinear mapping, f_i, of its preceding value, and some function, g_i, of the preceding activities at a set of different sites. If there are no interactions between the activities at different sites, the whole system is simply N independent mappings, f_i, and we have $x_i(n+1) = f_i\big(x(n)\big)$. If there are interactions, these can be local, global or in between these extremes and specified by some specific connectivity matrix.

If the connections are local, an element at site i interacts with some elements in its vicinity; these could be the nearest neighbours, or sites from a larger vicinity. For a one-dimensional lattice, the nearest neighbours of i are simply the sites at $i \pm 1$. In two- and higher dimensional lattices the neighbourhood must be specified, e.g., a von Neuman 4- or Moore 8-neighbour neighbourhood for a rectangular lattice in the plane. The connections can be unidirectional or symmetrical, and different weights can be associated with the different connections.

An example of a two-dimensional, nearest neighbour diffusively coupled CML is given as

$$x_{i,j}(n+1) = (1-\epsilon)f\big(x_{i,j}(n)\big) + \frac{\epsilon}{m} \sum_{p,q} \big(f(x_{p,q}(n))\big) \qquad (1)$$

where $p, q \in \mathrm{Nhd}(i, j)$, the neighbourhood of the element (i, j), m is the number of neighbours and n is a discrete time step. For investigating patterning and irregularity in spatially extensive systems, different local couplings and nonlinear functions, f, can be used. With f given by a logistic map $f(x) = 1 - ax^2$, a nearest neighbour, CML, as illustrated in Plate 18, is called the logistic CML and exhibits three main phases of behaviour [Kane89]:

> For small values of the nonlinearity parameter, a, there are frozen random domains, in which the lattice is broken into domains of different sizes. The larger domains show chaotic dynamics and the smaller domains repetitive, close to simple periodic dynamics. The domain size and locations depend on the initial conditions and are frozen — they do not change with time;

> With an increase in a there is pattern selection. The larger domains are lost, and the overall picture is of a large number of similar-sized domains, all exhibiting simple repetitive dynamics;

> Further increases in a give spatio-temporal intermittency and chaos.

Thus, the simple logistic lattice exhibits phase transitions and provides a caricature of turbulent flows. Any analogies with neural systems are remote. But it is tempting to identify the domains of the pattern selection phase with local neural assemblies, within which local coherence is dynamically maintained by the behaviour of local circuit neurones. Such dynamically maintained local coherence, manifest as synchronisation of bursting activity of neurones, is found in the visual cortex under conditions where visual binding (the unification of separate features of an object into a unified whole) occurs [Eckh91; Mate91]. Here the synchronisation is explained by a weak local coupling of oscillatory systems representing the individual neurones. Bifurcations and chaos in coupled oscillator model neurones are considered below.

Connections in the nervous system are not simply local but can extend over distance, forming a network with a specific hierarchical architecture that allows hierarchical dynamics [Hold91c]. These architectures fall between the extreme cases of local and global coupling, such as the completely coupled map lattice. In a *completely coupled map lattice* (CCML) the activity of any one element, x_i, depends on the preceding activities of all the elements of the lattice. A simple example is

$$x_i(n + 1) = (1 - \epsilon)f\big(x_i(n)\big) + \frac{\epsilon}{N} \sum_{j=1}^{N} f\big(x_j(n)\big) \tag{2}$$

in which there is a mean field global feedback. Kaneko [Kane90] classified the attractors for this example using the notion of cluster, which is the set of elements for which $x_i(n) = x_j(n)$ for all n. The state of the CCML can then be classified by the number of clusters, k, and the number of elements, N_k, in each cluster. Possible states of the CCML range from the entire system as one synchronised cluster (as in oscillating fireflies [Miro90]) to a large number of small clusters. There need not be a simple spatial relationship between elements of the same cluster, since the behaviour is produced by the connectivity, not by local interactions.

A phase diagram can then be constructed in terms of these cluster categories, with areas in the $\epsilon - a$ plane of:

coherent phase, with almost all initial conditions giving a coherent attractor;

an ordered phase, with almost all initial conditions giving a small number of attractors;

a partially-ordered phase, with almost all initial conditions giving a mixture of a few large clusters and a large number of small clusters;

a turbulent phase, with all the attractors having a large ($\simeq N$) number of clusters.

Since clusters are defined as coherent sets of elements, it seems plausible that the neurobiologically interesting behaviours correspond to transient behaviours in the partially ordered phase. However, real neural nets have both short- and long-range coupling and a specific architecture. Although it is possible to explore the behaviours of the limiting short-range (nearest neighbour) and long-range (global) models by systematic simulation, exploring intermediate architectures that have a mixture of short- and long-range interactions requires a more structured approach, as offered by the theory of synchronous concurrent algorithms [Thom89].

Single Nerve Cells

The background activity of a single neurone is irregular. This irregularity can be stochastic, due to asynchronous inputs from large numbers of other cells, or chaotic, generated by the nonlinear dynamics of the neural membrane.

Electrical recordings of patterned (period doubled) and irregular (bursting) activity recorded from single molluscan neurones are shown in Figure 1. The irregularity is identified as chaotic either by following how it develops, e.g., by a period doubling cascade, or by reconstruction and quantification of attractors [Hold86]. A three-variable system of nonlinear ordinary differential equations that simulates period doubling and bursting behaviour of molluscan neurones is the Hindmarsh-Rose equations [Hind84]

$$\frac{dx}{dt} = y - ax^3 + bx^2 - z + I$$

$$\frac{dy}{dt} = c - dx^2 - y$$

$$\frac{dz}{dt} = r[s(x - x_1) - z] \tag{3}$$

where x represents the membrane potential, y a recovery variable, z an adaptation variable and I a steady applied current.

In Figure 2 the time series, $\{x(t)\}$, and trajectories in the three-dimensional state space, $\{x, y, z\}$, for period doubling and irregular bursting are illustrated.

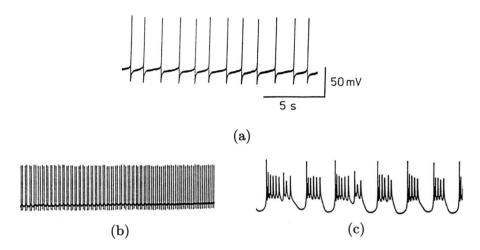

Figure 1. Period doubling and irregular bursting in a snail neurone. (a) Normal background discharge; (b) doublet discharge induced by K^+-channel blocker; (c) irregular bursts induced by menthol.

An examination of the bifurcation structure of this system provides insights on the general mechanisms of burst development [Hold91d].

Fractal Cell Structures

Ever since the work of Ramon y Cajal, the neurone has been established as the clearly defined structural building block of the nervous system. The silhouette images produced by silver staining methods suggest a network of neurones, precisely connected, against an amorphous background. Images produced by transmission electron microscopy show neural tissue to be densely packed, with little extracellular space, and most of the dendritic and somatic surface of neurones to be covered with specialised synaptic contacts.

The number of morphologically identified types of neurones is limited, and one of the aims of cellular neurophysiology is to relate the electrophysiological functioning of neurones to their structure. These branching structures can be quantified by estimating their fractal dimension, D, from

$$n(r) \cong r^D \qquad (4)$$

where n is the number of branches within a sphere, centred on the cell body within a radius, r. Diffusion-limited growth processes provide a means of simulating branching structures.

In diffusion-limited aggregation (DLA) we place a 'seed' at the centre of a two-dimensional lattice space. Then, starting from a random point on the lattice space which is far from the seed, we let a particle move randomly on the plane. When the moving particle comes close to the seed, it stops moving and sticks

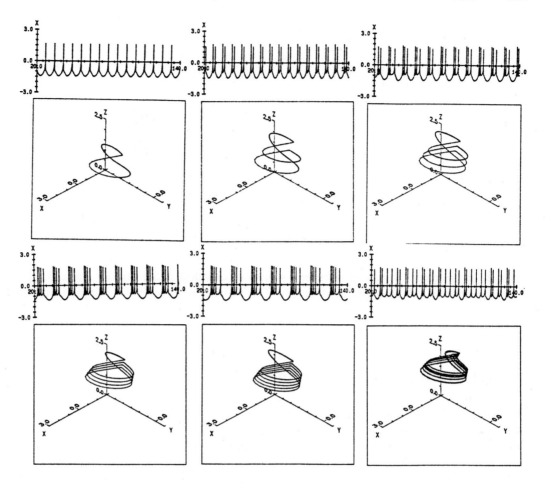

Figure 2. State space and time series for Hindmarsh-Rose equations.

to the seed. In a similar way, another moving particle is introduced and the process continued until an aggregation is formed. This random growth process generates dendritic structures that resemble the projection of neuronal dendrites in the plane (see Figure 3). Thus, DLA in three dimensions might be used to simulate the formation of dendritic trees (see Figure 4). However, the process of DLA bears no resemblance to the process of neurite growth and bifurcation. The fractal dimension, D, of the structure formed by DLA is related to the dimension of the lattice, d, by [Meak86a]

$$D = \frac{d^2 + 1}{d + 1} \qquad (5)$$

and so one might anticipate a constant fractal dimension of 2.5 for different dendritic trees. Experimentally estimated fractal dimensions for neurones range from 2.1 to 2.7 [Schi90] and show directional anisotropy. This agreement is fortuitous, as other models for dendritic growth, such as the diffusion limited growth model [Meak86b], also have $D = 2.5$ for a 3-d lattice. In reality, the

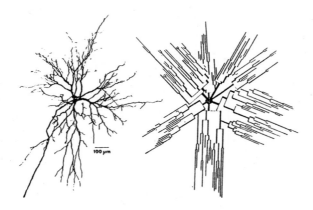

Figure 3. Branching dendrites and their trees.

growth of neurites occurs at different stages of development, and so there might be time-dependent changes in effective D. Thus, the branching pattern at the dendritic periphery would have a different fractal dimension than closer to the cell body.

Neural Networks: Coupling and Chaos

Although the structural unit of the nervous system is the neurone, the functional unit of the vertebrate brain is an assembly of neurones, all with similar functionality and acting in concert. The assembly is a dynamic concept; a neurone can participate in different assemblies at different times, and the assembly is characterised by some coherence in activity. A simple form of coherence is synchronisation, not so much as in phase-locked nonlinear oscillators but as a loose synchronisation of irregular, bursting activity (see [Hold91e]).

If we consider two second-order nonlinear oscillators, each capable of a simple limit cycle oscillation, coupling (which turns two two-variable systems into a single four variable system) allows the possibility of chaos. Neurones are complicated devices, describable by fairly high order differential systems. Coupling of oscillatory systems that may have patterned periodic, or even chaotic, behaviour, as seen in Figure 2, leads to either an increase or a decrease in the complexity of the behaviour. This is illustrated by coupling systems given by Eq. (3) to give a linearly coupled system

$$\frac{dx_1}{dt} = y_1 - ax_1^3 + bx_1^2 - z_1 + I + \epsilon z_2$$

$$\frac{dy_1}{dt} = c - dx_1^2 - y_1$$

$$\frac{dz_1}{dt} = r[s(x_1 - x_1) - z_1]$$

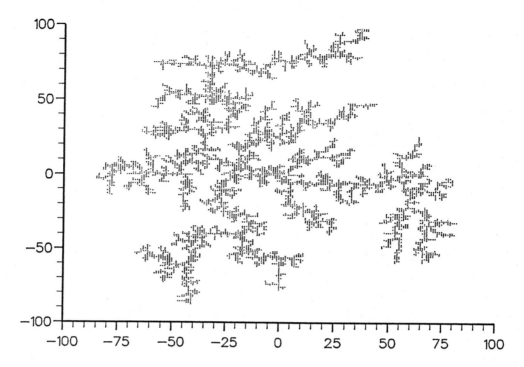

Figure 4. DLA constructed branching network that simulates the structure of a neurone.

$$\frac{dx_2}{dt} = y_2 - ax_2^3 + bx_2^2 - z_2 + I + \epsilon z_1$$

$$\frac{dy_2}{dt} = c - dx_2^2 - y_2$$

$$\frac{dz_2}{dt} = r[s(x_2 - x_1) - z_2] \tag{6}$$

A state space projection of irregular bursting is illustrated in Figure 5, and a bifurcation diagram of the behaviour of one cell as the coupling coefficient ϵ is increased is illustrated in Figure 6.

The Whole Brain: EEGs

Ideas from nonlinear dynamics have permeated clinical neurophysiology [Dvor91; Alba87; Free75], and so there is a need for algorithms that are efficient, straightforward to use, and that provide consistent estimates of measures whose clinical significance can be assessed by longitudinal, experimental or population studies. Some measures that we are investigating, using both experimental and clinical data, are the generalized dimensions and entropies for single and for multiple channel recordings of massed neural data.

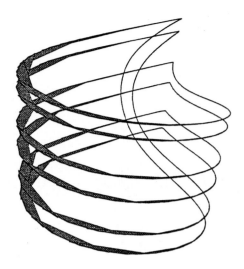

Figure 5. The attractor for two coupled Hindmarsh-Rose equations in state space.

For an m-dimensional phase space divided into a lattice of hypercubes of size l^m, if P_i is the probability that the trajectory of the attractor passes through the ith hypercube, then the generalized dimensions are defined as

$$D_q = \frac{1}{q-1} \lim_{l \to 0} \lim_{N \to 0} \frac{1}{\ln l} \ln \sum_{i=1}^{N} P_i^q \tag{7}$$

The generalized dimensions are written as

$$D_q = \lim_{l \to 0} \lim_{N \to \infty} \frac{1}{\ln l} \ln C^q(l) \tag{8}$$

where $$C^q = \left\{ \frac{1}{N} \sum_{i=1}^{N} \left[\frac{1}{N} \sum_{j=1}^{N} H\big(l - |\vec{x}_i - \vec{x}_j|\big) \right]^{q-1} \right\}^{1/q-1} \tag{9}$$

C^q is called the generalized correlation integral, which distinguishes it from the correlation integral proposed by Grassberger and Procaccia [Gras83].

We can also extend the definition of the Kolomogorov entropy to generalized entropies, which take the form [Eckm85, p. 647]

$$K_q = \lim_{l \to 0} \lim_{N \to \infty} \lim_{m \to \infty} \frac{-1}{q-1} \frac{1}{m\Delta t} \ln \sum_{i_1, \cdots, i_m} P_{i_1, \cdots, i_m}^q \tag{10}$$

where $P_{i_1, \cdots, i_m}$ is the joint probability for the trajectory on the attractor to visit the hypercubes, $i_1, i_2, \ldots, i_m$, in the phase space. Δt is the sampling time interval, and l is the length of the cubes. By using the joint probability instead of the simple probability, we obtain the formula for generalized entropies which is similar to the generalized dimensions.

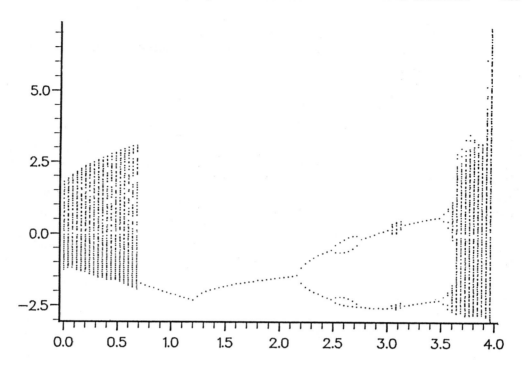

Figure 6. Bifurcation diagram for the two coupled Hindmarsh-Rose equations with the changing of the coupling strength.

We start with a single experimental time series, $x(t)$, $x(t + \Delta t)$, $x(t + 2\Delta t)$, $\cdots$, $x(t + n\Delta t)$, which is sampled at regular and discrete time intervals, Δt, from the value of a state variable. The time series, $x(t)$, is manifestly one-dimensional and represents a projection $\pi : R^M \to R$ from the full state vector, $\vec{X}(t) \in R^M$, and as such provides incomplete information for the dynamical system. Using the lagging method, we create a vector, $\vec{x} \in R^M$

$$\vec{x}(t) = \Big(x(t), x(t + \tau), \cdots, x\big(t + (m - 1)\tau\big)\Big) \qquad \tau = n\Delta t, \, n = 1, 2, \ldots \quad (11)$$

where the delay time, τ, and the embedding dimension, m, are the parameters for the embedding procedure. Here $\vec{x}(t)$ contains much more information about the system than does $x(t)$, and acts as a mapping, $\pi^m : R^M \to R^m$, from the full state, $\vec{X}(t)$, to the reconstructed $\vec{x}(t)$. Takens [Take81] and Mañé [Mane81] proved that when $m > 2D + 1$, where D is the fractal dimension of the attractor, t, this procedure does give a reliable reconstruction of the attractor from an infinitely long single time series.

In the computation of the generalized dimensions and entropies, there are a number of redundant computations. We describe some techniques that avoid these repeated computations and reduce data space that is required. As an example, we use the following procedures to compute the correlation dimension from an experimental time series.

The classical method to compute the correlation integral is purely based on the statistics of the pairwise distance proposed by Grassberger and Procaccia [Gras83], which takes the form

$$C_2(l) = \frac{1}{N^2} \sum_{i=1}^{N} \sum_{j=1, j\neq i}^{N} H(l - |\vec{x}_i - \vec{x}_j|) \tag{12}$$

Estimating the correlation dimension, D_2, requires a knowledge of $C_2(l)$ over a region of correlation distance, l, for example from $l_{\min}$ to $l_{\max}$. If we reconstruct an m-dimensional attractor from an N-points time series, and divide the correlation region into K subcorrelation regions related to K correlation distances, then the computation time for computing Eq. (12) is $O(K \times m \times N^2)$. The required data space is $O(m \times N)$. In practice we note that the following techniques reduce the computation time from $O(K \times m \times N^2)$ to $O(1/2 \times N^2)$, and reduce the required data space from $O(m \times N)$ to $O(N)$.

First, considering the symmetry in the pairwise distance, Eq. (12) is rewritten as

$$C_2(l) = \frac{2}{N^2} \sum_{i=1}^{N} \sum_{j>i}^{N} H(l - |\vec{x}_i - \vec{x}_j|) \tag{13}$$

Next, for convenience we use the supreme norm, so that the magnitude of a vector is the maximum of its Cartesian components. Instead of computing $|\vec{x}_i - \vec{x}_j|$, we use a quick sorting program to find out its maximum component. Then we calculate the correlation integrals for K selected correlation distances concurrently. The correlation integral for a specified correlation distance, l_i, is the total number of pairs whose distance are less than l_i. If the distance between two points is d, and

$$l_{i-1} < d \leq l_i \tag{14}$$

then
$$C_2(l_k) = C_2(l_k) + 1 \qquad k = i \quad i+1, \cdots, K \tag{15}$$

In this way, the computation time is reduced K-fold.

There are still some redundant computations. Suppose we have a time series, $x(1), x(2), \cdots, x(8)$, and we use the time delay method to reconstruct a three-dimensional attractor. The computation of the correlation integral consists of the computations

$$
\begin{array}{lllll}
|\vec{x}_1 - \vec{x}_2| & |\vec{x}_1 - \vec{x}_3| & |\vec{x}_1 - \vec{x}_4| & |\vec{x}_1 - \vec{x}_5| & |\vec{x}_1 - \vec{x}_6| \\
|\vec{x}_2 - \vec{x}_3| & |\vec{x}_2 - \vec{x}_4| & |\vec{x}_2 - \vec{x}_5| & |\vec{x}_2 - \vec{x}_6| & \\
|\vec{x}_3 - \vec{x}_4| & |\vec{x}_3 - \vec{x}_5| & |\vec{x}_3 - \vec{x}_6| & & \\
|\vec{x}_4 - \vec{x}_5| & |\vec{x}_4 - \vec{x}_6| & & & \\
|\vec{x}_5 - \vec{x}_6| & & & &
\end{array}
\tag{16}
$$

Considering the components of each vector, the required computations are

$$|\vec{x}_1 - \vec{x}_2|: \quad x(1) - x(2) \quad \underline{x(2) - x(3)} \quad \underline{x(3) - x(4)}$$
$$|\vec{x}_1 - \vec{x}_3|: \quad x(1) - x(3) \quad \underline{x(2) - x(4)} \quad \underline{x(3) - x(5)}$$
$$|\vec{x}_1 - \vec{x}_4|: \quad x(1) - x(4) \quad \underline{x(2) - x(5)} \quad \underline{x(3) - x(6)}$$
$$|\vec{x}_1 - \vec{x}_5|: \quad x(1) - x(5) \quad \underline{x(2) - x(6)} \quad \underline{x(3) - x(7)}$$
$$|\vec{x}_1 - \vec{x}_6|: \quad x(1) - x(6) \quad \underline{x(2) - x(7)} \quad \underline{x(2) - x(8)}$$

$$|\vec{x}_2 - \vec{x}_3|: \quad \underline{x(2) - x(3)} \quad \underline{x(3) - x(4)} \quad \underline{x(4) - x(5)}$$
$$|\vec{x}_2 - \vec{x}_4|: \quad \underline{x(2) - x(4)} \quad \underline{x(3) - x(5)} \quad \underline{x(4) - x(6)}$$
$$|\vec{x}_2 - \vec{x}_5|: \quad \underline{x(2) - x(5)} \quad \underline{x(3) - x(6)} \quad \underline{x(4) - x(7)}$$
$$|\vec{x}_2 - \vec{x}_6|: \quad \underline{x(2) - x(6)} \quad \underline{x(3) - x(7)} \quad \underline{x(4) - x(8)}$$

$$|\vec{x}_3 - \vec{x}_4|: \quad \underline{x(3) - x(4)} \quad \underline{x(4) - x(5)} \quad \underline{x(5) - x(6)}$$
$$|\vec{x}_3 - \vec{x}_5|: \quad \underline{x(3) - x(5)} \quad \underline{x(4) - x(6)} \quad \underline{x(5) - x(7)}$$
$$|\vec{x}_3 - \vec{x}_6|: \quad \underline{x(3) - x(6)} \quad \underline{x(3) - x(7)} \quad \underline{x(3) - x(8)}$$

$$|\vec{x}_4 - \vec{x}_5|: \quad \underline{x(4) - x(5)} \quad \underline{x(5) - x(6)} \quad \underline{x(6) - x(7)}$$
$$|\vec{x}_4 - \vec{x}_6|: \quad \underline{x(4) - x(6)} \quad \underline{x(5) - x(7)} \quad \underline{x(6) - x(8)}$$

$$|\vec{x}_5 - \vec{x}_6|: \quad \underline{x(5) - x(6)} \quad \underline{x(6) - x(7)} \quad \underline{x(7) - x(8)} \tag{17}$$

The underlined computations are done at least two and some three, or m, times. Now let us construct an $N \times (N - m - 1)$ matrix, which takes the form

$$\begin{bmatrix} x(1) - x(2) & x(1) - x(3) & x(1) - x(4) & x(1) - x(5) & x(1) - x(6) \\ x(2) - x(3) & x(2) - x(4) & x(2) - x(5) & x(2) - x(6) & x(2) - x(7) \\ x(3) - x(4) & x(3) - x(5) & x(3) - x(6) & x(3) - x(7) & x(3) - x(8) \\ x(4) - x(5) & x(4) - x(6) & x(4) - x(7) & x(4) - x(8) & 0 \\ x(5) - x(6) & x(5) - x(7) & x(5) - x(8) & 0 & 0 \\ x(6) - x(7) & x(6) - x(8) & 0 & 0 & 0 \\ x(7) - x(8) & 0 & 0 & 0 & 0 \end{bmatrix} \tag{18}$$

In the matrix (Eq. 18), we find every component of the computations in Eq. (17). Generally speaking, in the ith column, from the jth row, the following three elements are the components of the computation of $|\vec{x}_j - \vec{x}_{i+j}|$, e.g., with $i = 1$, $j = 3$, the following three components are $x(3) - x(4)$, $x(4) - x(5)$, $x(5) - x(6)$, that is, $|\vec{x}_3 - \vec{x}_4|$. Detailed study of the matrix (Eq. 18) shows that there is no relationship between columns. Each time, we only use a column of the matrix to do the related computation $|\vec{x}_j - \vec{x}_{i+j}|$. Thus, instead of an $N \times N$ matrix, we use an array, $z(N)$, to store the elements in the used column.

To summarize these techniques we use the following procedures to compute the correlation integral for an m-embedding attractor:

(1) Open an array, $z(N)$, which is used to store the elements in a column of the matrix of Eq. (18);

(2) Divide the relationships between all pairs of points into K classes which are related to the K selected correlation distances;

(3) Fill $z(j)$ with the ith column of the matrix; the element is then

$$z(j) = \big| [x(j) - x(j+i)] \big| \qquad j = 1, 2, N - i \qquad (19)$$

(4) In the ith column, find the maximum of each m group of elements of $z(j)$; assign it to one of the K classes specified in step 2 and update the related correlation integral;

(5) Repeat steps (3) and (4) until the computations cover all of the columns of the matrix.

In the above procedure, the required data space is $O(N)$, and the computation time is $O(1/2 N^2)$.

Multichannel recordings are obtained, in general, from a grid of equispaced points, for example in a rectangular lattice. In physical situations the problem is to identify spatially coherent structures. In the analysis of electroencephalographic data, the problems are more (a) to identify spatial coherences which indicate a local functional structure; (b) spatial differences in behaviour, which can be used to map different functional regions of the brain and (c) by using information from different sites, to obtain consistent measures and monitor changes in these measures produced by pharmacological interventions, or pathological processes.

An alternative to the lagging method is the multichannel method proposed by Eckmann and Ruelle [Eckm85, p. 647]. Instead of reconstructing an attractor from a single time series, the phase space spanned by simultaneous measurements of the same variable at different sites also constitutes an embedding. This construction has the advantage of covering the system spatially and thus incorporates better statistics.

We start with m-channels time series, $x_i(t)$, $x_i(t + \Delta t)$, $\cdots$, $x_i(t + n\Delta t)$ $(i = 1, 2, \cdots, m)$, which are recorded from a state variable concurrently at m different sites. The multichannel method consists of taking each channel as one component of the vector $\vec{x}(t)$, that is

$$\vec{x}(t) = [x_1(t), x_2(t), \cdots, x_m(t)] \qquad (20)$$

In implementing the multichannel method, we have a problem of how to decide the distance between two different recording sites. The distance between them determines the correlation between the recorded two time series. The computation result shows that with m channels from a local region, the correlation dimension gives a lower value because of a stronger correlation while giving a slightly higher value if we use m channels in a more expanded region [Dvor90].

We used both single and multichannel time series to reconstruct an attractor. Then we quantified the strange attractor for the electroencephalogram (EEG) recorded from a severely epileptic woman, where spike wave activity was induced by hyperventilation. The standard position of EEG recording electrodes over the surface of the scalp is illustrated in Figure 7, with 10–20 recording systems and a Goldman reference electrode.

The results of single channel (25 seconds of data sampled at 200 Hz, recorded from position Fp1) and multichannel (all 19 channels, 25 s of data sampled at 200 Hz) analysis are shown in Figure 8. In both cases, the measures are computed from a reconstructed attractor of less than 5000 points. The results from a single time series are seen in Figure 8a. Figure 8b shows the results from the multichannel time series.

The projections of the reconstructed attractors both have the same appearance, thus any clinical assessment based on attractor shapes applies to attractors reconstructed by either method. The eigenspectra, obtained by singular value decomposition, both have only four eigenvalues significantly greater than the plateau value. Thus, although 19 recording channels are routinely obtained in standard clinical recordings, reconstruction and quantification of an attractor (rather than the detection of regional differences in behaviour) requires a smaller number of channels.

The correlation exponent, or dimension D_2, defined in Eq. (8) was computed using 8-channel subsets of the 19-channel, unipolar 10–20 recording scheme, with Goldman reference electrode. The six subsets are listed in Table 1.

Properties of a clinically useful measure are that (a) it is consistent among a group of normal persons under standard conditions and (b) it does differ between normal and abnormal persons. Thus, the correlation exponent was computed from data obtained from these six sets of recording sites for healthy subjects

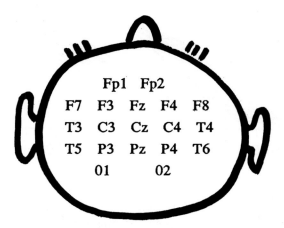

Figure 7. The map of the standard recording sites for the clinical EEG.

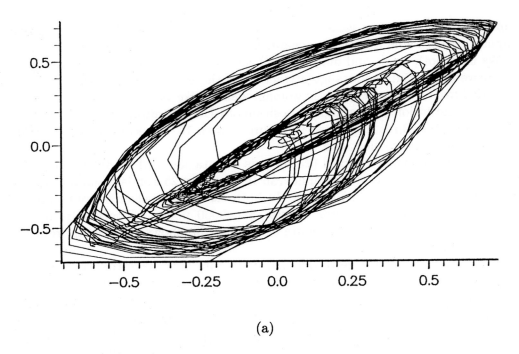

(a)

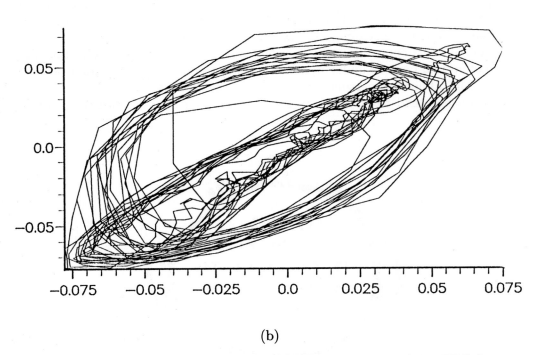

(b)

Figure 8. Reconstructed EEG attractors. (a) Single recording of the EEG from an epileptic subject at rest; (b) multichannel recording of the EEG from the same subject.

Table 1. Positions of leads for subsets 1–6.

Subset 1			Subset 2			Subset 3			
	Fp1			Fp2		Fp1		Fp2	
F7	F3		F4	F8	F7	F3	Fz	F4	F8
T3	C3		C4	T4			Cz		
T5	P3		P4	T6					
	01		02						

Subset 4					Subset 5			Subset 6		
						Fp1			Fp2	
					F7	F3	Fz	Fz	F4	F8
	Cz				T3	C3			C4	T4
T5	P3	Pz	P4	P6	T5	P3			P4	T6
	01		02							

(a) and (b) and for (c), the epileptic subject. These results are presented in Table 2. The values for the epileptic are consistently lower than those for the normal subjects.

Thus, efficient coding allows the practical estimation of generalized dimensions and entropies from experimental and clinical neurophysiological data. From the viewpoint of experimental neuroscience, spatial differences in these measures is of interest; from the viewpoint of clinical neuroscience, consistency of the measures is of prime importance. The similarity between measures obtained from single channel and multichannel recordings obtained from neighbouring regions allows consistent estimates to be obtained from relatively short recordings. Since the two approaches measure different features (dynamics versus space correlation) of the same object, and since the numerical results are close, this supports the assumption that time and space processes within the brain are highly coordinated.

Acknowledgments. This work was supported by a grant under the Cognitive Science Initiative, MRC SPG 9017859. The electroencephalographic results were presented as a poster, "Reconstruction and Quantification of Attractors from Single and Multi-channel Neural Signals," by A.V. Holden and H. Zhang (Leeds);

Table 2. Correlation dimension estimates for (a) and (b) normal subjects; (c) epileptic subject.

Recording site	Correlation dimension		
	Subject a	Subject b	Subject c
1	4.19 ± 0.06	4.4 ± 0.1	3.42 ± 0.09
2	4.27 ± 0.07	4.4 ± 0.1	3.63 ± 0.08
3	3.97 ± 0.03	4.6 ± 0.2	3.3 ± 0.06
4	4.18 ± 0.03	4.18 ± 0.07	3.24 ± 0.07
5	4.11 ± 0.05	4.45 ± 0.06	3.3 ± 0.1
6	4.18 ± 0.06	4.3 ± 0.1	3.6 ± 0.1

I. Dvorak, M. Palus and J. Wackermann (Prague Psychiatric Centre); and F.L. Li (Physics Department, University of Science and Technology of China, Hefei), at the IUTAM and NATO ARW on Interpretation of time series from nonlinear mechanical systems, University of Warwick, August 1991.

REFERENCES

[Alba87]
> Albano, A.M., Mees, A.I., de Guzman, G.C., and Rapp, P.E., Data requirements for reliable estimation of correlation dimensions, in *Chaos in Biological System*, Degn, H., Holden, A.V., and Olsen, L.F., Eds., NATO ASI Series, New York: Plenum Press, Vol. 138, pp. 207–220, 1987.

[Dvor90]
> Dvorak, I., Takens versus multichannel reconstruction in EEG correlation exponent estimates, *Phys. Lett. A*, Vol. 151, pp. 225–233, 1990.

[Dvor91]
> Dvorak, I., and Holden, A.V., Eds., *Mathematical Approaches to Brain Functioning Diagnostics*, Manchester, UK: Manchester Univ. Press, 1991.

[Eckh91]
> Eckhorn, E., Schanze, T., and Reitobeck, H.J., Neural mechanisms of flexible feature linking in the visual system, in [Dvor91].

[Eckm85]
> Eckmann, J-P., and Ruelle, D., Ergodic theory of chaos and strange attractors, *Rev. Modern Physics*, Vol. 57, No. 3, pp. 617–656, 1985.

[Free75]
> Freeman, W.J., *Mass Action in the Nervous System*, New York: Academic Press, 1975.

[Gerh90]
> Gerhardt, M., Schuster, H., and Tyson, J.J., A cellular automata model of excitable media, *Physica*, Vol. 46D, pp. 392–415, 1990.

[Gers60]
> Gerstein, G.L., and Kiang, N.Y.-S, An approach to the quantitative analysis of electrophysiological data from single neurones, *Biophys. Jour.*, Vol. 1, pp. 15–28, 1960.

[Gras83]
> Grassberger, P., and Procaccia, I., Characterisation of strange attractors, *Phys. Rev. Lett.*, Vol. 50, p. 346–349, 1983.

[Harr86]
> Harrison, S.A., and Scott, J.W., Olfactory bulb response to order stimulation: Analysis of response pattern and intensity relationships, *Jour. Neurophysiol.*, Vol. 56, pp. 1571–89, 1986.

[Hind84]
> Hindmarsh, J.L., and Rose, R.M., A model for neuronal bursting using three coupled first order differential equations, *Proc. Roy. Soc. London Ser. B*, Vol. 221, p. 87, 1984.

[Hold86]
Holden, A.V., Ed., *Chaos*, Manchester, UK: Manchester Univ. Press, 1986.

[Hold88]
Holden, A.V., Spatial-temporal patterns of activity in eural systems: Simulation and analysis, in *Biomathematics and Related Computational Problems*, Ricciardi, L.M., Ed., Dordrecht, Netherlands: Kluwer Academic Publishers, 1988.

[Hold89]
Holden, A.V., and Matsumoto, G., Patterned and irregular activity in excitable media, in *Biomathematics and Related Computation Problem*, Christiansen, P., and Parmentier, R.D., Eds., Manchester, UK: Manchester Univ. Press, 1989.

[Hold91a]
Holden, A.V., Tucker, J.V., and Thompson, B.C., The computational structure of neural systems, in [Hold91e].

[Hold91b]
Holden, A.V., Tucker, J.V., Thompson, B.C., Withington, D., and Zhang, H., Theoretical framework for synchronisation, coherence and chaos in real and simulated neural networks, in *Complex Dynamics in Neural Network: Approaches to Neurocomputing*, Clanke, J.W., and Taylor, J.G., Eds., Heidelberg: Springer-Verlag, 1991.

[Hold91c]
Holden, A.V., Structural, functional and dynamical hierarchies in neural networks, in *A Chaotic Hierarchy*, Baier, G., and Klein, M., Eds., Singapore: World Scientific, 1991.

[Hold91d]
Holden, A.V., and Fan, Y.-S., From simple to complex oscillatory behaviour via intermittent chaos in the Rose-Hindmarsh model, *Chaos, Solitons and Fractals*, Vol. 2, 1991.

[Hold91e]
Neurocomputers and Attention Vol. 1, *Neurobiology, Synchronisation and Chaos*, Holden, A.V., and Kryukov, V.I., Eds., Manchester, UK: Manchester Univ. Press, 1991 .

[Kane86]
Kaneko, K., Turbulence in coupled map lattice, *Physica*, Vol. 18D, pp. 475–476, 1986.

[Kane89]
Kaneko, K., Pattern dynamics in spatio-temporal chaos. Pattern selection, diffusion of defect and pattern competition intermittency, *Physica*, Vol. 34D, pp. 1–41, 1989.

[Kane90]
Kaneko, K., Clustering, coding, switching, hierarchial ordering and control in network of chaotic elements, *Physica*, Vol. 41D, pp. 137–172, 1990.

[Kaue88]
Kauer, J.S., Real-time imaging of evoked activity in local circuits of salamander olfactory bulb, *Nature*, Vol. 331, pp. 166–8, 1988.

[Laut73]
Lauterburn, P.C., Image formation by induced local interactions. Examples employing nuclear magnetic resonance, *Nature*, Vol. 242, pp. 190–1, 1973.

234   Arun V. Holden, Julie Hyde and Henggui Zhang

[Mane81]
Mañé, R., On the dimension of the compact invariant sets of certain non-linear maps, in *Dynamical Systems and Turbulence* (Warwick), Rand, D.A., and Young, L.-S., Eds., Berlin: Springer-Verlag, 1981.

[Mark86]
Markus, M., Müller, S.C., Plesser, Th., and Hess, B., Characterisation of order and disorder in spatial patterns, in *Chaos in Biological System*, Degn, H., Holden, A.V., and Olsen, L.F., Eds., NATO ASI Series, New York: Plenum Press, Vol. 138, pp. 295–304, 1986.

[Mark91]
Markus, M., Krafczyk, M., and Hess, H., Randomized automata for isotropic modelling of two- and three-dimensional waves and spatial temporal chaos in excitable media, in *Nonlinear Wave Processes in Excitable Media*, Holden, A.V., Markus, M., and Othmer, H.G., Eds., New York: Plenum Press, 1991.

[Mate91]
Mateef, S., Bohdanecky, Z., Ehrenstein, W.H., Hohnsbein, J., and Yakimoff, N., Motor responses to real and extrapolated motion: A new visual anisotropy, in [Dvor91].

[Meak86a]
Meakin, P., A new model for biological pattern formation, *Jour. Theoretical Biology*, Vol. 118, p. 101, 1986.

[Meak86b]
Meakin, P., Computer simulation of growth and aggregation processes, in *On Growth and Form*, Stanley, H.E., and Ostrowsky, N., Eds., Dordrecht, Netherlands: Martinus Nijhoff Publishers, 1986.

[Miro90]
Mirollo, R.E., and Strogatz, S.H., Synchronization of pulse-coupled biological oscillators, *SIAM Jour. Appl. Math.*, Vol. 50, pp. 1645–1662, 1990.

[Phel82]
Phelps, M.E., Mazziota, J.C., and Huang, S.C., Study of cerebral function with positron computed tomography, *Jour. Cerebral Blood Flow and Metab.*, Vol. 15, pp. S1–11, 1982.

[Schi90]
Schierwagen, A.K., Scale-invariant diffusive growth: A dissipative principle relating neuronal form function, in *Organizational Constraints on the Dynamics of Evolution*, Smith, J.M., and Vida, G., Eds., Manchester, UK: Manchester Univ. Press, 1990.

[Sher46]
Sherrington, C.S., *Man and His Nature*, Cambridge, UK: Cambridge Univ. Press, 1946.

[Take81]
Takens, F., *Detecting Strange Attractors in Turbulence*, Lecture Notes in Mathematics, 898, p. 366 in *Dynamical Systems and Turbulence* (Warwick), Rand, D.A., and Young, L.-S., Eds., Berlin: Springer-Verlag, 1981.

[Thom89]
Thompson, B.C., and Tucker, J.V., Synchronous concurrent algorithms, Technical

report, Department of Mathematics and Computer Science, University College of Swansea, 1992.

[Toff87]

Toffili, T., and Margolus, N., *Cellular Automata Machine*, Cambridge, MA, USA: MIT Press, 1987.

[Toff91]

Toffili, T., and Margolus, N., Programmable matter: Concepts and realization, *Physica*, Vol. 47D, pp. 263–272, 1991.

[Wolf84]

Wolfram, S., Universality and complexity in cellular automata, *Physica*, Vol. 10D, pp. 1–35, 1984.

The Dynamic Behaviour of Road Traffic Flow:

Stability or Chaos?

David Jarrett and Zhang Xiaoyan

Abstract

This paper is a report on work in progress on a project concerned with models of road traffic flow. Results for two such models are described and illustrated. One model is the classical car-following model. A number of numerical simulations were carried out, but no evidence of chaos was found. The other model concerns trip distribution. Here a dynamic formulation of the model results in some solutions which appear chaotic, and evidence of a period-doubling sequence of bifurcations is found.

Introduction

The motion of road traffic on a road network or on a single link of a network (a stretch of road between junctions) can be considered as a dynamic system. At a microscopic level, the system can be described in terms of variables such as the position and velocity of each vehicle. At a more macroscopic level, important variables include the total number of trips between two zones, the rate of traffic flow (the number of vehicles per unit time passing a fixed point), traffic density (the number of vehicles per lane and kilometre) and average speed. Dynamic models of road traffic flow describe how these variables change with time, possibly in response to external demands. These might be expressed, for instance, as the need for certain numbers of individuals or goods to be in particular places at particular times. The concepts of traffic equilibrium and its stability receive much attention; they are important both for understanding the behaviour of road traffic, and in traffic management and planning. Equilibrium and stability are desirable objectives for road traffic flow but are not always achieved. In dense traffic, where drivers follow each other very closely, small disturbances like the acceleration or deceleration of one vehicle might be preserved or amplified along the line of vehicles or over time, suggesting that there can be sensitive dependence on initial conditions. These phenomena can raise problems in traffic management, and can even result in accidents.

To the casual observer, road traffic flow appears inherently stochastic. However, many theoretical models of traffic flow are deterministic. Thus, it is appropriate to investigate these models and observed traffic flow for chaotic behaviour. This paper is a report on work in progress on a project concerned with nonlinear dynamic models of road traffic flow. One model being investigated is the car-following model, which describes the microscopic behaviour of congested traffic moving along a link. Two other recent studies investigated whether there is chaos in this model, but reached apparently different conclusions. This model and its solutions are considered in the next section. Macroscopic models being investigated include traffic assignment models and trip distribution models. Traffic assignment models are multi-dimensional discrete-time systems, in which the flows on the routes in the road network are iterated. In each iteration, the flows are diverted to 'cheaper routes' as perceived by drivers. Trip-distribution models are similar in form to assignment models, with the observables being the number of trips between given origin and destination zones. These models are considered later in the paper.

Computer systems are already widely used for the control of traffic signals, to move traffic efficiently through urban areas. Currently under development are systems for automated route guidance, and artificial intelligence systems in cars. One important application of this project is to investigate whether the introduction of such systems into the driving process, with the intention of improving traffic quality and efficiency, can lead to instability, or even chaos, in the motion of individual vehicles or the distribution of traffic over the system.

The Car-following Model

The motion of a line of vehicles on a crowded road link without overtaking is described by the car-following model [Leut88: Wilh73]. This model is based on the assumption that a driver responds to the motion of the vehicle immediately in front. In the simplest model, the acceleration of the following car is assumed to be proportional to the difference between its speed and that of the car in front; this model is linear. More complex models are nonlinear and allow the acceleration of the following car to depend both on its own speed and on the relative spacing of the two cars. In all cases, a time delay is built into the equations. The driver does not react immediately to changes in relative speed or spacing.

Consider a line of cars numbered from 1 (the leading car) to N (the last car) (Figure 1). Let $x_n(t)$ denote the position of car n at time t. Then the equations of the model are

$$\ddot{x}_n(t) = \alpha[\dot{x}_{n-1}(t-\tau) - \dot{x}_n(t-\tau)] \qquad n = 2, 3, \cdots, N$$

Here, α is a function of the current speed of car n, and its distance from car $n-1$ at the time $(t-\tau)$

$$\alpha = c \frac{\left(\dot{x}_n(t)\right)^m}{\left[x_{n-1}(t-\tau) - x_n(t-\tau)\right]^l}$$

In these equations, dots denote time derivatives. τ is a constant, representing the reaction time of the driver of the following car. c is a positive parameter; m and l are nonnegative parameters, not necessarily integers. The linear model corresponds to α constant, with $m = l = 0$. In general, α is called the *sensitivity*.

Many stability studies of traffic flow on a road link are based on this model. Most recently, there have been two studies about possible chaotic behaviour in the car-following model. Disbro and Frame [Disb90] claim that chaos can definitely occur in the car-following process. Their conclusion is based on showing that the first Lyapunov exponent is positive for certain values of the parameters, but they give no plots or other evidence of a strange attractor. On the other hand, in an exploratory study Kirby and Smith [Kirb91] found no evidence of chaos in car following.

From a mathematical point of view, the car-following equations have a number of interesting features. Firstly and most importantly, they are a system of delay-differential equations and therefore have an infinite-dimensional phase space. Initial conditions must be specified as functions $x_n(t)$ over the interval $-\tau \leq t \leq 0$. The mathematical analysis of such equations is difficult. However, finite-dimensional attractors exist for systems of delay-differential equations; some such systems are believed to possess finite-dimensional strange attractors (see [Farm82]). Secondly, for given initial conditions, solutions do not necessarily exist for all $t \geq 0$; for $l > 0$ the equations have a singularity where $x_{n-1}(t - \tau) = x_n(t - \tau)$, corresponding to a collision between vehicles $n - 1$ and n at time $(t - \tau)$. Such collisions can occur quite easily. Similarly, for m noninteger the equations make no sense if the speed of any vehicle becomes negative. Thirdly, where the solutions $x_n(t)$ exist for all positive t, they in general are unbounded: the cars eventually reach any given point on the road. It is also possible for the speed of one or more vehicles to increase without limit.

Note that the motion of each car is influenced directly by only the car immediately in front; the motion of the first car is taken as given. The equations

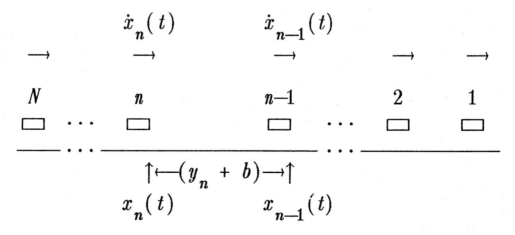

Figure 1. The car-following model.

can therefore be solved numerically one by one. However, progress can be made analytically by writing the equation for car n as

$$\frac{\ddot{x}_n(t)}{\dot{x}_n(t)^m} = c \, \frac{\dot{x}_{n-1}(t-\tau) - \dot{x}_n(t-\tau)}{\left[x_{n-1}(t-\tau) - x_n(t-\tau)\right]^l}$$

These equations can be integrated once (see [Leut88], p. 140).

Further analysis of the model is most easily carried out by re-expressing the model in terms of relative quantities so the solutions can remain bounded. Denote the spacing between adjacent cars by

$$y_n(t) = x_{n-1}(t) - x_n(t) - b \qquad n = 2, 3, \cdots, N$$

where b is interpreted as the minimum headway (see Figure 1). Then

$$\dot{y}_n(t) = \dot{x}_{n-1}(t) - \dot{x}_n(t)$$
$$\ddot{y}_n(t) = \ddot{x}_{n-1}(t) - \ddot{x}_n(t)$$

Let $x_1 \equiv x_1(t)$, $y_n \equiv y_n(t)$, $y_n^\tau \equiv y_n(t-\tau)$. Then the model becomes

$$\ddot{y}_2 = \ddot{x}_1 - c(\dot{x}_1 - \dot{y}_2)^m \, \frac{\dot{y}_2^\tau}{(y_2^\tau + b)^l}$$

$$\ddot{y}_n = c(\dot{x}_1 - \dot{y}_2 - \cdots - \dot{y}_{n-1})^m \, \frac{\dot{y}_{n-1}^\tau}{(y_{n-1}^\tau + b)^l}$$

$$- c(\dot{x}_1 - \dot{y}_2 - \cdots - \dot{y}_n)^m \, \frac{\dot{y}_n^\tau}{(y_n^\tau + b)^l} \qquad n = 3, 4, \cdots, N$$

These equations are solved numerically using a Runge-Kutta algorithm, modified for dealing with the delay time in the equations. The motion of a line of cars can be simulated, with the movement of the first car being treated as an input, that is

$$x_1(t) = ut + \frac{a}{\omega^2} \sin \omega t$$

Thus, the speed of the first car fluctuates about a constant, u. For $a = 0$ the equations are autonomous; for $a \neq 0$ there is a sinusoidal forcing term. This model has been simulated for selected combinations of values of the parameters m and l, for both the autonomous and the forced model.

If there is no forcing term, then typically there are stable equilibria, where the relative speed is zero and the relative spacing is constant. The limiting relative spacing depends on the initial conditions. There is a continuum of fixed points — note from the equations that if the relative speed becomes zero then the relative spacing remains constant. If the sensitivity, as determined by the parameter, c, is small, then most solutions converge to an equilibrium without oscillation. However, unbounded solutions can exist if the initial conditions are far from equilibrium. As the sensitivity increases, oscillations begin to occur.

For initial conditions close to an equilibrium, these oscillations damp down as the solution converges. If the initial conditions are further from equilibrium, then the solutions break down: they oscillate with increasing amplitude until the speed of the last car becomes negative. The basins of attraction of the equilibria become smaller as the sensitivity increases. In between the two cases, a periodic attractor (limit cycle) exists in the case $m = 0$ and $l = 2$ for a small range of values of the parameter, c. A solution converging to this attractor is shown in Figure 2. The period is approximately 4τ. This appears to be independent of the initial conditions, the value of c and the number of cars — only the amplitude of the oscillations depends on these factors. The basin of attraction of this periodic attractor is very small. A small change in the initial conditions results in a long transient, but the solution eventually tends to an equilibrium or breaks down.

When the forcing term is introduced, the solutions behave in a very similar way to those of the autonomous equations. The equilibria are replaced by stable periodic solutions with the same period as the forcing term. The amplitudes of these solutions depend on the initial conditions, sensitivity and the position of the car in the line. For initial conditions not close to a stable solution, the solutions diverge and break down, with long transients. Again, the basins of attraction of the periodic attractors become smaller as the sensitivity is increased. Where the unforced equations have a periodic attractor, the forced equations have a more complex behaviour. This is illustrated in Figure 3. However, this

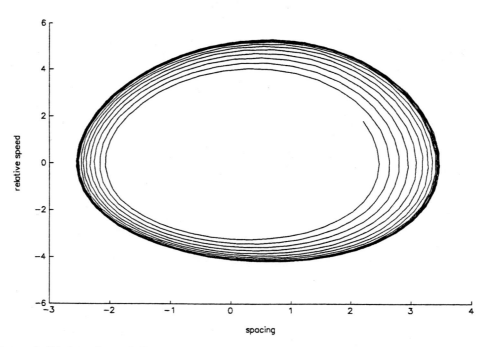

Figure 2. Unforced car-following model, periodic attractor, with $N = 4$, $m = 0$, $l = 2$, $\tau = 1$, $c = 155.3$ and $u = 15$. Relative speed and spacing of third and fourth cars.

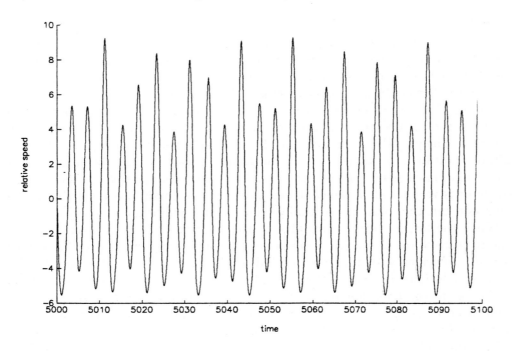

(a)

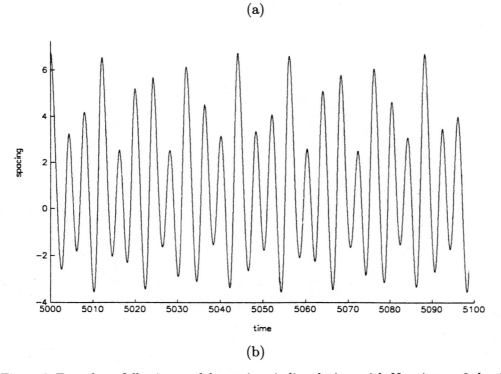

(b)

Figure 3. Forced car-following model, quasi-periodic solution, with $N = 4$; $m = 0$, $l = 2$, $\tau = 1$, $c = 165.3$; $u = 15$, $\omega = 1$, $a = 0.5$. (a) Relative speed; (b) relative spacing; (c) relative speed against delayed relative speed (delay = reaction time) of the third car to the fourth car.

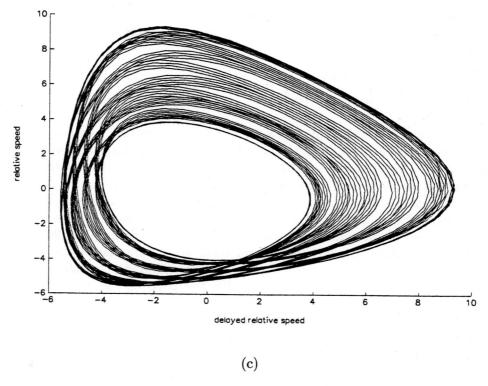

(c)

Figure 3. (*Continued.*).

solution is not chaotic; it appears to be quasi-periodic, or possibly periodic with a very long period.

When the solutions oscillate, a small deviation in the initial conditions tends to be amplified along the line of cars, although it can damp down with time. Thus, any breakdown in the equations occurs only with the last car in the line. Removing car N averts the breakdown. However, a similar situation is bound to occur for car $N-1$ at a larger deviation from the equilibrium or an increased sensitivity. Thus, it is felt that the number of cars has little effect on the qualitative form of the solution.

In none of the investigations carried out so far has any evidence of chaos in the car-following model been found. Of course, no general conclusion can be reached from a finite number of numerical experiments. However, chaos does not appear to occur typically in the model. From a practical point of view, the existence of solutions leading to collisions is probably more important than the existence of chaotic solutions, and indicates the need for care if the car-following equations are used in any method for the automatic control of cars.

There is another study of chaos in road traffic flow by Kühne [Kuhn91], based on a fluid approximation model. In contrast to the car-following model, which treats vehicles individually, the fluid model describes traffic behaviour by macroscopic quantities such as flow rate, traffic density and average speed. Kühne investigates a truncation of the fluid equations; he finds a chaotic attractor and computes the first Lyapunov exponent. The present authors have not yet investigated this model.

The Trip Distribution Model

The aim of the trip distribution model is to determine the number of trips between each pair of zones given the number of trips originating and terminating in each zone. One of the most widely used models is the gravity model, which assumes that the number of trips between zones depends on the number produced at and attracted to each zone, and on the travel cost between zones. Most formulations of this model are static, where the travel costs are assumed to be independent of the number of trips. Dendrinos and Sonis [Dend90] give a dynamic formulation in which the travel costs are a function of the number of trips between zones. At each stage of the iteration, the number of trips is generated using the costs associated with the trips of the previous stage. Dendrinos and Sonis suggest that this iteration can be chaotic, but they do not specify ranges of parameters for which this might be the case.

The dynamic trip distribution model takes the form

$$x_{ij}(t+1) = k(t)f\big(c_{ij}(t)\big)$$

where $x_{ij}(t)$ is the relative number of trips from zone i to zone j, normalised so that $\sum\sum x_{ij}(t) = 1$, and $c_{ij}(t)$ is the travel cost from zone i to zone j, given the trips $x_{ij}(t)$. Dendrinos and Sonis suggest taking

$$c_{ij}(t) = c_{ij}^0\left[1 + \alpha\left(\frac{x_{ij}(t)}{z_{ij}}\right)^\gamma\right]$$

where c_{ij}^0 is the uncongested travel cost, z_{ij} is the relative capacity and α and γ are constants.

$f(c_{ij})$ is a function which relates the number of trips to the travel costs. Three types of function have been suggested (see [Ortu90]):

$$
\begin{array}{llll}
\text{(a)} & f(c_{ij}) & = & \exp(-\beta c_{ij}) & \text{(exponential)} \\
\text{(b)} & f(c_{ij}) & = & c_{ij}^{-n} & \text{(power)} \\
\text{(c)} & f(c_{ij}) & = & c_{ij}^n \exp(-\beta c_{ij}) & \text{(combined)}
\end{array}
$$

where β and n are positive constants. For (a) and (b) the number of trips is a decreasing function of cost, while in (c) the number of trips first increases and then declines as cost increases.

The model as formulated above is unconstrained: it cannot guarantee that the number of trips originating from or terminating at a given zone has a value

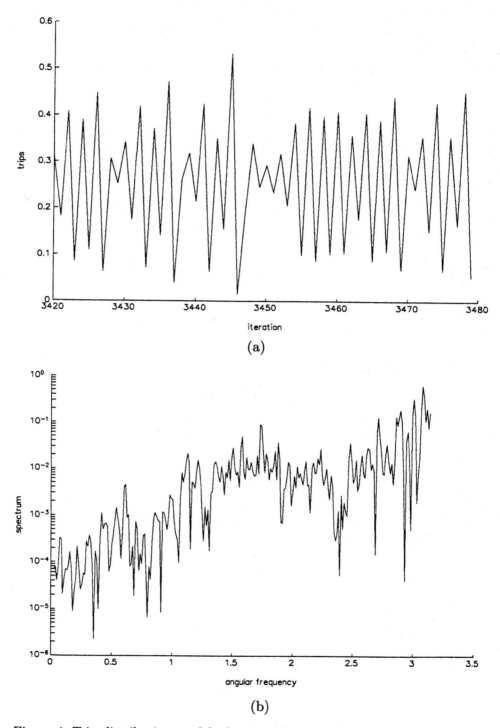

Figure 4. Trip distribution model, chaotic solution with two origins and two destinations, $\alpha = 1$, $\gamma = 1$; $n = 8$, $\beta = 3.25$. (a) Number of trips from origin 1 to destination 2; (b) power spectrum.

which is predetermined. In fact, the numbers become totally different from the starting values after a few iterations. Constraints can be incorporated but are not investigated here. This model has been investigated with two or three origin and destination zones, using each of the three forms of cost functions. In most cases there is a stable fixed point or periodic orbit. However, for the combined cost function, evidence of a period-doubling sequence of bifurcations has been found. If α and γ are fixed at 1, then for appropriate values of n the period changes from 2 to 4 to 8 to 16 as β is gradually increased. Eventually, the sequence becomes irregular and appears chaotic, with a continuous power spectrum. Figure 4 shows such a solution for the three-dimensional model with two origins and two destinations. Lyapunov exponents for this solution were calculated using the algorithm of Eckmann and Ruelle [Eckm85], and were found to be approximately 0.2, −0.02 and −0.7, respectively. A bifurcation diagram for this model is shown in Figure 5. The apparent discontinuity seems to be because there are two or more periodic attractors for some parameter values.

Related models concern traffic assignment. Given the trips $\big(x_{ij}(t)\big)$, the models attempt to estimate the flow on each link of a road network. The assignment of flows to different links is a dynamic process; in each iteration the flows are diverted to 'cheaper routes' as perceived by drivers. When the flow on each link tends to a constant value, it is said to converge to an equilibrium state. Horowitz [Horo84] pointed out that even in a two-route system this equilibrium might not be stable, that is, the equilibrium might not be reached or approached from arbitrary initial conditions. The authors are currently investigating these models and hope to report on them elsewhere.

Conclusion

In this paper two different traffic models were investigated for the presence of chaotic solutions. No evidence of chaos was found in the car-following model, although other authors have indicated that chaos can be found in related models. However, chaotic solutions were found in a dynamic trip-distribution model. It is clear that other traffic models might have chaotic solutions, and the authors hope to report on these in a later paper.

Acknowledgments. The authors thank Professor C.C. Wright for comments on an earlier draft of this paper. The second author is grateful to Middlesex University for financial support.

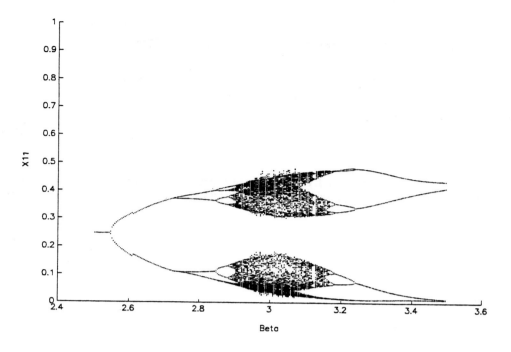

Figure 5. Trip distribution model, bifurcation diagram with two origins and two destinations; $\alpha = 1$, $\gamma = 1$; $n = 7$. The vertical axis is the number of trips from origin 1 to destination 1.

REFERENCES

[Dend90]
    Dendrinos, D.S., and Sonis, M., *Chaos and Social-Spatial Dynamics*, New York: Springer-Verlag, 1990.

[Disb90]
    Disbro, J.E., and Frame, M., Traffic flow theory and chaotic behaviour, *Transportation Research Record*, Vol. 1225, pp. 109–115, 1990.

[Eckm85]
    Eckmann, J-P., and Ruelle, D., Ergodic theory of chaos and strange attractors, *Rev. Modern Physics*, Vol. 57, No. 3, pp. 617–656, 1985.

[Farm82]
    Farmer, J.D., Chaotic attractors of an infinite-dimensional dynamical system, *Physica*, Vol. 7D, pp. 366–393, 1982.

[Horo84]
    Horowitz, J.L., The stability of stochastic equilibrium in a two-link transportation network, *Transportation Research*, Vol. 18B, pp. 13–28, 1984.

[Kirb91]
    Kirby, H.R., and Smith, M.J., Can chaos theories have transport applications?, 23rd Annual Conf. of the Universities Transport Studies Group, University of Nottingham, 1991.

[Kuhn91]

Kühne, R.D., Chaotic behaviour of traffic flow, Preprint, 1991.

[Leut88]

Leutzbach, W., *Introduction to the Theory of Traffic Flow*, Berlin: Springer-Verlag, 1988.

[Ortu90]

Ortúzar, J.deD., and Willumsen, L.G., *Modelling Transport*, Chichester, UK: Wiley, 1990.

[Wilh73]

Wilhelm, W.E., and Schmidt, J.W., Review of car following theory, *Transportation Engrng. Jour.* (ASCE), Vol. 99, TE4, pp. 923–933, 1973.

No Evidence of Chaos But Some Evidence of Multifractals in the Foreign Exchange and the Stock Markets

J.C. Vassilicos, A. Demos and F. Tata

Abstract

There have been a number of claims to have discovered chaos in economic time series. This paper presents investigations of the continuous tick-by-tick Dollar/DM foreign exchange spot rate for one week, and a daily returns series from the New York Stock Exchange for over a century, both containing more than 20,000 data points. Three mathematical tests fail to find any signs of chaotic behaviour. The suggestion is that earlier announcements of chaos in such series may have been due to researchers using series with too few data points. Preliminary evidence is found for a 'multifractal' structure of the very high frequency Forex (Foreign Exchange) fluctuations.

Introduction

In a series of three Discussion Papers [Tata91a, 91b; Vass90] we showed how difficult it is to find evidence for chaos in both the stock and the foreign exchange markets. We used three series: the continuous tick-by-tick Dollar/Deutsche Mark and Dollar/Swiss Franc foreign exchange rates, for one and three weeks, respectively, and a daily returns series from the New York Stock Exchange, for over one century, all of which have over 20,000 quotations. We applied the two most powerful and most popular tests for chaos based on the Lyapunov exponents and the correlation dimension, and a shuffle test. Although we found some indication of a 'hidden structure' in the series from the shuffle test, we failed to find any signs of chaotic behaviour. The number of data points used in our study was, to our knowledge, the largest ever in studies of chaos in economic series. We suggested that earlier announced findings of chaos in economics may have been due to time series that were too short. In particular, we demonstrated how the tests for chaos can give positive answers, e.g., positive Lyapunov exponents, when subsamples with smaller numbers of data points are used, and how these Lyapunov exponents in fact converge to zero when the number of data points is increased.

The first part of this paper is a summary of the results obtained by Vassilicos and Tata [Tata91a, 91b; Vass90]. Having failed to detect any convincing traces of chaos, but having nevertheless obtained some evidence of structure in the Forex (Foreign Exchange) series from the shuffle test, we initiate a study of the fractal and multifractal properties of the Forex series. The second part of this paper is a report of the preliminary results obtained in that direction. A more complete study will appear in the summer of 1992 at the London School of Economics in the form of an FMG Discussion Paper by Demos and Vassilicos [Demo92].

The correlation dimension of a chaotically evolving system is a lower bound to the fractal dimension of the strange attractor in the phase space of the system [Gras83]. This strange attractor has fractal characteristics, and so has the one-dimensional time series generated by it. The graph, or time plot, seen as a line in a two-dimensional plane has a fractal geometry and a nontrivial fractal dimension.

Random walk models of, e.g. the Forex series, where the level of the foreign exchange rates is determined by a straightforward random walk, are alternative models to the deterministic ones which generate chaos. In these models the exchange rates are driven by news events, which represent random exogenous variables — exogenous in the sense that they are not part of an internal mechanism which drives the price fluctuations. The branches of a tree move because of the wind, which is 'exogenous' to the tree, and therefore 'news' to it, whereas a chaotic model of the motion of trees would assume the existence of a simple deterministic, 'nonlinear' engine within the tree (endogenous) which generates chaotic motion by a simple mechanism of feedback of the motion of the tree upon itself.

These random walk models generate fractal, but not multifractal, price fluctuations. Chaotic models generate fractal, and sometimes multifractal, fluctuations too. The fractal character of the signals may not be able to distinguish whether the mechanisms generating the signal are stochastic or deterministic. In fact, we rule out the possibility of chaos anyway *because we could not find it.* (Some of the most conclusive experiments in physics are those experiments where nothing was found. For example, in their now famous experiment of 1887 Michelson and Morley attempted to measure the velocity of the earth relative to the ether, but found nothing that was significantly different from zero. It was subsequently correctly assumed that the ether did not exist, and this assumption led to Einstein's theory of relativity.) But if we are to assume that price fluctuations are both stochastic and have a structure, e.g., correlations between today's price variations and yesterday's prices, then it is important to find ways that distinguish between such fluctuations and simple random walk models. We propose to use the multifractal formalism to that effect.

Random walk models assume that price changes, e.g. stock returns, do not depend on previous prices, e.g. stock prices, and that the market is efficient. This means that prices reflect instantly all new relevant information, all 'news'. Examples of such models are the arbitrage pricing theory and the Black and Scholes options pricing model.

Quite often though, exchange rates are subject to relatively large changes even if no significant news hits the market, except for the fact that the movement of the exchange rate itself is news. Even more difficult to explain by a simple random walk theory are sudden crashes as in October 1987, when a one day fall of more than 500 points on the Dow Jones Industrial Average was recorded.

Related to the previous qualitative comments are recent quantitative results which indicate that the kurtosis of the distribution of high frequency exchange rate variations is of the order of 10 times greater than the variance. This provides strong evidence against the random walk theory where this distribution is Gaussian (see Dassios and Demos [Dass91] and references therein). Low frequency exchange rate fluctuations are closer, though, to a random walk behaviour.

It is in the high frequencies that the departure from Gaussianity is significant, and it is for these frequencies that more sophisticated models which incorporate structural information are needed. Thus, testing for chaos in the Forex market was predominantly interesting at the high and medium frequency ranges. It may be, though, that the high frequency variations have multifractal properties. If so, the multifractal formalism provides a concise way to describe the distribution of high frequency exchange rate variations. Low frequency variations, being Gaussian, have some well-known fractal properties but no multifractal characteristics.

We next describe the data sets we used. The third and fourth sections correspond to the chaos side of this paper, and the fifth to the multifractal side. Finally, we present our conclusions.

The Data Sets

Two different types of data were used in the chaos investigation. The first data set consists of daily, and therefore aggregate, returns of the New York Stock Exchange over a period of more than one century. Specifically, the time series spans a period from February 1885 to December 1988. This data set, 29,137 observations in all, consists of three subdata sets of daily returns:

Dow Jones returns between February 3, 1885 and January 3, 1928;

from January 4, 1928 through to July 2, 1962, the daily returns from the S and P composite portfolio;

from July 3, 1962 to December 31, 1988, the daily returns in the CRSP-value-weighted portfolio. More information on this data set is found in [Schw90].

The second and third data sets differ from the first one insofar as no aggregation of any kind has been done. Both contain tick-by-tick exchange rate data as they are announced (advertised) on Reuter's FXFX page. The resolution is therefore maximum, in the sense that the slightest fluctuation of price is conserved in the data set (high frequency variations; the previous data set of daily stock returns is a medium frequency one). Reuter's FXFX page includes both the 'ask' and the 'bid'. We performed our experiments with the 'ask' rather than with the average between both the 'ask' and the 'bid' because we wanted to preserve the slightest small-scale fluctuation in the data. The time series are the Dollar/Swiss Franc spot exchange rate, from April 9, 1989 to April 29, 1989 (32,200 data points); and the Dollar/Deutsche Mark spot exchange rate, from April 9, 1989 to April 15, 1989 (20,408 data points). For more information on these data sets, the method of filtering the data set from obvious dialing errors and about similar data sets extracted from Reuter's FXFX page, see Goodhart and Figliuoli, and Goodhart and Demos [Good91, 88].

The fact that both the 'bid' and the 'ask' are quoted, and that they usually only differ by the last digit, indicates the care with which these quotes are given. The data set carries, therefore, an exceptionally low level of noise. One can also find in Goodhart and Figliuoli [Good88] an argument based on the dealers' and the banks' reputation, supporting the claim that the indicative price quotes on Reuters screens are reliable.

A typical exchange rate is a number with four decimal digits. In our Dollar/ Deutsche Mark data set it is always strictly between 1 and 2. A typical such exchange rate is, for example, 1.8873.

In the multifractal analysis reported here we only use the *quotation times* of the Dollar/Deutsche Mark quotations. Work on the combined quotation/quotation times series is now under way but is not included in this paper (see forthcoming paper by Demos and Vassilicos [Demo92]). The Reuters FXFX page contains both the price quotations and the times when announcement of these quotations are made. In the case of the Dollar/Deutsche Mark, announcements are so frequent that often more than three of them are made within a minute. The Reuter's data is tick-by-tick, but the distribution of these ticks is not necessarily homogeneous and certainly not regular. We are using data from all week days from April 10, 1989 until June 30, 1989. Specifically, we are only looking at the quotation times of Asian mornings, i.e., between 1:00 A.M. and 4:00 A.M. British Summer Time, when the most important market in operation is the one in Japan, and both New York and Europe are still dormant.

The Search For Chaos

PHASE SPACE RECONSTRUCTION

In essence, the mathematical result used in all tests for chaos in time series is the following [Take85]: The n-dimensional time series, constructed with successive n consecutive quotes of the one-dimensional series, represents a trajectory in n-dimensional space. This is similar to the trajectory of the state of the system, assumed chaotic, generating the 1D time series as this state evolves in phase space. In practice, one never knows a priori the dimension of the phase space, so one does not know which number n to choose for this reconstruction. We tried all numbers n from 1 to 10, and we calculated the largest Lyapunov exponent and the correlation dimension corresponding to each of these 'reconstructions', or simply constructions.

THE LARGEST LYAPUNOV EXPONENT

We used Wolf et al.'s algorithm for the determination of the largest Lyapunov exponent; see [Wolf85] and [Tata91b] for explanations and details. We calculated the largest Lyapunov exponent for a variety of values of most parameters involved. In the case of stock returns, a total of 409,230 exponents were computed. In particular, it is important to say that we did our calculations for the entire data sets, and then for two subsamples of the data sets. The results are presented in Figure 1 for the stock returns and Figure 2 for the Dollar/Deutsche Mark exchange rate. It is clear from Figure 1 that the largest Lyapunov exponent for the stock returns is zero, the asymptotic value of the Lyapunov exponent (LYAP) as the number of points on the time axis (NPT) tends to large values in Figure 1. As shown in the figure, the calculation has been repeated for subsamples containing 5,000 and 15,000 data points.

Figure 2 is particularly interesting, because it illustrates how the results depend on the number of data points used. Had we based our investigation on the subsample with 15,000 data points, we might have concluded that the largest Lyapunov exponent is marginally positive, and therefore that chaos might well exist in Forex data. The calculation repeated with 20,408 data points gives, though, a different result; the largest Lyapunov exponent is now found to be marginally negative. The only conclusion we can draw is that there is in these results no indication of chaos whatsoever.

THE CORRELATION DIMENSION

For a detailed account of what we are doing here, see [Tata91a, 91b; Vass90] (and references therein). We calculate the correlation integral, $C_n(r)$, the number of pairs of n-dimensional 'reconstructed' data points that are at a distance, r, from each other, divided by the number of all possible pairs in each n-dimensional

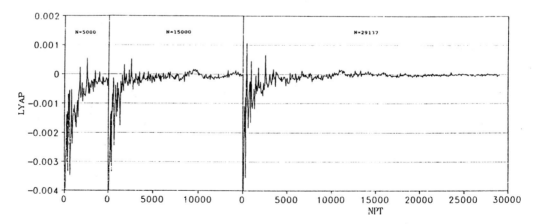

Figure 1. Lyapunov exponent for New York Stock Exchange data from samples of 5,000 and 15,000 points and the full set of 29,137 data points.

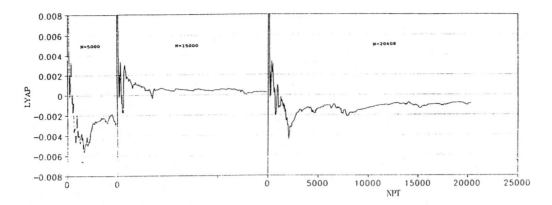

Figure 2. Lyapunov exponent for Dollar/Deutsche Mark data from samples of 5,000 and 15,000 points and the full set of 20,408 data points.

'reconstructed' space, $n = 1, 2, \cdots, 10$. If the data is the result of chaotic dynamics, then $C_n(r) \sim r^{d_n}$ and the power, d_n, reaches a saturation limit, d, as n increases.

Numerical results by Ramsey and Yuan [Rams89] and some general theoretical considerations indicate that for as long as the sample size is too small for an accurate determination of d_n to be possible, d_n decreases as the number of data

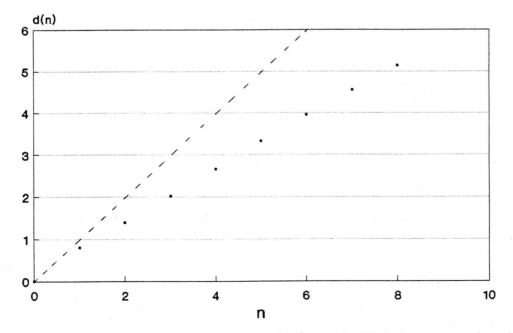

Figure 3. Correlation dimensions for 4,584 Dollar/Deutsche Mark data points; dotted line indicates random walk behaviour.

points in the sample increases. Figure 3 shows results obtained with 4,584 Dollar/Deutsche Mark Forex quotes. It is interesting to note that after shuffling the values of d_n coincide with the dotted line indicating the random walk behaviour on this graph. Clearly no saturation, and therefore no evidence of chaos, exists. To strengthen this point, we repeated the calculations with a larger number of data points. Figure 4 shows the results for 20,000 quotes. Beyond 10,000 quotes, d_n is found to no longer decrease with increasing sample size, and according to Ramsey and Yuan we can infer that our value of d_n is quite accurate when more than 10,000 Dollar/Deutsche Mark quotes are used. Saturation is also not seen in Figure 4. Figure 5 shows results for the Dollar/Swiss Franc spot exchange rates, and again, with 32,200 data points, no evidence of chaos is found. To our knowledge this is the largest and highest quality data set ever used in a search for chaos in economic series.

The Lack of Evidence for Chaos in Economic Data

In the past six years various economic time series have been tested for low-dimensional chaos; see Tata and Vassilicos [Tata91b] for a list of examples. The results of these studies differ; some claim evidence of chaos, others find no such evidence. A priori these results are not inconsistent, because they apply to different markets. However, all these studies (with the exception of one which we will discuss in the sequel) are performed on less than 1,000 data points.

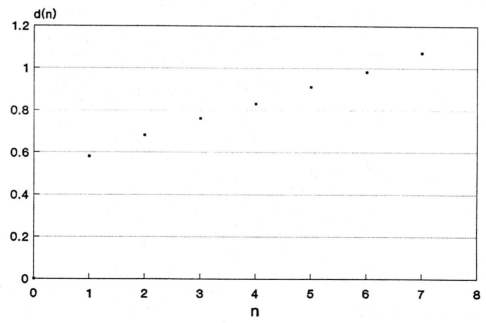

Figure 4. Correlation dimensions for 20,000 Dollar/Deutsche Mark data points.

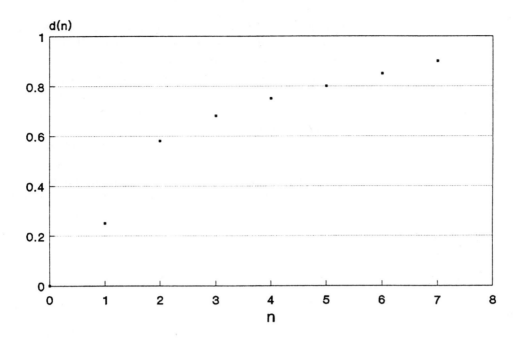

Figure 5. Correlation dimensions for 32,200 Dollar/Swiss Franc data points.

According to Wolf et al. [Wolf85], to detect a chaotic attractor of dimension 3, at least 1,000 to 30,000 data points are needed. Ramsey and Yuan [Rams89] found that 5,000 data points is a lower bound for the detection of chaos on some simple dynamical systems known to display chaotic behaviour in certain regimes. Finally, specifically for the correlation dimension test, Smith [Smit88] showed that if the data set is small, d_n appears to converge towards a finite value, d, even in the absence of chaos.

Scheinkman and LeBaron [Sche89] claimed the existence of economic chaos on the basis of 5,200 daily stock returns which are a subset of the 29,137 daily stock returns that we used in the present study. In effect, they aggregate their series to obtain a weekly returns series in order to reduce the noise level. Quality of the data is an additional requirement, as is the quantity of the data, for a successful detection of chaos. This leaves them with 1,040 data points; they perform the various tests for chaos on that weekly series. On a data set which incorporates the sample used by Scheinkman and LeBaron [Sche89], we demonstrated in the previous section, and more fully in our previous papers, that when we use smaller and smaller samples of the data set, the largest Lyapunov exponent can be different from 0. Our smallest sample had 5,000 quotations. For a straightforward critique of Scheinkman and LeBaron's 1989 evidence for chaos, see [Ruel90].

We therefore believe that all the previous investigations of chaos in economic time series were not fit to demonstrate the presence of chaos. In all, there exists no convincing evidence of chaos in economics to date, despite thorough examination of at least two markets, the Foreign Exchange and the Stock Exchange.

The High Frequency Multifractal Structure of Quotation Times

As was implied in the introduction, Forex price variations are increasingly non-Gaussian as the frequencies sampled are higher. Multifractal distributions have this property, and they apply to signals with scaling characteristics (see [Fris91; Fede88]), as the ones studied here may well have, e.g., see Peters [Pete89] for a study of the fractal property of capital markets. In fact, multifractal statistics originated, in part, from the study of fully developed turbulence in fluids, where a similar and quite well-documented phenomenon called intermittency exists. The statistics of turbulent velocity fluctuations are also increasingly non-Gaussian, since the frequency or wave number of these fluctuations is higher. Multifractals were used recently to describe, account for and even model intermittent turbulent velocity fluctuations (see [Vass92; Fris91] and references therein).

Here we report the preliminary phase of our research on multifractals in the Forex markets, and only consider the series of quotation times, t_n. n is an integer indicating the order in the succession of announcements, and t_n are the times of these announcements. In this respect the questions we ask here are reduced to two:

Is the set of points, t_n, on the time axis a fractal set, i.e., is the distribution in time of these announcements characterised by some sort of scaling? In other words, is there a statistical similarity between the distribution of groups of points t_n, these groups having a given time span, and the distributions of subgroups or of the points themselves within the extent of one of these groups?

If the t_n are indeed distributed in some fractal way, is this fractal distribution homogeneous? That is, is this distribution fractal or is it multifractal in the sense that different fractal scalings may apply at different times?

For a discussion of what one can conclude from the use of fractal and multifractal algorithms we refer, respectively, to [Vass91] and [Vass92]. We will return to this question briefly at the end of this section.

The algorithm we use is as follows (see [Fede88] for further explanations): We cover the time axis with a grid of points separated by a fixed distance, ϵ, from each other. We label each interval between grid points with an integer, i, and calculate the total number of announcements, μ_i, that lie within the interval i. Then compute the quantity

$$N_q(\epsilon) = \sum_i \mu_i^q \qquad (1)$$

for various integers q; here $q = 0, 2, 3, 4$. When $q = 0$, this quantity is nothing but the number of boxes of size ϵ needed to cover the points t_n. When the distribution of t_n is fractal in some sense, K-fractal in the terminology of Vassilicos and Hunt [Vass91], then $N_0(\epsilon) \sim \epsilon^{-D_0}$ for ϵ small enough (though larger than the average distance between the points t_n) and $0 < D_0 \le 1$. D_0 is called the fractal dimension and characterises the fractal scaling structure of the set. When D_0 is close to 0, the points t_n do not fill the time axis at any scale at which the time axis can be resolved. In fact when $D_0 = 0$, the points t_n are essentially distributed regularly, in a statistical sense. When $D_0 = 1$, the fractal is said to be space filling, because it fills the time axis at all relevant scales without regularity.

If there exists a power D_0 characterising the scaling property of $N_0(\epsilon)$, there also exist powers τ_q such that

$$N_q(\epsilon) \sim \epsilon^{-\tau_q} \tag{2}$$

for ϵ small enough and for integer values of q. Note that $\tau_1 = 0$, and that the generalised dimensions, D_q, are defined by

$$D_q = \frac{\tau_q}{1-q} \tag{3}$$

It is possible to show [Fede88] that $1 \geq D_0 \geq D_1 \geq D_2 \geq \cdots \geq 0$. When the set is a homogeneous fractal, i.e., it has the same scaling behaviour at all times, then $0 \neq D_0 = D_1 = D_2 = \cdots$, etc. If this is not the case, then the set is 'multifractal', or, in other words, not a homogeneous fractal. Before shedding more light on the meaning of these concepts, we now present some preliminary results.

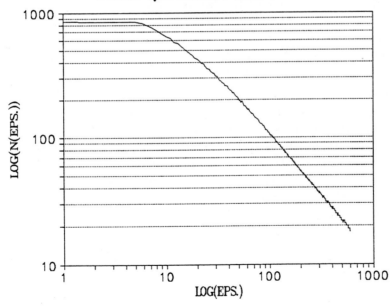

Figure 6. A typical log-log plot of $N_0(\epsilon)$ against ϵ for quotation times in the Forex market.

Figure 6 shows a typical log-log plot of $N_0(\epsilon)$ versus ϵ. The curve on this graph can be fitted very well with a power law, $N_0(\epsilon) \sim \epsilon^{-\tau_0}$, $\tau_0 = 0.88 \pm 0.004$, over a range between $\epsilon = 6$ sec and $\epsilon = 600$ sec, to within 99.8% of the 594 entries on the graph. Many graphs similar to Figure 6 were obtained by covering more than 80 Asian mornings from 1:00 A.M. to 4:00 A.M. British Summer Time. The graphs have one-dimensional grids of intervals of length ϵ between 6 and 600 seconds. Every one of these graphs was fitted very well with a power law, and thus well-defined values of τ_0 were obtained for each of these days. A wide variability was observed from day to day, with τ_0 fluctuating between 0.53 and 0.9. Figure 6 corresponds to only one of these mornings.

An example of a result for $q = 2$ (see Eq. 2), i.e., a log-log plot of $N_2(\epsilon)$ versus ϵ, is given in Figure 7. Remarks similar to those for Figure 6 can be made for this figure: a very well-defined power law is observed, again in the range between 6 sec and 600 sec, with, in the case of Figure 7, $\tau_2 = -0.87 \pm 0.002$ to within 99% of the entries on the graph. This implies, from Eq. (3), that $D_2 = 0.87 \pm 0.002$, which is strictly smaller than $D_0 = 0.88 \pm 0.004$, from Figure 6. Both graphs are from the same Asian morning.

Figure 8 shows the values of D_q for four values of q. This figure corresponds to a different Asian morning than Figures 6 and 7, thus illustrating the variability of the generalised dimensions, D_q, from day to day. On the other hand, the black boxes in Figure 8 give the magnitude of the statistical errors on the values of D_q

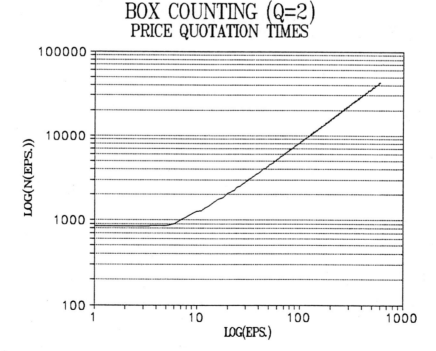

Figure 7. A typical log-log plot of $N_2(\epsilon)$ against ϵ for quotation times in the Forex market.

for a given day, thus indicating how well-defined these dimensions are within an Asian morning.

A fractal is homogeneous only if D_q is the same for all q, which we have not observed in any of the 80 or so Asian mornings we studied. When the fractal is not homogeneous, D_q is strictly decreasing with increasing q, as is the case here (see Figure 8). We conclude, therefore, that the high frequency distribution of quotation times has a multifractal structure within time intervals of less than 10 minutes (6 to 600 seconds).

This conclusion implies one of two things, or in principle even both: either the quotation times are multifractal in the Hausdorff sense (H-fractal [Vass92, 91]), in which case they should be viewed as distributions in time of different fractal sets of points, like the Cantor set of different Hausdorff dimensions [Fede88]. Or they are 'multifractal' in the sense discussed by Vassilicos ([Vass92], 'multispiral'). In that case the set of quotation times consists of different accumulating patches of points with different Kolmogorov capacities, or box dimensions [Vass91]. For example, the generalised dimensions, D_q, of the set of point intersections with the t-axis of a function, $p(t) = \sin(t^{-a})$, $0 < a$, which is an accumulating oscillation towards $t = 0$, are $D_q = 1/(1 + a) \neq 0$. A superposition of different such functions with different values of a gives nontrivial values of D_q, such that D_q is strictly decreasing with increasing q.

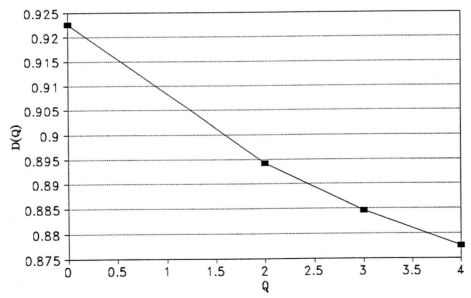

Figure 8. Generalised dimensions D_0, D_2, D_3 and D_4 of quotation times during a typical morning in the Forex market.

Figure 9a shows Dollar/Deutsche Mark spot exchange rate fluctuations within an interval of three hours on June 14, 1989, between 1:00 A.M. and 4:00 A.M. British Summer Time. As it is, it reminds one of a Weierstrass function [Fede88], and therefore has fractal and maybe even multifractal properties in the Hausdorff sense. But the multifractal behaviour we identified is not within such large time intervals; Figure 9b shows a blow up of an interval of slightly less than 25 minutes within Figure 9a. Accumulating oscillations seem to exist at these time scales. A subsequent blow up of a time interval of roughly 10 minutes within Figure 9b, seen in Figure 9c, seems to strengthen this observation. It is indeed within time intervals of less than 10 minutes that we observed the multifractal structure of quotation times. Our results may reflect very high frequency oscillatory changes of prices following private or maybe even public news (see [Good89]). This is an hypothesis to be tested in the future. Also, the structure of the entire time series of spot rates (not only the quotation times — see Figure 9a) may well have a multifractal structure in a different sense (Hausdorff?), characterising the market at lower frequencies. This question is addressed in the forthcoming paper by Demos and Vassilicos [Demo92].

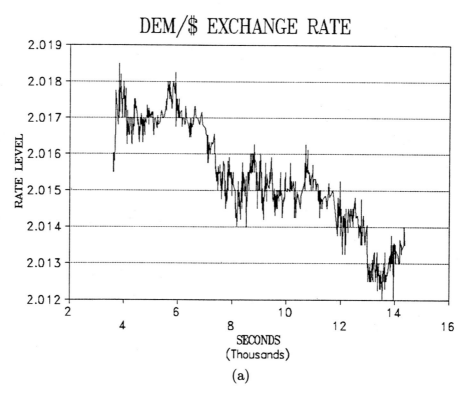

(a)

Figure 9. Dollar/Deutsche Mark exchange rates for June 14, 1989 over different intervals. (a) A three hour interval; (b) a 25 minute interval; (c) a 10 minute interval.

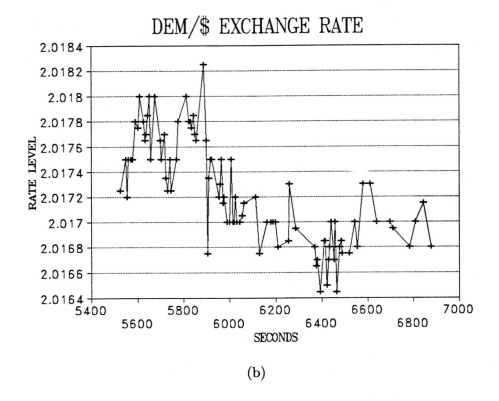

(b)

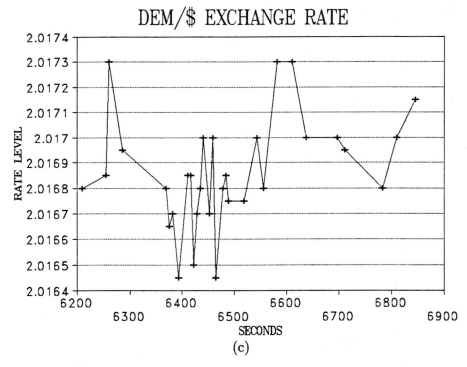

(c)

Figure 9. (*Continued.*)

Conclusion

It has been suggested that the departure from Gaussianity of the high and medium frequency fluctuations in Forex prices may be due to low-dimensional deterministic chaos. We pointed out that tests for chaos require an enormous number of data points, and that previous studies of chaos in economic data from various markets failed to comply with this requirement. We then presented a summary of our own results, obtained from the largest, to our knowledge, data sets in any study of chaos in economic series to date. Three data sets were used, which hold from 20,000 to 32,000 entries each, from the Forex and the stock markets. No evidence of chaos was found.

Rather than attempting an explanation of the high frequency non-Gaussian character of Forex price fluctuations, we initiated a study of whether, and to what extent, multifractals can describe and characterise the type of non-Gaussianity found in these fluctuations. Here we report preliminary results indicating that the set of quotation times of the Dollar/Deutsche Mark spot exchange rates has a multifractal structure within time intervals of less than 10 minutes. This structure may be a reflection of very high frequency oscillatory changes of prices from one local equilibrium to another following private, or perhaps even public, news. More work is under way [Demo92].

Acknowledgments. We thank Professor C.A.E. Goodhart for making the Reuters data available to us, for his interest and support, and for numerous discussions that have had a clear imprint in our research. This work has been done under the auspices of the Financial Markets Group of the London School of Economics.

REFERENCES

[Dass91]
  Dassios, A., and Demos, A., Some econometric tests on real time forex market data, Discussion Paper in Financial Economics, Birkbeck College, May 1991.

[Demo92]
  Demos, A., and Vassilicos, J.C., The multifractal structure of high frequency forex price fluctuations, Financial Markets Group Discussion Paper, London School of Economics, submitted for publication.

[Fede88]
  Feder, J., *Fractals*, New York: Plenum Press, 1988.

[Fris91]
  Frisch, U., From global scaling, *à la* Kolmogorov, to local multifractal scaling in fully developed turbulence, *Proc. Roy. Soc. London Ser. A*, Vol. 434, pp. 89–99, 1991.

[Good88]
  Goodhart, C., and Figliuoli, L., Every Minute Counts In Financial Markets, Preprint . . . . . London School of Economics, 1988.

264   J.C. Vassilicos, A. Demos and F. Tata

[Good89]
Goodhart, C.A.E., 'News' and the foreign exchange market, Paper presented at the Manchester Statistical Society, 17 October 1989.

[Good91]
Goodhart, C.A.E., and Demos, A., Reuter's screen images of the foreign exchange market: The yen/dollar and the sterling/dollar spot market, *Jour. Int. Securities Markets*, Vol. 5, pp. 35–41, 1991.

[Gras83]
Grassberger, P., and Procaccia, I., Characterisation of strange attractors, *Phys. Rev. Lett.*, Vol. 50, pp. 346–349, 1983.

[Pete89]
Peters, E., Fractal structure in the capital markets, *Financial Analysis Jour.*, Vol. 45, July/August, pp. 32–37, 1989.

[Rams89]
Ramsey, J.B., and Yuan, H.-J., Bias and error bars in dimension calculations and their evaluations in some simple models, *Phys. Lett. A*, Vol. 134, No. 5, pp. 287–297, 1989.

[Ruel90]
Ruelle, D., Deterministic chaos: The science and the fiction, *Proc. Roy. Soc. London Ser. A*, Vol. 427, pp. 241–248, 1990.

[Sche89]
Scheinkman, J.A., and LeBaron, B., Nonlinear dynamics and stock returns, *Jour. of Business*, Vol. 62, No. 3, pp. 311–337, 1989.

[Schw90]
Schwert, G.W., Indexes of United States stock prices from 1802 to 1987, *Jour. of Business*, Vol. 63, pp. 399–426, 1990.

[Smit88]
Smith, L.A., Intrinsic limits on dimension calculations, *Phys. Lett. A*, Vol. 133, No. 6, pp. 283–288, 1988.

[Take85]
Takens, F., Distinguishing deterministic and random systems, in *Nonlinear Dynamics and Turbulence*, Barenblatt, G.I., Ioss, G., and Joseph, D., Boston: Pitman, 1985.

[Tata91a]
Tata, F., Is the foreign exchange market characterised by nonlinearity?, Financial Markets Group Discussion Paper 118, London School of Economics, 1991.

[Tata91b]
Tata, F., and Vassilicos, J.C., Is there chaos in economic time series? A study of the stock and the foreign exchange markets, Financial Markets Group Discussion Paper 120, London School of Economics, 1991.

[Vass90]
Vassilicos, J.C., Are financial markets chaotic? A preliminary study of the foreign exchange market, Financial Markets Group Discussion Paper 86, London School of Economics, 1990.

[Vass91]
Vassilicos, J.C., and Hunt, J.C.R., Fractal dimensions and spectra of interfaces

with application to turbulence, *Proc. Roy. Soc. London Ser. A*, Vol. 435, pp. 505–534, 1991.

[Vass92]

Vassilicos, J.C., The multispiral model of turbulence and intermittency, in *Topological Aspects of the Dynamics of Fluids and Plasmas*, Moffatt, H.K., Zaslavsky, G.M., Tabor, M., and Comte, P., Dordrecht, Netherlands: Cluwer Academic Publishers, 1992.

[Wolf85]

Wolf, A., Swift, J.B., Swinney, H.L., and Vastano, J.A., Determining Lyapunov exponents from a time series, *Physica*, Vol. 16D, pp. 285–317, 1985.

Spatio-temporal Evolution of Disturbances in Boundary Layer Transition

Jonathan J. Healey

Abstract

A wind tunnel experiment is performed in which the boundary layer over a flat plate is excited using a loudspeaker embedded near the leading edge of the plate. Hot wire anemometry is used to study the evolution of the disturbances as they convect downstream. A phase portrait reconstruction technique is applied to the data sets taken from successive downstream locations. The boundary layer is assumed to behave like a nonlinear transfer function, which in turn is modelled as a chain of coupled nonlinear oscillators. Radial basis functions are used to fit parameters to the oscillators directly from the experimental data.

Introduction

The drag on a solid object moving through a fluid is much greater when the fluid is turbulent than when it is laminar. There are innumerable practical applications of this fact, and yet relatively little is known of the fundamental principles which govern the transition from a laminar to a turbulent flow. It may be that chaos theory is relevant to this process.

In low viscosity fluids such as air or water, where relatively high Reynolds number flows are often obtained, the concept of the boundary layer, first originated by Prandtl [Pran04], is very important. The fluid must satisfy a 'no-slip' boundary condition when it is in contact with a solid surface. At high Reynolds numbers most of the fluid travels at the speed of the free stream, and only the fluid close to the solid is slowed appreciably. It is this thin layer of fluid clothing the solid's surface which is called the boundary layer, and it is the boundary layer which contributes substantially to the drag.

Nonlinear partial differential equations which describe the boundary layer can be derived from the Navier-Stokes equations in the limit of large Reynolds number, Re.[†] The simplest case to study is the boundary layer with zero pressure gradient, e.g., over a flat plate. Blasius [Blas08] was the first to obtain the steady

---

[†]This derivation is not given here but is well established in the literature.

laminar solution to the flat plate boundary layer equations. However, although the laminar Blasius profile can be confirmed experimentally at low Re,[†] at higher Re this steady solution gives way to time-dependent turbulent flow.

Linear stability analysis is the study of the behaviour of small perturbations from a given solution. For example, consider the simple pendulum consisting of a weight attached to a rigid rod which is free to rotate in a vertical plane about one end (with damping). When the pendulum hangs vertically downwards, it is in a linearly stable equilibrium state; that is, if it is given a small angular displacement then it tends to return to its original position. If the damping is small, then the motion is an exponentially decaying harmonic oscillation. This is shown using the familiar linearisation, $\sin \theta \approx \theta$. When the pendulum is hanging vertically upwards, it is in a linearly unstable state. Any arbitrarily small angular displacement grows exponentially, and the pendulum falls.

A linear stability analysis was first performed on the Blasius solution by Tollmien [Toll29] and Schlichting [Schl33]. Their work predicted that for Re > Re_c, where Re_c is a critical Reynolds number, there exists a finite range of wave numbers which are linearly unstable and so are expected to grow exponentially. It was not until Schubauer and Skramstad [Schu47] were able to build a wind tunnel with sufficiently low free stream turbulence intensity that the Tollmien-Schlichting waves were observed experimentally. Confusion concerning the exact nature of the instability was finally resolved by Gaster [Gast62], who showed that the waves grow exponentially in space but not in time, i.e., the instability is *convective* rather than *absolute*.

The Tollmien-Schlichting mechanism explains the selective amplification of wave numbers for infinitesimal disturbances. However, as the disturbances grow the effects of nonlinearity become more significant. Ultimately, turbulent flow is obtained which is strongly nonlinear and highly unpredictable. Thus, if we are to understand the transition process from laminar to turbulent states, it is necessary to use data analysis techniques that describe the nonlinear spatial convective nature of the boundary layer.

In this paper we present a method for analysing experimental data in a way that incorporates the essential features outlined above. In the next section we describe the experimental arrangement, including how controlled, reproducible disturbances are introduced into the boundary layer. A brief summary of the experimental results is then presented. The experimental time series are interpreted by projecting them onto a reconstructed phase space. A novel technique employing radial basis functions is used to fit nonlinear models to the reconstructed attractors from neighbouring streamwise locations in the boundary layer. This method, which enables us to capture the spatial evolution of disturbances as well as the temporal behaviour, is described in the section on data analysis techniques. The results of analysing the experimental data sets in this way are then presented, and in the final section the conclusions are given.

[†]The laminar profile is not confirmed explicitly here but is well established in the literature.

The Experiment

EXPERIMENTAL ARRANGEMENT

The experiments were carried out on a flat plate which was mounted vertically in the 0.914 m × 0.914 m working section of Gaster's small closed-return research wind tunnel in Cambridge. The wind tunnel was designed to have extremely low levels of background turbulence so that the behaviour of controlled excitations would not be masked. This was achieved through the use of a 5 mm-deep paper honeycomb followed by four fine mesh screens. The r.m.s. turbulence intensity at the inlet of the working section was 0.008% of the free stream velocity, 18 m/s, within the frequency range 4–4000 Hz. The plate and flap arrangement were set up to achieve an essentially zero pressure gradient over the region where measurements were made.

A hot wire anemometer was mounted on a computer-controlled traversing system attached to the side panel of the tunnel, enabling three-dimensional movement of the probe. The electrical signal generated by a DISA 55M01 constant temperature anemometer unit was processed by a low-noise pre-amplifier and band pass filter of range 4–4000 Hz. The resulting signal was then digitised by a 12-bit Analogue to Digital (A–D) converter, fitted with a further computer-controlled amplification stage.

The excitation of the flow was provided by a small buried loudspeaker that communicated with the boundary layer by a small hole 200 mm from the leading edge on the centre line of the plate. Some noise was inevitably generated by the presence of the driving hole, but by interposing some felt material between the loudspeaker and the hole this was reduced to an acceptable level.

Motivated by the work of Gaster [Gast90], we chose for our excitation signal a sine wave with added white noise. The frequency of the sine wave was 200 Hz, placing it within the band of amplified Tollmien-Schlichting waves. The noise was obtained by adding computer-generated random numbers to the sine wave, and thus was exactly reproducible (they were calculated using an algorithm from Press et al. [Pres86]). The purpose of adding this noise was to 'drown out' the ubiquitous low-level background noise, effectively making the broad band component of the signal reproducible. This is important because Gaster [Gast90] demonstrated that breakdown can occur through the nonlinear coupling of the fundamental driving frequency and the broad band excitations always present.

The A–D converter collecting the data was phase locked with the D–A converter driving the loudspeaker with the computer-generated signal. A sample frequency of 8192 Hz was used, giving approximately 40 points per cycle of the sine wave. This high frequency is necessary to obtain good phase portrait reconstructions (see the section on data analysis techniques).

EXPERIMENTAL PROCEDURE

The experiment basically consisted of collecting hot wire signals from various locations directly downstream from the source. All the hot wire signals were obtained with the wire located at a nondimensional distance, $\eta = 1.5$, from the plate. η is equal to $1.72\sqrt{xU/\nu}$, where x is the distance from the leading edge, U is the free stream speed and ν is the kinematic viscosity. This value of η corresponds to the strongest maximum of the Tollmien-Schlichting eigenfunctions, i.e., the distance from the plate at which the amplitude of the Tollmien-Schlichting waves is greatest.

The hot wire anemometer signals were taken at 50 mm intervals from 300 mm to 1100 mm from the leading edge of the plate. At each station, sixty realisations were averaged to improve the signal-to-noise ratio. This is possible because the signals are highly reproducible, thus random fluctuations can be reduced. The standard deviation of the different realisations is monitored to check that a satisfactory level of reproducibility is maintained.

Experimental Results

The ensembled time series are close to sinusoidal over the upstream part of the plate, but further downstream the time series become increasingly modulated and complicated (see Figure 1). Power spectra were calculated at each x position and plotted as an isometric graph (see Plate 19).

The fundamental 200 Hz component is clearly visible, as are its first harmonic and a subharmonic broad band. In Figure 2 the linear stability of the wave

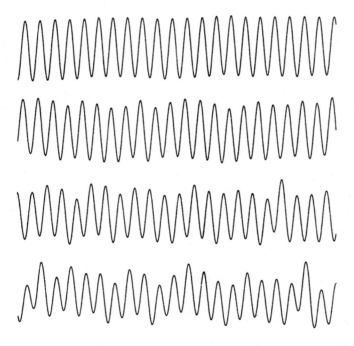

Figure 1. Hot wire signals taken at different streamwise locations showing the progressive increase in complexity.

number–Reynolds number parameter space is shown. The wave number and Reynolds number are both made nondimensional with respect to the boundary layer displacement thickness and so increase down the plate as the boundary layer grows. The region enclosed within the neutral stability curve, NN', is unstable, while the area outside is stable. A 200 Hz disturbance propagates along the ray AB shown in Plate 19, and a 400 Hz disturbance propagates along the ray CD. The points A and C correspond to the location of the driving hole, and the crosses correspond to the locations at which measurements were made.

At the driving hole, a 200 Hz signal decays while the 400 Hz signal grows. The forcing mechanism is itself likely to be nonlinear, and any harmonic distortion is amplified by the boundary layer close to the hole. However, at the first measuring sites a 200 Hz signal is now amplified; it is the 400 Hz signal which decays. The behaviour of the spectra for the data nearest the leading edge is thus consistent with the linear theory. The 200 Hz signal is observed to grow in amplitude, and the first harmonic, arising from nonlinear distortion at the driving hole, is observed to decay rapidly.

Beyond the first few measurement positions, the first harmonic starts to grow. This is clearly incompatible with the linear theory and represents a regime where the effects of nonlinearity are becoming significant. Further downstream, the broad band component increases in amplitude. This is consistent with the linear theory, and one sees from Figure 3 that the broad band component starts to become dominant. However, unlike some of the spectra observed by Gaster

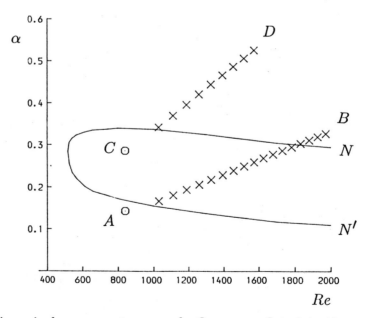

Figure 2. Dimensionless parameter space for flow over a flat plate; the wave number is measured along the vertical axis, the Reynolds number along the horizontal axis. 'O's mark the location of the driving hole, and 'x's mark the measurement stations.

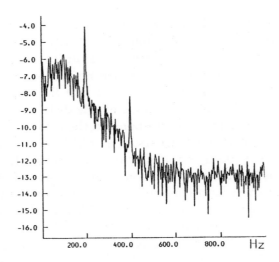

Figure 3. Power spectrum from furthest down the plate.

[Gast90], the broad band is not arranged symmetrically about the fundamental frequency, suggesting that the nonlinearity in this case is 'weak'.

Power spectra can become difficult to interpret when nonlinearities are important. For example, the simple set of nonlinear ordinary differential equations

$$\dot{x} = -y - z$$
$$\dot{y} = x + ay$$
$$\dot{z} = b + xz - cz \qquad (1)$$

known as the Rossler model (see [Ross76]), has an irregular chaotic solution for parameter values $a = b = 0.2$, $c = 5$. The power spectrum for the x solution shown in Figure 4 consists of broad band components punctuated by harmonics of the fundamental frequency. This complicated power spectrum belies the simplicity of the Rossler model.

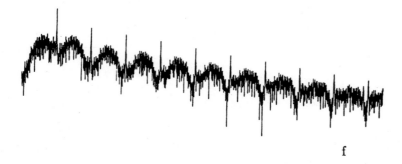

Figure 4. Power spectrum from the Rossler model.

The appropriate representation of a nonlinear evolution is in its phase space. The phase space is defined so that each axis corresponds to an independent variable describing the state of the system. The instantaneous state of the system is therefore represented by a point in phase space, and its evolution corresponds to a trajectory in phase space. The flow of points in phase space, and the geometry of the distribution of these points, characterise the dynamics of the system under study. For instance, the flow in phase space obtained by treating the state variables (x, y, z) in the Rossler model as position vectors when plotted (see Figure 5) gives a much clearer insight into the behaviour than the corresponding power spectrum shown in Figure 4. The object shown in Figure 5 is called a phase portrait.

Many new techniques for the analysis of irregular signals from deterministic systems have been developed in the field of nonlinear dynamical systems theory. In the next section we discuss an important technique for reconstructing phase space. This technique then forms the basis for an approach developed specifically for problems in which convective instability, such as in the boundary layer, plays an important role.

Data Analysis Techniques

PHASE PORTRAIT RECONSTRUCTION

Takens [Take81] was the first to prove that, provided certain generic conditions are met, it is possible to reconstruct a multidimensional phase portrait from a single time series. Such a phase portrait is related to the true phase portrait by a smooth invertible mapping, and hence the important geometric information is preserved. The method he prescribes is to place a window over n elements of the time series, $\{x_i\}_{i=1}^{N}$. The elements of the window then form the components of a position vector in the reconstructed phase space

$$\vec{x}_i = (x_i, x_{i+1}, x_{i+2}, \ldots, x_{i+n-1})^T \tag{2}$$

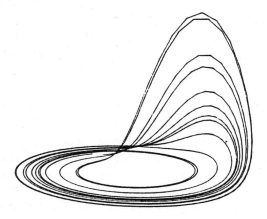

Figure 5. Phase portrait of the Rossler model.

n should be large enough that the window 'sees' a significant portion of the time series. The first minimum of the autocorrelation function provides a convenient time scale over which the elements in the position vector are decorrelated. It is plausible that such a vector characterises the state of the system, since it captures the instantaneous evolution; for a deterministic system the evolution is uniquely determined by its state.

However, in order to produce a phase portrait like the one shown in Figure 5, the time series must be highly sampled or the lines connecting the points will be long and the phase portrait will be jagged in appearance. Experience indicates that a smooth portrait is obtained provided the sample frequency is of order 40 times that of the highest frequency component that is of interest.

The Nyquist sampling criterion says that a sample frequency of twice the highest frequency component captures all the available information. Hence, there is a significant redundancy in our over-sampled time series. This is expressed by saying that the matrix of position vectors (the trajectory matrix)

$$[X] = \begin{bmatrix} x_1 & x_2 & x_3 & \cdots & x_n \\ x_2 & x_3 & x_4 & & x_{n+1} \\ \vdots & & & & \\ x_i & x_{i+1} & x_{i+2} & & x_{i+n-1} \\ \vdots & & & & \\ x_{N-n+1} & x_{N-n+2} & x_{N-n+3} & & x_N \end{bmatrix} \tag{3}$$

is rank deficient. The 'method of delays' overcomes this problem by arbitrarily deleting columns from X. A typical n-dimensional position vector is then of the form $(x_i, x_{i+\tau}, x_{i+2\tau}, \ldots, x_{i+(n-1)\tau})^T$.

The method of delays is the easiest phase portrait reconstruction technique to implement, but when dealing with experimental data it has certain limitations. Different projections yield identical phase portraits, e.g., a plot of x_i versus $x_{i+\tau}$ yields the same portrait as a plot of $x_{i+\tau}$ versus $x_{i+2\tau}$. A more serious consequence is that since the noise is isotropic the arbitrary deletion of columns does not improve the signal-to-noise ratio.

A method proposed by Broomhead and King [Broo86] elegantly solves the problem of rank deficiency of the trajectory matrix. The rank of a rectangular matrix is properly determined by using 'singular value decomposition' (SVD) (see Press et al. [Pres86]). SVD gives three matrices, two of which are relevant here: a diagonal matrix with nonnegative diagonal elements (the singular values), and a square orthonormal matrix whose columns (the singular vectors) span the row space of the rectangular matrix. The singular values give a measure of the energy associated with each singular vector. If the matrix is singular, then at least one of the singular values is zero and the corresponding singular vector(s) span the null space of the original matrix. The effects of noise prevent the trajectory matrix from being strictly rank deficient, but it nonetheless is ill-conditioned because of the high sample frequency. SVD is used to determine the basis of smallest dimension which contains the most information. This basis is then orthogonal to the directions spanned only by noise. Hence, in the resulting basis the data has an optimal signal-to-noise ratio. It is this systematic treatment of experimental noise which makes the method of Broomhead and King so attractive.

The singular vectors can be thought of as representing wave forms which occur frequently in the time series and can be interpreted in terms of the principle axes of inertia of the distribution of points (see [Heal91] for further discussion). A graph of the singular values and singular vectors obtained from a hot wire time series is shown in Figure 6. There are a small number of singular values significantly above the noise. The first two are of almost equal energy, and the corresponding singular vectors look like a pair of sine and cosine waves. They have a period equal to half the window length and hence have a frequency of 200 Hz, since the window length is equal to the first minimum of the autocorrelation function. This most energetic pair is associated with the fundamental driving frequency of the excitation forcing the boundary layer. The additional singular vectors have shapes reminiscent of successively higher-order polynomials.

The energy of each singular vector is proportional to the square of the corresponding singular value. Thus, over 99.9% of the energy of the time series is contained within the first three singular vectors. Figure 7a shows the original time series. Figures 7b–d show the time series obtained by projecting onto the first, first two and first three singular values. Figures 7b and c are similar to

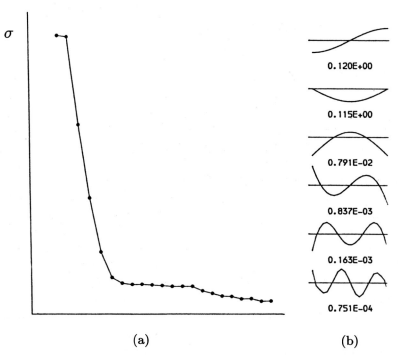

(a)   (b)

Figure 6. Singular values and singular vectors obtained from a hot wire time series. (a) The singular values on a log plot; (b) the first six singular vectors.

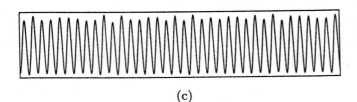

(a)

(b)

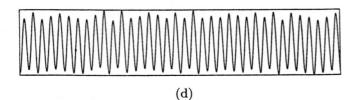

(c)

(d)

Figure 7. Example of the filtering effects of SVD. (a) The experimental time series; the time series reconstructed from the (b) first, (c) first + second and (d) first + second + third singular vectors.

one another, and both are clearly filtered versions of the original time series — the extrema have been rounded off. However, Figure 7d very closely resembles the original time series, confirming that the first three singular values do indeed capture the significant components of the time series.

The three-dimensional phase portrait is shown in Figure 8a. The basic circling motion is a consequence of the nearly sinusoidal nature of the time series. A Poincaré section through this phase portrait is shown in Figure 8b. There is no evident structure. Thus, the phase portrait seems to give no further insight into the behaviour of the boundary layer. The difficulty occurs because the boundary layer is excited by a nonperiodic, random forcing. Although the forcing is reproducible, from the point of view of dynamical systems it is nondeterministic; hence, the response of the boundary layer is also nondeterministic. 'Natural' transition is also fed by small stochastic disturbances. What is needed is an understanding of the way in which these disturbances evolve in time and space as they propagate through the boundary layer. As discussed in the section on experimental results, their evolution is well understood when the amplitudes are small and the linear theory applies. We now describe a method for studying the nonlinear evolution of disturbances.

COUPLED NONLINEAR OSCILLATORS

The boundary layer can be thought of as a nonlinear transfer function which takes one signal as an input (the forcing) and then generates an output signal (a hot wire time series). The transfer function must be extremely rich and complicated, since it can give rise to turbulence. As such it poses a daunting problem to analyse. However, it can be decomposed into a set of smaller transfer functions, each of which modifies the signal in a less drastic way.

The boundary layer is divided up into a chain of black boxes, each of which is regarded as an oscillator taking a signal from an upstream location as its forcing, and whose solution is the signal at some downstream location. Thus, the ith oscillator takes the output of the $(i-1)^{\text{th}}$ oscillator as its forcing, and its own output is the forcing for the $(i+1)^{\text{th}}$ oscillator. If the oscillators are all linear, then the accumulative effect of N such oscillators is also linear. But if nonlinear oscillators are chosen, then the combined effect can be very strongly nonlinear, with the potential for highly complicated behaviour, including chaos. Such a chain, in principle, is capable of describing the nonlinear spatio-temporal

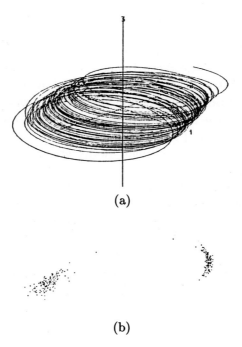

(a)

(b)

Figure 8. The three-dimensional phase portrait; (a) The reconstructed phase portrait; (b) a Poincaré section through the 3D phase portrait.

evolution of disturbances in the boundary layer, and indeed any other flow in which convective instability plays a major role.

Casdagli [Casd89] gives a review of methods for constructing nonlinear models which operate in the domain of the phase space reconstructed from a single time series. The novel variation here is that the nonlinear models are constructed from a *pair* of time series, which are taken from neighbouring streamwise locations in the boundary layer.

Consider, for example, the forced Duffing equation

$$a\ddot{x} + b\dot{x} + c_1 x + c_3 x^3 = F \cos \omega t \tag{4}$$

Given a model (the LHS) and the forcing (the RHS), the problem is then to find the solution, $x(t)$. Here we solve the *inverse* problem where, given the solution, $x(t)$, and the forcing, $f(t)$, we must deduce the parameters of the model. This is feasible, since for any given (unknown) oscillator we know the forcing and the solution — they are the upstream and downstream hot wire data sets, respectively.

The solution data set is projected onto an optimised set of basis vectors calculated from the singular value decomposition of the trajectory matrix to give a set of position vectors, $\vec{x}_i$. The forcing data set is then projected onto the same basis to give a set of position vectors $\vec{y}_i$. A model of the form

$$\vec{x}_{i+1} = \vec{f}(\vec{x}_i) + \vec{y}_{i-k} \tag{5}$$

where
$$\vec{x}, \vec{y}, \vec{f} \in \mathcal{R}^m \tag{6}$$

and m is the embedding dimension (three, in this case). k is a phase lag accounting for the time taken for the disturbance measured at the upstream location to convect to the downstream location. The function, $\vec{f}$, describes the temporal evolution, i.e., the next point depends on the current point. The inclusion of the forcing term, $\vec{y}$, models the spatial evolution, i.e., what happens at one location depends on what happened at an upstream location.

A vexed question is: what nonlinear model should be chosen? There is an infinite number of choices, many of which can turn out to be inappropriate to the data. In addition, we do not want an exact fit, we want a fit that averages out the effect of noise. There are many possible approaches, but a type of nonlinear model that gives much flexibility is that of 'radial basis functions'. Radial basis functions can be thought of as a generalisation of splines to higher dimensions. They have good localisation properties, and under certain circumstances they exactly reproduce particular types of function (see [Powe90, 85]) for details.

Basically, the function is made up from a sum of functions which are each radially symmetric about a different point

$$f_j(\vec{x}_i) = \sum_{l=1}^{p} \omega_{lj} \phi\Big(\|\vec{x}_i - \vec{x}_l\| \Big) \qquad \phi : \mathcal{R}^+ \mapsto \mathcal{R} \tag{7}$$

where $\| \cdot \|$ denotes the Euclidean norm and $\{\vec{x}_l\}_{l=1}^p$ is a set of p centres. This is analogous to constructing an arbitrary potential from a set of point charges (this case corresponds to a radial basis function, $\phi(r) = 1/r$). Radial basis functions are a powerful tool in multidimensional analysis because they are so easily extended to arbitrary dimension. Thus, substituting Eq. (7) into Eq. (5) and rearranging gives

$$(\vec{x}_{i+1} - \vec{y}_{i-k})_j = \sum_{l=1}^{p} \omega_{lj}\, \phi\left(\|\vec{x}_i - \vec{x}_l\|\right) \tag{8}$$

There are N such simultaneous equations for the N data points $\vec{x}_i$ and $\vec{y}_i$. In matrix form they are written

$$\underbrace{[X]}_{N \times m} = \underbrace{[\Phi]}_{N \times p}\, \underbrace{[\Omega]}_{p \times m} \tag{9}$$

where the LHS of Eq. (8) is the ij^{th} element of the LHS of Eq. (9).

It is not known a priori what functional form ϕ should take, but often used are the choices

$$\phi(r) = r^3$$
$$\phi(r) = r^2 \ln r$$
$$\phi(r) = \left(r^2 + a^2\right)^{1/2}$$
$$\phi(r) = \left(r^2 + a^2\right)^{-1/2} \tag{10}$$

Here we tried all four functions to see if there is any significant difference between them for our particular application. The solution of Eq. (9) is given by

$$[\Omega] = [\Phi]^+\, [X] \tag{11}$$

where $[\Phi]^+$ is the pseudoinverse of $[\Phi]$ and is calculated from its singular value decomposition, i.e.

$$[\Phi] = [S]\, [\Sigma]\, [C]^T \implies [\Phi]^+ = [C]\, [\Sigma]^{-1}\, [S]^T \tag{12}$$

where $[C]$ and $[S]$ are orthonormal and $[\Sigma]$ is diagonal with elements σ_i. If $[\Phi]$ is singular, then $[\Sigma]^{-1}$ is replaced by $[\Sigma]^+$, whose elements are given by

$$\sigma_i^+ = \begin{cases} \sigma_i^{-1} & \text{if } \sigma_i \neq 0 \\ 0 & \text{if } \sigma_i = 0 \end{cases}$$

When analysing experimental data, $[\Phi]$ never is exactly singular but can be ill-conditioned, so it is convenient to introduce a level of tolerance, ε, and use

$$\sigma_i^+ = \begin{cases} \sigma_i^{-1} & \text{if } \sigma_i > \varepsilon \\ 0 & \text{if } \sigma_i < \varepsilon \end{cases}$$

The use of SVD provides a least-squares solution which is ideally suited to this type of over-determined and yet near-singular problem (see [Crut87]).

It is important that the method be robust with respect to noise. If there are enough free parameters ($p = N$) then it is possible to produce an exact fit (if the centres are suitably chosen) between the model and the data. However, the parameters of such a model are very sensitive to the effects of noise, and it can give an extremely poor representation of the true dynamics. This overfitting manifests itself by causing $[\Phi]$ to be rank deficient, i.e., there exist degeneracies amongst the columns of $[\Phi]$.

One solution is to increase ε so that, for example, only the first r singular values are used. This reduces the number of independent parameters and so, in effect, reduces the number of centres used. Or we can simply choose fewer centres in the first place and have $p < N$. If fewer centres are chosen then the actual distribution of centres can become important — if centres are sparse in a particular region of interest, then the model is disadvantaged. In addition, even if fewer centres are used $[\Phi]$ can still be rank deficient. In practise, both r and p are varied in order to find a good fit.

To test the quality of the fit, a model is deduced from the first 2000 data points from the forcing and solution time series. Then the model is iterated for the next 2000 points of the forcing, and the r.m.s. error between the actual solution and the predicted solution is calculated. Thus, the error index is calculated using an independent test of the model.

Previous workers, e.g., Farmer and Sidorowich [Farm87], reported difficulties with iterating a fitted model many times — small errors in the model can grow exponentially, and the predicted time series diverges from the true time series. There are two features of our method which overcome this problem. First, the 2000 points used to construct the model are chosen so as to include the section where the driving excitation is turned on, i.e., both forcing and solution data sets have a constant section followed by a short 'rise time' as the oscillation sets in, and then a section where forcing is at full strength. In this way the model experiences transients and explores the phase space surrounding the attractor, thus emphasising the asymptotic nature of the data. Secondly, the presence of the forcing in the iterated model is often observed acting to constrain the generated output and prevent it from diverging.

Nonetheless, divergent models are sometimes created, often when too high a rank, r, is chosen for $[\Phi]$. These models are dismissed as 'bad' models, and another choice of p and r is made. If up to p centres are chosen, then of order p^2 models have to be calculated to find the best model, i.e., the one which has minimum error index and best predicts the evolution of an unseen data set. This rapidly becomes computationally prohibitive, especially if we wish to analyse many different data sets and to investigate different types of radial basis function (Eq. 10).

However, the study of radial basis functions as interpolants was originally motivated by the problem of minimising a multivariable function which is expensive to compute (see [Powe85]). The problem of finding the most suitable nonlinear function which smooths out the effects of noise is thus expressed as minimising the error index with respect to p and r (the column dimension and rank of the pseudointerpolant matrix, $[\Phi]$, respectively). The procedure is to calculate the error index for values of (p, r) up to p_{max} and for $r \leq p$, where p and r are incremented in steps of 3, thus reducing by a factor of 9 the number of models to be calculated. Radial basis functions are then fitted to the surface defined by treating the error index as a height over the p, r plane. A search is then made for the minimum value of the radial basis function approximation to the error index for integer values of p, r. The true value of the error index is then calculated at this point; and the radial basis function interpolant is then recalculated, including the new estimate for the minimum. This iterative process is repeated until the true minimum of the error function is located.

Use of this interpolation technique significantly reduces computation time — only a relatively sparse initial search is made, and then successive estimates tend to cluster around the minimum. If the radial basis function interpolant throws up a spurious estimate that is far from the true minimum, then this is quickly corrected when the true value of the function at this point is included in the interpolation scheme. An exact interpolation is required, so centres are placed at all of the points on the p, r plane, where the error function was calculated. We chose $\phi(r) = (r^2 + a^2)^{1/2}$ where a is the order of the separation of points; other choices are also possible, but this one works satisfactorily.

We were able to set $p_{max} = 100$. For this value of p the minimum value of the error index was not sensitive to the actual distribution of points, although its location on the p, r plane can vary. In addition, we experimented using polynomial functions to augment the space of functions spanned by the radial basis functions (see [Powe85]).

Analysis of Hot Wire Signals

The techniques presented in the previous section have been applied to the data sets discussed in the section on experimental results. Here we treat the linear model obtained from using no centres and first-order polynomial functions only as providing the 'bench mark' against which the nonlinear models should be tested. The linear model simply attempts to adjust the phases and amplitudes of the harmonic components present. However, it should not be confused with the more familiar spectral linear transfer function, where the complex Fourier transform of the output signal is divided by the transform of the input signal. In such a representation, the N data points from each signal are replaced by N transfer function coefficients — $N/2$ spectral amplitude ratios, $a(\omega)$, and $N/2$ phase differences, $\phi(\omega)$. There is no compression of information, but the method is operationally useful provided the system being modelled is truly linear.

The linear models generated by the method used for coupled nonlinear oscillators contain very few coefficients and can be thought of as fitting simple curves, which give the functional dependence of a and ϕ vs. ω. Hence there is a large compression of information, but the output generated by the model is not identical to the true output.

A comparison between an experimental time series and the time series generated using an upstream data set to force a linear model deduced from the data is shown in Figure 9. At the left hand side a section of the time series showing the switching on of the driving excitation is seen. Figure 9a shows how well this transient section is modelled. The two time series then diverge a little, but, as can be seen from Figure 9b, they remain close for some time.

When nonlinear models are constructed using radial basis functions the error indices are improved by $\lesssim 15\%$. This is a relatively modest improvement and reflects the fact that the flow is only weakly nonlinear. Nonetheless, the technique is not confined to linear or weakly nonlinear data sets, and current work is dedicated to exploring its limits of applicability.

Conclusions

Experiments were performed in a low turbulence intensity wind tunnel. Hot wire anemometry was used to study the evolution of controlled disturbances which could be introduced into the boundary layer near the leading edge of a flat plate. A novel signal processing technique was presented which uses new ideas currently being developed in dynamical systems theory. The approach is based on treating the boundary layer as a chain of coupled nonlinear oscillators which operate in the domain of reconstructed phase spaces. Radial basis functions are used for the oscillators, and their coefficients are determined from pairs of upstream and downstream data sets using singular value decomposition.

Radial basis functions are used again to evaluate how best to average out the presence of experimental noise — they are used to minimise an error index which judges an oscillator's ability to predict an unseen data set. The method has been shown to work successfully in the case of a weakly nonlinear nearly-sinusoidal driving excitation.

Work is now starting on a new series of experiments where different types of forcing will be used. Of particular interest is an excitation consisting of a set of impulses, or delta functions. Each impulse has a broad band Fourier spectrum and so explores the full range of linear behaviour. In addition, the impulses will have varying amplitudes enabling the exploration of nonlinear phenomena as well. Ultimately it is our intent to make simultaneous measurements at a set of streamwise locations. In this way it may be possible to model the irregular chaotic dynamics observed before full turbulence ensues.

Acknowledgments. This work has benefited immeasurably from discussions with Professor M. Gaster and members of the Transition Research Group in Cambridge. I also express gratitude to Dr. D.S. Broomhead and Dr. L. Smith for their encouragement and interest shown in this project. This work was supported by the Science and Engineering Research Council (S.E.R.C.).

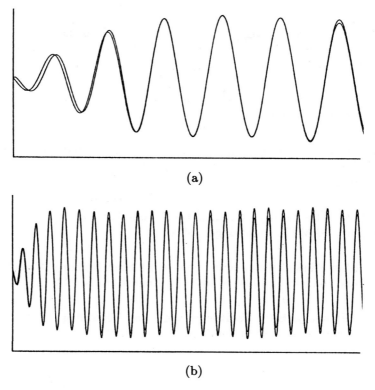

(a)

(b)

Figure 9. A comparison between an experimental time series and the time series obtained by iterating the model. (a) The first 250 records; (b) the first 1000 records.

REFERENCES

[Blas08]
  Blasius, H., Grenzschichten in Flüssigkeiten mit kleiner Reinbung, *Zeit. Math. Phys.*, Vol. 56, pp. 1–37 (English transl. in NACA TM1256), 1908.

[Broo86]
  Broomhead, D.S., and King, G.P., Extracting qualitative dynamics from experimental data, *Physica*, Vol. D20, p. 217, 1986.

[Casd89]
  Casdagli, M., Nonlinear prediction of chaotic time series, *Physica*, Vol. D35, pp. 335–356, 1989.

[Crut87]
  Crutchfield, J.P., and McNamara, B.S., Equations of motion from a time series, *Complex Systems*, Vol. 1, pp. 417–452, 1987.

[Farm87]
  Farmer, J.D., and Sidorowich, J.J., Predicting chaotic time series, *Phys. Rev. Lett.*, Vol. 59, No. 8, pp. 845–848, 1987.

[Gast62]
  Gaster, M., A note on the relation between temporally-increasing and spatially-increasing disturbances in hydrodynamic stability, *Jour. Fluid Mechs.*, Vol. 14, pp. 222–224, 1962.

[Gast90]
Gaster, M., The nonlinear phase of wave growth leading to chaos and breakdown to turbulence in a boundary layer as an example of an open system, *Proc. Roy. Soc. London Ser. A*, Vol. 430, pp. 3–24, 1990.

[Heal91]
Healey, J.J., "Qualitative Analysis of Experimental Time Series", Ph.D. dissertation, Oxford University, 1991.

[Powe85]
Powell, M.J.D., Radial basis functions for multivariable interpolation: A review, *Proc. IMA Conf. on 'Algorithms for the Approximation of Functions and Data'*, RMCS Shrivenham, 1985.

[Powe90]
Powell, M.J.D., 'The Theory of Radial Basis Function Approximation in 1990', Internal Report, DAMTP, Cambridge, 1990.

[Pran04]
Prandtl, L., Uber Flüssigheitbewegung bein sehr kleiner Reibung, *Proc. 3rd Inter. Math. Congress*, Heidelberg 1904, p. 484–491, English transl. NACA TM452, 1928.

[Pres86]
Press, W.H., Flannery, B.P., Teukolsky, S.A., and Vetterling, W.T., *Numerical Recipes*, Cambridge, UK: Cambridge Univ. Press, 1986.

[Ross76]
Rossler, O.E.. An equation for continuous chaos, *Phys. Lett. A*, Vol. 57, pp. 397–398, 1976.

[Schl33]
Schlichting, H., Zür entstehung der turbulenz bei der Plattenströmung, *Nachr. Ges. Wiss. Goett., Math. Phys.*, pp. 181–208, 1933.

[Schu47]
Schubauer, G.B., and Skramstad, H.K., Laminar boundary layer oscillations and stability of laminar flow, National Bureau of Standards paper 1772. Reprint of confidential NACA Report dated April 1943 (later published as NACA War-time Report W-8) and *JAS*, Vol. 14, pp. 69–78, 1947; see also NACA Rep. 909, 1947.

[Take81]
Takens, F., *Detecting Strange Attractors in Turbulence*, Lecture Notes in Mathematics, 898, p. 366 in *Dynamical Systems and Turbulence* (Warwick), Rand, D.A., and Young, L.-S., Eds., Berlin: Springer-Verlag, 1981.

[Toll29]
Tollmien, W., Über die entstehung der turbulenz, *Nachr. Ges. Wiss. Goett.*, pp. 21–44 (English transl. NACA TM 609, 1929.

Chaotic Motion of a Rotor System With a Bearing Clearance

Richard D. Neilson and Diane H. Gonsalves

Abstract

Clearance in mechanical systems can be caused by a variety of phenomena, including wear or poor tolerance of parts. In dynamic systems the presence of such clearances generally is to introduce strong nonlinearities in the form of discontinuous stiffnesses. These, in turn, give rise to the possibility of impacts and chaotic responses over regions of the parameter space.

This paper describes the numerical investigation of the response of a rotor system which has a bearing clearance effect. Initially the mathematical model of the system, consisting of two discontinuously nonlinear equations of motion, is presented, and the numerical techniques used to solve these are described. Benchmarks for the various computer systems used for the simulations are presented.

A number of chaos techniques were used to investigate the system, including spectral analysis, bifurcation diagrams, Poincaré maps and Lyapunov exponents. Examples of phase plane diagrams and Poincaré maps for periodic, quasi-periodic and chaotic responses of the system are given, along with bifurcation diagrams and spectral data showing the regions over which these different motions exist.

Introduction

In many mechanical systems, clearance between moving parts is present. This can be a design feature to ensure adequate passage of lubricants or allow relative motion between adjacent parts, but it can also be induced by wear or poor tolerance of manufactured parts. No matter how such clearances occur within systems, they can introduce strong nonlinearities into the equations governing the motion of the system. In general, these are likely to be of the form of discontinuous stiffnesses, as shown in Figure 1, although other effects, e.g. changes in damping, can also occur. The presence of these nonlinearities has implications on the response of the system which can be unforeseen if simple linear models are used.

In recent years a number of researchers have investigated the response of systems with such clearance effects. Work on the effects of clearances on the 'rattling' of unloaded gear wheels in gearboxes was undertaken by Pfeiffer [Pfei88a, 88b, 84] and by Kunert and Pfeiffer [Kune89]. This included the study of chaotic

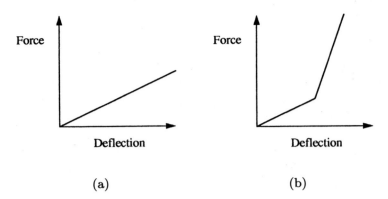

Figure 1. Stiffness characteristics. (a) Linear; (b) nonlinear.

phenomena [Pfei88b] and stochastic modelling of the system [Kune89]. Investigations into the response of rotor systems with clearance have also been reported. In the main, these have centred around 2-degree of freedom dynamical models of the rotor and the study of periodic and quasi-periodic motion [Kim90; Ehri88; Day85; Chil82]. Kim and Noah [Kim90], in reporting their investigation of a rotor system, noted the possibility of chaotic motion. One of the authors has also published numerical and experimental data on 4- and 6-degree of freedom systems [Neil88a, 88b, 88c, 87]. Although the possibility of chaos in the response of these systems was noted [Neil88a, 87, 86], the complexity of these systems and high dimension of the phase space (9 and 13 dimensions, respectively) restricted the ease of investigating such complex phenomena. As a consequence, the numerical investigation of a simpler 2-degree of freedom model which allows asymmetry of the clearance is presented here.

Mathematical Model of a Rotor System with Clearance

One of the simplest models which can be obtained for a rotor system is the Jeffcott model, which describes the motion of a rigid rotor on an elastic support, or a disk mounted centrally on a flexible shaft. The equations of motion for this system are

$$m\ddot{x} + c\dot{x} + k_1 x = m\rho\Omega^2 \cos\Omega t$$
$$m\ddot{y} + c\dot{y} + k_1 y = m\rho\Omega^2 \sin\Omega t$$

These are linear equations governing the motion of the rotor or disk. In the presence of clearance, however, these equations become modified to include the discontinuously nonlinear terms. For the case under consideration here, it is assumed that the rotor is suspended within an elastically supported ring with a radial clearance, g, between the ring and the outer surface of the rotor, as shown in Figure 2.

In modelling the clearance effect, certain assumptions and simplifications have been made. These include assuming that the ring can be represented by stiffness

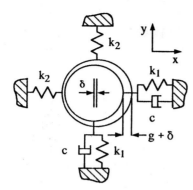

Figure 2. Dynamic model of a rotor system with clearance.

only, and that there are no inertia effects. Secondly, the effect of dry or sliding friction between the massless ring and the rotor has been neglected at this stage. Introducing this would modify the effective stiffness in the two directions during contact.

To allow for possible asymmetry in the system, the ring can be offset by an amount, δ, relative to the original equilibrium position of the rotor. Obviously, if δ exceeds the radial clearance, g, then when at rest the rotor is continuously in contact with the ring and possibly offset from its original position. The equations of motion governing the motion of the rotor while in contact are

$$m\ddot{x} + c\dot{x} + k_1 x + k_2(x - \delta) - k_2\left\{ \frac{g(x - \delta)}{\sqrt{(x - \delta)^2 + y^2}} \right\} = m\rho\Omega^2 \cos\Omega t$$

$$m\ddot{y} + c\dot{y} + k_1 y + k_2 y - k_2\left\{ \frac{gy}{\sqrt{(x - \delta)^2 + y^2}} \right\} = m\rho\Omega^2 \sin\Omega t$$

or alternatively, the system can be summarised as

$$\ddot{x} + 2\nu\omega_1\dot{x} + \omega_1^2 x = \Omega^2\rho\cos\Omega t$$

$$\ddot{y} + 2\nu\omega_1\dot{y} + \omega_1^2 y = \Omega^2\rho\sin\Omega t$$

for $R \leq g$ and

$$\ddot{x} + 2\nu\omega_1\dot{x} + \omega_1^2 x + \omega_2^2\left\{ (x - \delta)\left(1 - \frac{g}{R}\right) \right\} = \Omega^2\rho\cos\Omega t$$

$$\ddot{y} + 2\nu\omega_1\dot{y} + \omega_1^2 y + \omega_2^2\left\{ y\left(1 - \frac{g}{R}\right) \right\} = \Omega^2\rho\sin\Omega t$$

for $R > g$, where

$$\omega_1 = \sqrt{\frac{k_1}{m}}$$

$$\omega_2 = \sqrt{\frac{k_2}{m}}$$

$$R = \sqrt{(x - \delta)^2 + y^2}$$

and the two sets of equations are valid only for the ranges of motion specified. The equations have not been nondimensionalised, since part of the project is to compare the simulations presented here with the results of on-going experimental work. In the following cases, $\rho = 6.067 \times 10^{-5}$ m.

Numerical Solution Techniques

Because of the discontinuous form of the equations of motion for the system, the feasibility of obtaining closed form analytical or even approximate solutions is reduced. Furthermore, since the purpose of the investigation was to study chaotic motion for which no closed form solution could be sought, recourse was made to numerical solution of the equations of motion.

The discontinuous nature of the equations, however, also leads to difficulties in the numerical techniques used to solve for the response. Because the two sets of equations of motion govern the system only for particular ranges of motion, the system must be solved in a piecewise manner, using the appropriate equations depending on the current state of the system. Within usual numerical integration techniques, the functions evaluated to produce the solution of the system can change within a single time-step of the integration if simple 'IF THEN' type switching techniques are utilised. Borthwick noted that this leads to a severe drop in the order of convergence of the method used [Bort84]. As a consequence, care must be exercised in finding precisely the time at which the equations of motion must be changed before continuing the solution using the revised equations of motion.

The computational methods used during this investigation were based on those described by Borthwick [Bort84] and subsequently developed by one of the authors [Neil86]. These are based on the classical fourth-order Runge-Kutta algorithm, with an additional midstep approximation given by

$$y_{n+1/2} = \frac{h}{4}\left(K_1 + K_2\right)$$

Although of lower-order accuracy, this is utilised in interpolation procedures to locate precisely in time the point of contact between the rotor and the massless ring.

A flow diagram of the logic used during a single time step is shown Figure 3. To check for the point of contact, a function called a discontinuity function, which has a zero value at the point of contact between the rotor and the ring, has been formulated. At the end of each time-step the program calls a subroutine, which checks if the value of the function has either changed sign or remained at a value close to zero. If either case is indicated, then a hierarchy of interpolation subroutines is called to establish the time of contact within a known spatial tolerance. In most cases, a tolerance of 10^{-9} m or smaller has been used. Within the structure, quadratic interpolation is used for well-conditioned cases, with linear interpolation being used if this fails. A bisection routine accounts for any

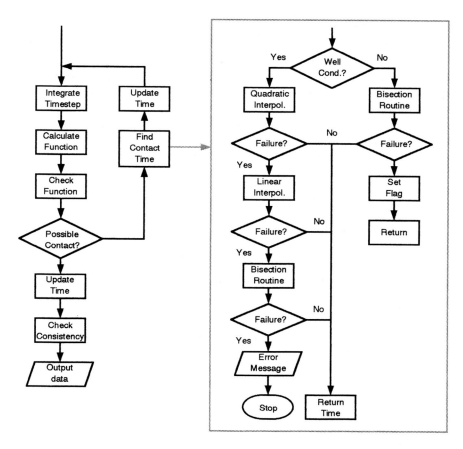

Figure 3. Flow diagram of the numerical simulation procedures.

badly conditioned sets of points, and also for cases where a local extremum is present within the time-step. A checking subroutine has also been incorporated into the main program, to check if the flags, which indicate which system of equations is being integrated, and the actual state of the system are consistent. If they get out of step, the program terminates before erroneous data is produced.

Computer Benchmarks

Because of the numerically intensive solution techniques employed, computational speed has been at a premium for this investigation. Benchmarks for the various machines available to run the simulations have been undertaken and are shown in Table 1. The results show the obvious advantage of utilising the HP720 platform, which has a substantial performance advantage over even the local mainframe machine (SUN 4/470). Reports suggest that the upgrade to HP-UX 8.05 will further increase floating point performance, since the current compilers are not optimised for the 720 chip set. In addition, the HP's graphics capability is being used extensively.

Table 1. Computer benchmarks.

Machine	CPU	Operating System	Dhrystones	Whetstones (kWIPS)		LinPacks (MFLOPS)	
				Single	Double	Single	Double
HP 330	68020/881	HP-UX 7.03	4300	1703	1434	0.11	0.1
HP 720	PA RISC	HP-UX 8.01	80600	32370	28570	9.25	8.8
Sun 4/470	SPARC	SunOs 4.1	31700	14370	12407	4.95	3.12
Sun IPC	SPARC	SunOs 4.1	21200	8970	6321	2.86	1.64

Numerical Simulations

To give an overview of the system response, a variety of simulations have been undertaken using the system described above. The responses were subjected to various diagnostic techniques. Basically, the work can be split into three main sections dealing with the variation of forcing frequency, damping ratio and stiffness ratio.

VARIATION OF EXCITATION FREQUENCY RATIO

In rotor systems which may run at various shaft speeds, one of the most important aspects of the response to investigate is how the response changes as the shaft speed is varied. A number of simulations have been undertaken for various values of the system parameters and for a range of shaft speeds. In the discussions which follow, the shaft speed is quoted in terms of the frequency ratio between the shaft speed and the linear natural frequency of the system.

Figure 4 shows the response of the system with a clearance of 10m and an offset, δ, of 10m. Although physically this is an impractical case, it is useful in

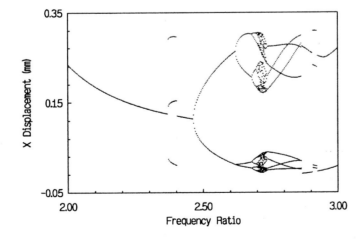

Figure 4. Bifurcation diagram for varying shaft speed, with $k_2/k_1 = 30$, $g = 10\,\mathrm{m}$, $\delta = 10\,\mathrm{m}$ and $\nu = 0.125$.

showing correlation between the rotor system and simpler single degree of freedom models, because, with this large radius of curvature of the ring, the motions
in the x and y directions become effectively uncoupled. The bifurcation diagram
shows the classical period doubling route through a series of flip bifurcations into
chaos, and then eventually stabilisation into a period two motion. Comparison
with a single degree of freedom model, which had been checked against published
data [Shaw83], shows good agreement in terms of the bifurcation points.

Of greater interest physically, however, are cases where the clearance is of a
size which is more likely to occur in real systems. Figure 5 shows the effect of a
reduction of the clearance to a value of $g = 0.5$ mm, while simultaneously maintaining contact with the ring by setting $\delta = 0.5$ mm. The resulting bifurcation
diagram shows a distinct change in form, with the motion changing from period
1 to an area where the points are dispersed across the phase space. A period
7 solution is then established over the range $2.52 < \Omega/\omega_1 < 2.57$. Beyond this
region a series of bifurcations occur, and the response changes back to filling
a region of the phase space before stabilising on a period 2 motion at about
$\Omega/\omega_1 = 2.6$. As the frequency ratio is further increased, a set of bifurcations
from period 2 to 4 and back to 2 are apparent. Figure 6 shows an expanded view
of the region from $2.44 < \Omega/\omega_1 < 2.64$, showing the transitions into and out of
the periodic regimes and the cascade of bifurcations more clearly.

Although the bifurcation diagrams give insights into where chaos can exist,
they are not definitive indicators of chaos. Consequently, the region of the parameter space which is filled and therefore may be chaotic has been subjected to
further analysis using spectral analysis, phase plane techniques, Poincaré maps
and Lyapunov exponents to distinguish what actual form the response has.

Figures 7–12 show examples of the response for two different shaft speeds.
Figures 7, 8 and 9 show the spectra, phase plane portraits and Poincaré sections
for $\Omega/\omega_1 = 2.48$. As can be seen from the spectrum, the motion is quasi-periodic

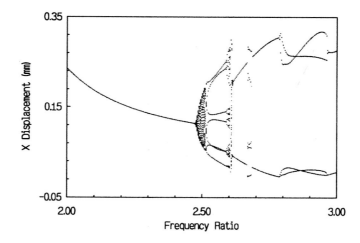

Figure 5. Bifurcation diagram for varying shaft speed over the range $2 < \Omega/\omega_1 < 3$,
with $k_2/k_1 = 30$, $g = 0.5$ mm, $\delta = 0.5$ mm and $\nu = 0.125$.

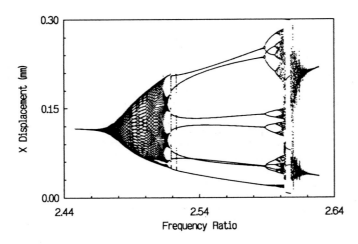

Figure 6. Bifurcation diagram for varying shaft speed over the range $2.44 < \Omega/\omega_1 < 2.64$, with $k_2/k_1 = 30$, $g = 0.5\,\text{mm}$, $\delta = 0.5\,\text{mm}$ and $\nu = 0.125$.

in nature, with a finite number of distinct spikes in the spectrum and with the characteristic closed loop on the Poincaré sections (Figure 9). Figures 10, 11 and 12 show the same data when $\Omega/\omega_1 = 2.55$. In this case, the very clear period 7 motion is obtained.

Calculation of the Lyapunov exponent for this system was complicated by two factors. First, because of the discontinuous nature of the equations, the system is nondifferentiable. Thus, the classical method of calculating the exponent cannot be used. In this case, the Lyapunov was estimated by first calculating a reference trajectory and then perturbing this at various points in the phase space. At each point the perturbed trajectory was allowed to propagate, and all four exponents were calculated. An average value for each was then obtained across the phase space. This is similar to the technique applied by Wolf et al. [Wolf85], except that, since all the phase space variables are available, there has been no need to reconstruct the attractor. Secondly, although the system is nonlinear in global

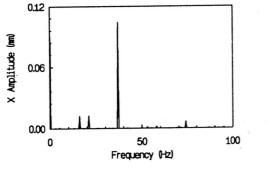
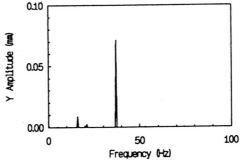

Figure 7. Spectra of the quasi-periodic response at $\Omega/\omega_1 = 2.48$, with $k_2/k_1 = 30$, $g = 0.5\,\text{mm}$, $\delta = 0.5\,\text{mm}$ and $\nu = 0.125$.

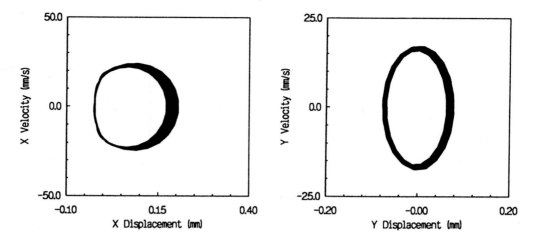

Figure 8. Phase plane portraits of the quasi-periodic response at $\Omega/\omega_1 = 2.48$, with $k_2/k_1 = 30$, $g = 0.5\,\text{mm}$, $\delta = 0.5\,\text{mm}$ and $\nu = 0.125$.

terms, during certain parts of the motion the system is linear and positively damped, i.e., it would give a negative exponent. As a result, care must be exercised in choosing the length of time over which the trajectories are allowed to propagate before estimating the exponent.

After further investigation, it appears that for this level of damping and gap virtually no chaotic motion exists over the frequency range. This is to some extent surprising, given the severity of the nonlinearity and the fact that impact systems in general have a propensity for exhibiting chaotic phenomena. Changes in system parameters were, therefore, made to the system to establish if chaos did occur, and if so in what regions of the parameter space.

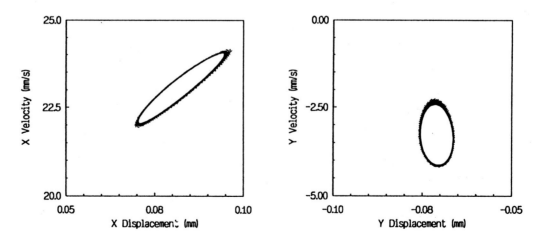

Figure 9. Poincaré sections of the quasi-periodic response at $\Omega/\omega_1 = 2.48$, with $k_2/k_1 = 30$, $g = 0.5\,\text{mm}$, $\delta = 0.5\,\text{mm}$ and $\nu = 0.125$.

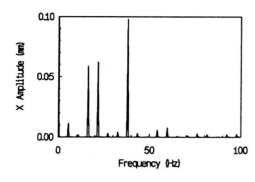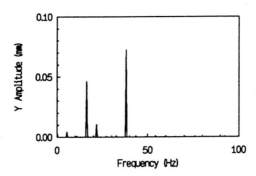

Figure 10. Spectra of the period 7 response at $\Omega/\omega_1 = 2.55$, with $k_2/k_1 = 30$, $g = 0.5\,\mathrm{mm}$, $\delta = 0.5\,\mathrm{mm}$ and $\nu = 0.125$.

VARIATION OF DAMPING RATIO

Damping is of great importance in determining the response of dynamical systems. In many physical systems it can also be difficult either to control or measure. This parameter has been subjected to investigations using bifurcation diagrams to give an overview of the form of the responses obtained.

Figure 13 shows the response when most of the system's parameters have been held at the same values but the damping has been reduced to $\nu = 0.1$. As can be seen, this change results in a distinct modification to the form of the response over the speed range. Although in the ranges $2 < \Omega/\omega_1 < 2.1$ and $2.7 < \Omega/\omega_1 < 3$ the response is basically the same, the region $2.12 < \Omega/\omega_1 < 2.23$ now has a dispersed structure before the period 1 regime is re-entered. Subsequently, at $\Omega/\omega_1 \approx 2.4$ period 3 motion is established with a series of bifurcations. A

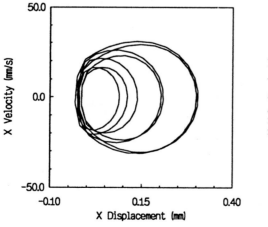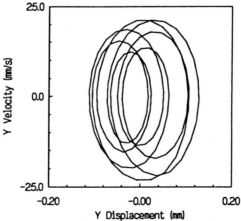

Figure 11. Phase plane portraits of the period 7 response at $\Omega/\omega_1 = 2.55$, with $k_2/k_1 = 30$, $g = 0.5\,\mathrm{mm}$, $\delta = 0.5\,\mathrm{mm}$ and $\nu = 0.125$.

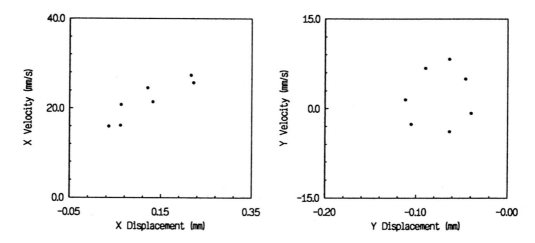

Figure 12. Poincaré sections of the period 7 response at $\Omega/\omega_1 = 2.55$ with $k_2/k_1 = 30$, $g = 0.5\,\text{mm}$, $\delta = 0.5\,\text{mm}$ and $\nu = 0.125$.

region of chaotic motion then exists over the range $2.55 < \Omega/\omega_1 < 2.65$. This was diagnosed through the use of Poincaré maps and Lyapunov exponent estimation.

Figures 14 to 16 show a sample of the chaotic motion at a value of $\Omega/\omega_1 = 2.555$. As expected, the spectra (Figure 14) show a wide band response with a clear spike at the excitation frequency, and, in the case of the x motion, two other large, well-defined spikes. The y motion has a single additional spike. The Poincaré maps (Figure 16), too, have the typical fractal pattern of a strange attractor. This is confirmed by the positive Lyapunov exponent ($\lambda = 0.106$) which differentiates it from being a strange but nonchaotic attractor [Kapi91]. Figures

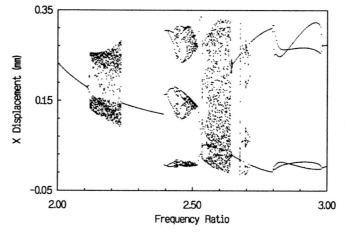

Figure 13. Bifurcation diagram with varying shaft speed, with $k_2/k_1 = 30$, $g = 0.5\,\text{mm}$, $\delta = 0.5\,\text{mm}$ and $\nu = 0.1$.

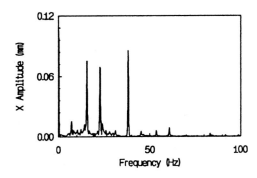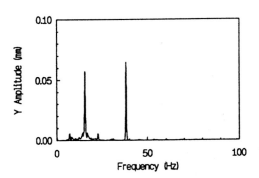

Figure 14. Spectra of the chaotic response at $\Omega/\omega_1 = 2.555$, with $k_2/k_1 = 30$, $g = 0.5\,\text{mm}$, $\delta = 0.5\,\text{mm}$ and $\nu = 0.1$.

17a–d show the variation in position and shape of this attractor throughout a forcing cycle at phases of 0°, 90°, 180° and 270°, respectively.

In order to assess the extent of the chaotic region within the parameter space, a series of bifurcation diagrams were produced using the damping ratio as the control parameter. Figure 18 shows the bifurcation diagram for the case where $\Omega/\omega_1 = 2.555$ and the damping ratio of the system has been varied from $0.075 < \nu < 0.125$. This case was chosen because it was known that chaotic motion occurred for $\nu = 0.1$. As can be seen, the chaotic motion exists over a large proportion of the parameter space, with stable period 5 and 7 motions and bifurcations present over the ranges $0.101 < \nu < 0.108$ and $0.121 < \nu < 0.125$.

Figures 19a–d show the form of the attractors over the range $0.075 < \nu < 0.1$ and at $\nu = 0.1125$. Despite the changes in damping level, the form of the

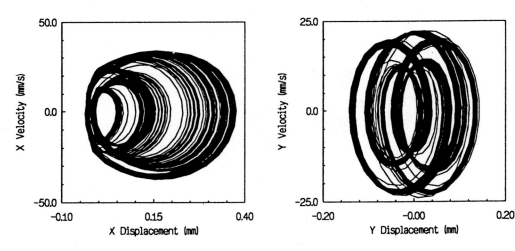

Figure 15. Phase plane portraits of the chaotic response at $\Omega/\omega_1 = 2.555$, with $k_2/k_1 = 30$, $g = 0.5\,\text{mm}$, $\delta = 0.5\,\text{mm}$ and $\nu = 0.1$.

attractor appears to change only gradually. The shape remains similar, but the dispersion of the trajectories decreases with increasing damping.

Another interesting aspect which became apparent during this phase of the work was the similarity in shape between some of the quasi-periodic attractors and the chaotic attractors, despite their being in different parts of the parameter space. Figure 20 shows the comparison between two of these attractors. Figure 20a is the chaotic response at $\Omega/\omega_1 = 2.555$, $\nu = 0.1125$ and $k_2/k_1 = 30$, while Figure 20b is a quasi-periodic motion obtained at $\Omega/\omega_1 = 2.5$, $\nu = 0.085$ and $k2/k1 = 36.6$.

The response is shown in a more concise form in Plate 20, which shows a three-dimensional view of the parameter space, where a bifurcation diagram has been plotted with varying damping and shaft speed along the axes. The view shows that the chaotic region extends across quite a large volume of the parameter space. In particular, at the lower damping levels large regions of chaos occur. From a practical standpoint this can be quite significant, since there are large regions where 'smooth running' of the rotor system is impossible.

VARIATION OF STIFFNESS RATIO

Another parameter which merits investigation in such systems is the stiffness ratio, i.e., the ratio of the initial stiffness of the elastic supports of the rotor to the secondary stiffness which is contacted. Although many investigators, e.g. [Shaw89; Whis87], utilise an impact model for convenience of analysis, this assumes an effectively infinite stiffness during the contact. In reality, any two surfaces coming into contact have some finite stiffness, even if this is very large. In addition, it is unlikely that chaotic or strange motion occurs with lower stiffness ratios, i.e., less severe nonlinearities. From a practical standpoint, it is important to be able to assess the regions within which approximate techniques,

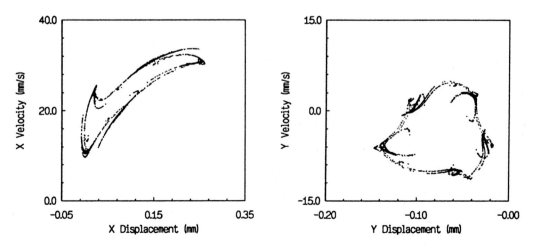

Figure 16. Poincaré sections of the chaotic response at $\Omega/\omega_1 = 2.555$, with $k_2/k_1 = 30$, $g = 0.5\,\text{mm}$, $\delta = 0.5\,\text{mm}$ and $\nu = 0.1$.

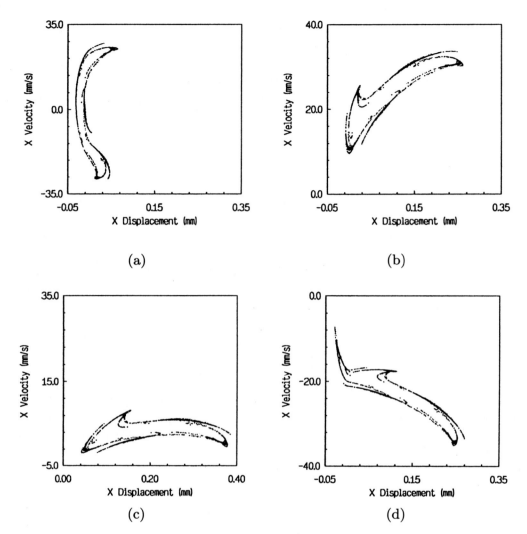

Figure 17. Poincaré sections of the response at $\Omega/\omega_1 = 2.555$, with $k_2/k_1 = 30$, $g = 0.5$mm, $\delta = 0.5$mm and $\nu = 0.1$ for (a) 0°; (b) 90°; (c) 180°; (d) 270° phase.

e.g., equivalent linearisation or harmonic balance, which assume certain forms of motion can be used to estimate the response of the system. Consequently, numerical tests have been undertaken to assess the effect of the stiffness ratio on the presence of chaos.

Figure 21 shows a bifurcation diagram in which the control parameter used was the stiffness ratio. The other parameters were fixed at the values shown. The shaft speed chosen ($\Omega/\omega_1 = 2.555$) is such that from the initial tests it was known that chaotic motion was present at a stiffness ratio of 30. As can be seen below, at a ratio of about 15.5 the motion is period 2, while above this there is a sudden transition into period 7 motion, followed by a series of flip bifurcations. A narrow band of unsteady motion occurs between $20 < k_2/k_1 < 23$, with a period

5 orbit established at $k_2/k_1 = 23$. Again, a series of bifurcations leads to chaos. Finally, a period 3 motion exists in the region around $33 < k_2/k_1 < 37$, with chaotic motion above about $k_2/k_1 = 39.5$. This is useful in showing that, for this level of damping, approximate solutions as used by Kim and Noah [Kim90] can be used for stiffness ratios less than 15. This is substantiated by the findings obtained from other numerical tests.

Discussion

Having established that a wide variety of responses can be elicited from a relatively simple nonlinear rotor system, an obvious issue which needs to be addressed from an engineering standpoint is whether the different types of response are more or less damaging to the system in terms of wear and fatigue. In general terms, the displacement of the rotor is approximately proportional to the stresses induced in the original supporting structure, while the deflection of the ring from its equilibrium position indicates the level of stress in the impacted structure. Although it is possible to look qualitatively at the responses and say whether chaotic motion results in larger deflections, as is the case when comparing Figures 15 and 11, some quantitative measure of damage is required. The next stage of this work is to subject the displacement time-histories from the numerical simulations and from current experimental investigations to standard cumulative fatigue damage criteria. It is hoped that this will lead to some assessment of whether chaotic motion is generally 'bad' for the system, or indeed possibly less damaging. Such results will be of use in life prediction of components, and also possibly in aspects of condition monitoring, particularly for large capital machinery, e.g., aeroengines [Carr90].

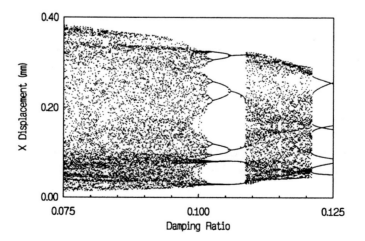

Figure 18. Bifurcation diagram with varying damping, with $k_2/k_1 = 30$, $g = 0.5$mm and $\delta = 0.5$mm.

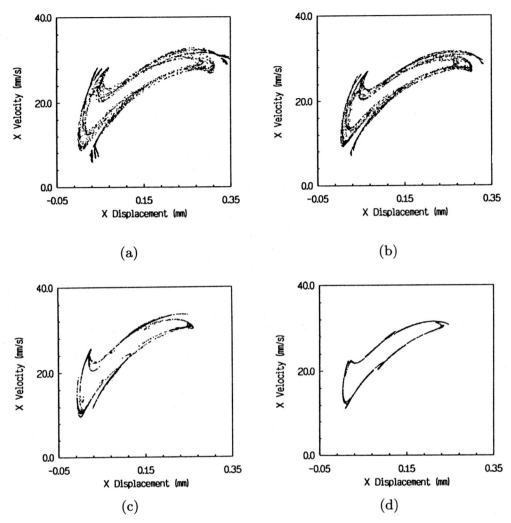

Figure 19. Poincaré sections of the response at $\Omega/\omega_1 = 2.555$, with $k_2/k_1 = 30$, $g = 0.5$mm, $\delta = 0.5$mm and (a) $\nu = 0.075$; (b) $\nu = 0.0875$; (c) $\nu = 0.1$; (d) $\nu = 0.1125$.

Conclusions

It is clear from the investigations that, assuming that the model used is representative, chaotic motion is possible in rotor systems which have discontinuous stiffnesses due to clearance effects. This has implications, as designs based on a linear model will not predict that there can be violent oscillations due to the impacts. In addition, small changes in the system parameters can change the response from chaotic to periodic or quasi-periodic. This is of importance in real systems, where designs may be validated numerically prior to production. In these cases, even if the full nonlinear model is used, care is necessary when

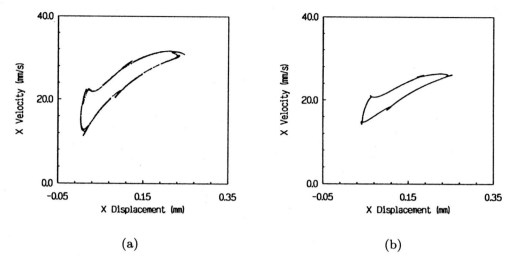

(a)   (b)

Figure 20. Poincaré sections, $g = 0.5$mm, $\delta = 0.5$mm, of (a) the chaotic response at $\Omega/\omega_1 = 2.555$, with $k_2/k_1 = 30$ and $\nu = 0.1125$; (b) the quasi-periodic response at $\Omega/\omega_1 = 2.5$, with $k2/k1 = 36.6$ and $\nu = 0.085$.

investigating the response in the region of parameter space around the design values to establish that no unwanted phenomena occur.

Acknowledgments. The authors acknowledge the support of the S.E.R.C., who funded this work under grant number GR/F 29158. In addition, they also express their appreciation to Professor A.D.S. Barr for his encouragement during this

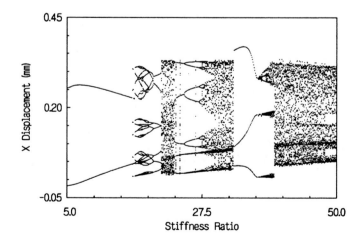

Figure 21. Bifurcation diagram with varying stiffness ratio for $\Omega/\omega_1 = 2.555$, $g = 0.5$mm, $\delta = 0.5$mm and $\nu = 0.1$.

work, and Dr. P.F. Smith for undertaking the computer performance benchmarks for the various systems.

REFERENCES

[Bort84]
    Borthwick, W.K.D., The numerical solution of discontinuous structural systems, *Proc. Second Int. Conf. on Recent Advances in Structural Dynamics*, University of Southampton, UK, pp. 307–316, 1984.

[Carr90]
    Carr, H.R., Joint study on the computerisation of in-field aero engine condition monitoring, *Proc. I. Mech. E. Seminar on Machine Condition Monitoring*, Institute of Mechanical Engineers, London, pp. 7–16, 1990.

[Chil82]
    Childs, D.W., Fractional frequency rotor motion due to nonsymmetric clearance effects, *A.S.M.E. Jour. Engng. Power*, Vol. 104, pp. 533–541, 1982.

[Day85]
    Day, W.B., Nonlinear rotordynamics analysis, NASA Report CR171425, 1985.

[Ehri88]
    Ehrich, F.F., High order subharmonic responses of high speed rotor in bearing clearance, *Jour. Vibration, Stress and Reliability in Design*, Vol. 110, pp. 9–16, 1988.

[Kapi91]
    Kapitaniak, T., Strange non-chaotic attractors, *Chaos, Solitons and Fract.*, Vol. 1, No. 1, pp. 67–77, 1991.

[Kim90]
    Kim, S.T., and Noah, Y.B., Bifurcation analysis for a modified Jeffcott Rotor with bearing clearances, *Jour. Nonlinear Dynamics*, Vol. 1, pp. 221–241, 1990.

[Kune89]
    Kunert, A., and Pfeiffer, F., Stochastic model for rattling in gear boxes, *Proc. IUTAM Symposium on Nonlinear Dynamics in Engineering Systems*, Stuttgart, F.R.G., pp. 233–240, 1989.

[Neil86]
    Neilson, R.D., "Dynamics of Simple Rotor Systems having Motion Dependent Discontinuities", Ph.D. Dissertation, University of Dundee, U.K.,1986.

[Neil87]
    Neilson, R.D., and Barr A.D.S., Spectral features of the response of a rigid rotor mounted on discontinuously nonlinear supports, *Proc. 7th World Congress on the Theory of Machines and Mechanisms*, Seville, Spain, 17-21 September 1987, pp. 1799–1803.

[Neil88a]
    Neilson, R.D., and Barr, A.D.S., Transition to chaos in the structure of the sideband spectral response of a rigid rotor mounted on discontinuously nonlinear elastic supports, Paper presented at the Euromech 252 Colloquium on Chaos Concepts in Mechanical Systems, Bergische University, Wuppertal, F.R.G., 1988.

[Neil88b]

Neilson, R.D., and Barr, A.D.S., Dynamics of a rigid rotor mounted on discontinuously nonlinear elastic supports, *Proc. I. Mech. E.*, Vol. 202, C5, pp. 369–376, 1988.

[Neil88c]

Neilson, R.D., and Barr, A.D.S., Response of two elastically supported rigid rotors sharing a common discontinuously nonlinear support, *Proc. I. Mech. E. 4th Int. Conf. on Vibrations in Rotating Machinery*, Heriot-Watt University, Edinburgh, UK, 12–14 September 1988, pp. 589–598.

[Pfei84]

Pfeiffer, F., Mechanische Systeme mit instetigen Ubergangen, *Ingenieur Archiv*, Vol. 54, No. 3, pp. 232–240, 1984.

[Pfei88a]

Pfeiffer, F., Seltsame Attraktoren in Zahnradgetrieben, *Ingenieur Archiv*, Vol. 58, No. 3, pp. 113–115, 1988.

[Pfei88b]

Pfeiffer, F., Application aspects of chaos concepts, Paper presented at the Euromech 252 Colloquium on Chaos Concepts in Mechanical Systems, Bergische University, Wuppertal, F.R.G., 1988.

[Shaw83]

Shaw, S.W., and Holmes, P.J., A periodically forced piecewise linear oscillator, *Jour. Sound and Vibration*, Vol. 90, No. 1, pp. 129–155, 1983.

[Shaw89]

Shaw, J., and Shaw, S.W., The onset of chaos in a two-degree-of-freedom impacting system., *A.S.M.E. Jour. Appl. Mech.*, Vol. 56, pp. 168–174, March 1989.

[Whis87]

Whiston, G.S., Global dynamics of a vibro-impacting linear oscillator, *Jour. Sound and Vibration*, Vol. 118, No. 3, pp. 395–429, 1987.

[Wolf85]

Wolf, A., Swift, J.B., Swinney, H.L., and Vastano, J.A., Determining Lyapunov exponents from a time series, *Physica* D, Vol. 16, pp. 285–317, 1985.

About the Editors
Applications of Fractals and Chaos

A.J. Crilly

Tony Crilly began his education in Sydney, Australia and later obtained under-graduate and master's degrees in mathematics from the University of Hull in the United Kingdom. He received his Ph.D. in the history of mathematics in 1981 from the Council for National Academic Awards. He has served as both secretary and treasurer of the British Society for the History of Mathematics and is currently a committee member. He is a Fellow of the Institute of Mathematics and its Applications and a member of the British Computer Society Computer Graphics and Displays Group. He has taught in the United States at the University of Michigan and recently spent two years teaching at the newly established City Polytechnic of Hong Kong. While in Hong Kong, he helped set up a department of Applied Mathematics and designed courses in Engineering Mathematics and Discrete Mathematics. His present interests lie in the geometry of computer graphics and in mathematical education. He is currently principal lecturer in the Faculty of Engineering, Science and Mathematics at Middlesex University. He is married with four children and lives in St. Albans, Hertfordshire.

R.A. Earnshaw

Rae Earnshaw is Head of Computer Graphics at the University of Leeds, with interests in graphics algorithms, human–computer interface issues, scientific vi-sualization, graphics standards, fifth-generation graphics software, workstations and display technology, mathematics of computer graphics, CAD/CAM, graph-ics system building and education issues. He has been a visiting professor at Illinois Institute of Technology, Chicago, USA, Northwestern Polytechnical Uni-versity, China and George Washington University, Washington DC, USA. He was a director of the NATO Advanced Study Institute on 'Fundamental Algo-rithms for Computer Graphics' held in Ilkley, England, in 1985, a co-chair of the BCS/ACM International Summer Institute on 'State of the Art in Computer Graphics' held in Scotland in 1986 and a director of the NATO Advanced Study

Institute on 'Theoretical Foundations of Computer Graphics and CAD' held in Italy in 1987. He is a member of ACM, IEEE, CGS, EG and a Fellow of the British Computer Society.

Dr. Earnshaw has authored and edited 15 books on graphics algorithms, computer graphics and associated topics and published a number of papers in these areas. He chairs the Scientific Visualization Group at the University of Leeds, is a member of the Editorial Board of The Visual Computer, vice-president of the Computer Graphics Society and chair of the British Computer Society Computer Graphics and Displays Group.

H. Jones

Huw Jones was brought up in South Wales and graduated from University College Swansea with a B.S. in Applied Mathematics in 1966. The following year he obtained a Diploma in Education from the same institution and, after a short period as a schoolmaster, has spent the rest of his working life as a lecturer in higher education in London. During this period, he obtained a Master of Science in Statistics from Brunel University, became a Fellow of the Royal Statistical Society, a member of the European Society for Computer Graphics and of the British Computer Society, currently being vice-chair of that society's Computer Graphics and Displays Group Committee. He is currently a principal lecturer in Computer Graphics and Human-Computer Interaction in the School of Mathematics, Statistics and Computing at Middlesex University, where he follows his research interest in fractal geometry and is head of the Master of Science in Computer Graphics and the Bachelor of Science in Human-Computer Interaction Design courses. He is married to Judy, a Mathematics teacher, and has a son, Rhodri, and a daughter, Ceri.

Contributors' Addresses
Authors' Addresses

Mr. M. Ali
Communications Research Group
Department of Electronic
        and Electrical Engineering
Kings College
Strand
London WC2R 2LS
United Kingdom

Dr. S.R. Bishop
Centre for Nonlinear Dynamics
        and Applications
University College
Civil Engineering Building
Gower Street
LONDON WC1E 6BT
United Kingdom

Dr. J.M. Blackledge
Department of Applied Computing
    and Mathematics
School of Mechanical Engineering
Cranfield Insitute of Technology
Cranfield
Bedford MK43 0AL
United Kingdom

Professor R.L. Devaney
Department of Mathematics
Boston University
111 Cummington Street
Boston
MA 02215
USA

Dr. J. Healey
Department of Engineering
University of Cambridge
Trumpington Street
Cambridge CB2 1PZ
United Kingdom

Dr. A.V. Holden
Department of Physiology
University of Leeds
Leeds LS2 9JT
United Kingdom

Professor K.J. Hsü
Geologisches Institut
ETH-Zentrum
CH-0892 ZURICH
Switzerland

Dr. M.D. Impey
Environmental Division
Intera Information Technologies Ltd.
Chiltern House
45 Station Road
Henley-on-Thames
Oxon RG9 1AT
England

Dr. L.F. Jardine
School of Electrical Engineering
        and Science
The Royal Military College of Science
Shrivenham, SWINDON
Wilts SN6 8LA
United Kingdom

Mr. D. Jarrett
Middlesex Business School
The Burroughs
Hendon
London NW11 7HU
United Kingdom

Dr. J.A. Kaandorp
University of Amsterdam
Department of Computer Science
Kruislaan 403
1098 SJ Amsterdam
Netherlands

Professor R.J. Lansdown
CASCAAD
Faculty of Art and Design
Middlesex University
Cat Hill
Barnet, Herts EN4 8HT
United Kingdom

Dr. R.D. Neilson
Department of Engineering
Fraser Noble Building
King's College
University of Aberdeen
Aberdeen AB9 2UE
Scotland

Dr. J.C. Vassilicos
Department of Applied Maths
     and Theoretical Physics
University of Cambridge
Silver Street
Cambridge CB3 9EW
United Kingdom

Dr. R.F. Voss
Thomas J. Watson Research Center
P.O. Box 218
Yorktown Heights
NY 10598
USA

Dr. G.H. Watson
SD-Scicon UK Ltd.
Station House
Camberley
Surrey GU15 3XH
United Kingdom

Editors' Addresses

Dr. A.J. Crilly
Department of Mathematics
Middlesex University
Trent Park   Cockfosters Road
Barnet
Herts EN4 0PT
United Kingdom

Dr. R.A. Earnshaw
Head of Graphics
University of Leeds
Leeds LS2 9JT
United Kingdom

Mr. H.Jones
School of Mathematics, Statistics
     and Computing
Middlesex University
Bounds Green Road
London N11 2NQ
United Kingdom

Index

Index

Springer-Verlag
and the Environment

We at Springer-Verlag firmly believe that an international science publisher has a special obligation to the environment, and our corporate policies consistently reflect this conviction.

We also expect our business partners – paper mills, printers, packaging manufacturers, etc. – to commit themselves to using environmentally friendly materials and production processes.

The paper in this book is made from low- or no-chlorine pulp and is acid free, in conformance with international standards for paper permanency.